"The principles discussed in *Supernutrition* have helped my family and me stay in great health. . . . *Supernutrition* will help each person be at his best."

—Sonny Jurgensen,
former all-star NFL quarterback

Until you experience the miracle of Supernutrition, you simply will not know the meaning of the word "alive." Richard A. Passwater's program is different from other vitamin therapy programs because it is personalized for individual needs, taking age, life-style, health problems, and food preferences into account. It is a balanced food and vitamin plan that clearly warns against vitamin misuse and overuse.

"Passwater marshals much new scientific evidence to support his ideas—few people know the world literature on this subject as well as he." —Raymond F. Chen, M.D., Ph.D.

SUPER-NUTRITION

Richard A. Passwater

PUBLISHED BY POCKET BOOKS NEW YORK

POCKET BOOKS, a Simon & Schuster division of GULF & WESTERN CORPORATION
1230 Avenue of the Americas, New York, N.Y. 10020

ISBN: 0-671-42172-7

First Pocket Books printing August, 1976

15   14   13   12   11   10   9   8

POCKET and colophon are trademarks of Simon & Schuster.

Printed in the U.S.A.

To My Wife
BARBARA
This book, as my life, is
dedicated to you

Acknowledgments

I am indebted to Dr. Hans J. Kugler, author of *Slowing Down the Aging Process,* for suggesting that I should write this book on nutrition. Dr. Kugler's argument that I could help more people with this book than I could by gerontological research alone overcame my earlier protests to the interruption in my research. This book reports on the work of many brilliant researchers as well as results from my own research. Therefore, I am indebted to the many discussions, suggestions, reviews, and reports from Dr. Dick Ahrens, Dr. Keith Brewer, Dr. Ray Chen, Dr. E. Cheraskin, Dr. Colin Chignell, Dr. Bill Driscoll, Dr. Doug Frost, Dr. Denham Harman, Dr. Abram Hoffer, Dr. Fred Klenner, Dr. Lionel Leong, Dr. Orville Levander, Dr. Dan Nebert, Dr. Kurt Oster, Dr. Linus Pauling, Dr. Ed Pinckney, Dr. Wilfred Shute, Dr. Evan Shute, Dr. Irwin Stone, Dr. Hans Weber, and Dr. Roger Williams.

I would also like to recognize the special help by those who tested the methods, specifically tested other details, and allowed me to draw upon their experience, with special thanks to George Allen, Lee Fryer, Ken Halaby, Sonny Jurgensen, Mort Katz, Cheryll Kloak, Pat McGrady, Jr., Fred Scott, Ron Sell, Harald Taub, and Helena Tuttle.

Preface for Physicians

Some physicians may be offended by this book on nutrition written by a nonphysician. The subject of food and food supplementation is highly controversial, and anyone who is confused about diet is told to "consult a physician." Doctors are proud to be considered fountainheads of nutritional information. Unfortunately, as one AMA official pointed out in the March–April 1974 issue of *Nutrition Today*, physicians do not generally know very much about the subject. Most medical schools do not teach nutrition as a separate subject, although bits and pieces of dietary information are presented in various courses of the medical curriculum. Physicians should not be surprised if, reading this book, they learn a lot of things not covered in medical school.

Physicians may be offended by this book because Passwater advocates the medically supervised taking of supplemental vitamins. Medical students are told that the giving of vitamins in a modern society serves only to provide a placebo effect, since diseases like rickets, beriberi, scurvy, pernicious anemia, and other hypovitaminoses rarely occur now, and are the only possible indications for vitamin administration. The basis of this attitude is what I would call the "two state" theory of health—either you are *sick*, or you are *well*. That is, if the patient does not have beriberi, there is no need to give thiamine.

The "two state" theory of health is encouraged by formal medical education, which stresses diagnosable diseases and their treatment. Doctors love to have patients with clear-cut diseases. But if the chief complaint consists of vague symptoms of depression, lack of energy, and strange aches and pains, the average physician begins to get a little annoyed. If the laboratory-test results are all normal, the patient is likely to be labeled a hypochondriac. The thinking in such cases is often: "since there is no evidence that the patient is *sick,* he must be *well.*"

The "two state" theory runs counter to common sense; health has many gradations, not just two. It seems obvious that the human organism is so complex that different systems could be functioning suboptimally without frank evidence of illness. There are great variations in the way we feel on different days, and there are great differences in the amount of energy that people possess. Passwater, in this book, states that vitamins and other dietary nutrients may be crucial in accounting for these differences.

In 1970, Linus Pauling shocked the world by publicizing evidence that vitamin C prevented and cured illnesses other than scurvy. He pointed out that the effect on the common cold appeared to demand a daily intake of upward of 1 gram of vitamin C—an amount much higher than that recommended by the established authorities. Controversy continues to swirl about Dr. Pauling and his ideas in spite of the fact that *all* the double-blind studies made to test his observations have supported him.

The significance of the Pauling incident reaches far beyond the controversy over vitamin C. For one thing, since the traditional teaching that vitamin C supplementation is ineffective turned out to be questionable, similar assumptions about other vitamins might also be incorrect. Additionally, the "two state" theory of health is undermined as follows: a person with low vitamin C intake may be said to be in poorer health than another who is more disease-resistant by virtue of an optimum vitamin C intake. Both persons would feel "well," yet one person is clearly "more well." Finally, the vitamin C experience shows that vitamins may have more than one action, and amounts in excess of the recommended daily allowance (RDA) may indeed be beneficial.

Passwater relies heavily on the lessons learned from the

vitamin C story; in fact, he goes beyond Pauling in one respect: Pauling theorized that the human body evolved in response to environmental conditions, and a desirable vitamin intake should probably resemble what is ingested by apes and other primates in nature. According to this evolutionary argument, Pauling found that modern man is most likely to be deficient in vitamin C. Passwater points out that man no longer lives in his "natural environment," and his body now has to cope with a variety of unnatural factors like carcinogens and other chemical pollutants. Thus, he argues, man may benefit from "unnaturally" large supplements of vitamins and nutrients, especially antioxidants like vitamins E and C.

Passwater marshals much new scientific evidence to support his ideas—few people know the world literature on this subject as well as he. His book will make fascinating reading for physicians and laymen interested in the latest ideas in nutrition.

Raymond F. Chen, M.D., Ph.D.
Research Biochemist
Bethesda, Maryland

Foreword to Scientists

More and more of my fellow researchers are discovering the role of nutrition, especially supernutrition, in preventing the dread diseases of our time. One of the most persuasive writers who has brought this connection to light is the biochemist Richard A. Passwater.

In my book, *Slowing Down the Aging Process* (Pyramid, 1973), I discuss Passwater's research in retarding aging, heart disease, and cancer. They may not seem related until you realize that, as Passwater has shown, they each involve free-radical pathology and antioxidant therapy. Modern man is deficient in the antioxidant nutrients, thus prone to epidemic diseases.

There are physicians who instinctively react negatively to the words "vitamin" or "nutrition." Part of this Pavlovian reflex is an "overkill" response to protect their patients against quackery, while another part arises from misinformation in the medical establishment itself, due to deficiencies in medical school training.

As more and more physicians realize the significance of the untapped resources of nutrition, they will increase their competence. This book is a good tutor. *Supernutrition* presents the facts from many laboratories for evaluation. It offers a program that the physician and patient can cooperate in to obtain optimum health. Some patients will find they need few, if any, supplements; others will find that they need them in quantities that seem large by former standards. Health improvement is monitored by objective and subjective clinical observations, while the supplement program is one in which supplements are progressively increased until the monitored parameters are maximized.

Supernutrition answers many of the questions that I am often asked during my television interviews. "How does a person know how many vitamins to take?" "How can I stay younger longer?" This book provides a practical guide for everyone. There are no exotic foods or unbalanced diets presented herein; rather, a middle path between the extremes of ignorance and faddism is given. Here is a program for the nutrition-conscious patient that physicians can endorse.

Hans Kugler, Ph.D.
Author of *Slowing Down
the Aging Process*
Torrance, California

Introduction

To read newspaper columns of medical advice, or similar articles in popular magazines, or, for that matter, most textbooks on nutrition, you would suppose that nutrition is one of the older branches of science and that just about everything to be known about it has long been established. People who would not presume to tell you how often to exercise without hedging and pointing out alternative possibilities do not hesitate to pontificate about your diet and how to regulate it.

The world is literally full of "experts" who can tell you to the calorie how much food you should eat, and can pinpoint to the milligram what your body requires of several dozen different essential nutrients. They can tell you with assurance exactly how to regulate your diet to avoid a heart attack, and will keep on telling you even after they have had their own heart attacks. They can tell you how much "protein" you need for health, regardless of its source, and assure you, with contempt for any differing opinions, that highly processed food is no different from natural food as long as it contains the same chemicals. In fact, the world is full of nonsense. Your ordinary nutritional expert is about as reliable as an expert on how to curb inflation or make a fortune in the stock market.

Yet even though the profound ignorance of experts is one of the hallmarks of our civilization, there are today, as there have always been, quieter and humbler people who are more interested in learning than they are in asserting the superiority of such knowledge as they possess.

Richard Passwater is one of this rare breed.

When you read *Supernutrition,* you will notice some remarkable things. It is a work of profound scholarship that has managed to dig out and organize hundreds of significant nutritional studies that had been buried because they were embarrassing to the opinions of the experts. You will find that the work has a monumental quality: there is no nutritional research, no matter how obscure or recent, that Passwater is not aware of or does not take into account. But most important, even though the author demonstrates that his knowledge is profound, he never loses the awareness that any facet of his knowledge may be changed tomorrow, that creative nutrition is one of the newest of scientific studies, that nothing about it is cut and dried.

That leavening of humility is one of the most helpful elements in a book whose purpose is anything but humble —a book that claims, in fact, to be able to demonstrate how we may become super-healthy by eating those foods that will make us so. The claim might seem extravagant, to say the least, if Passwater were not so careful to point out that he is far from being the ultimate authority, and that even though he can show most of us how to improve our health by improving our diets, newly emerging information is bound to refine and improve what he already knows. What he knows, in addition, is so carefully documented that it takes nothing more than an open mind to see that he must be right.

For example, look at heart disease. Some twenty years ago it became noticeable that diseases of the heart and circulatory system were the major killers of middle-aged people throughout Western civilization. Tens of thousands of laboratory and epidemiological studies were made, leading to some general conclusions about diet and heart disease. Essentially, these conclusions said that by sharply reducing one's intake of dietary cholesterol and subtituting polyunsaturates, one could gain the greatest measure of protection against atherosclerotic heart disease. The arguments for this position have been persuasive, and today the belief is widely, nearly universally held. Passwater points out, however, that even as more and more people carefully control their diets and avoid foods that contain cholesterol, switch from butter to margarine, and turn pale at the thought of an egg for breakfast, the rate of occurrence of heart disease keeps rising, making no exception of the millions who have trained themselves to avoid all the foods they really enjoy. They are struck down as impartially as those who make no effort whatsoever to protect themselves.

It takes no particular talent to recognize that if a theory does not work in practice, it cannot be right. Yet even that simple conclusion is going to be so shocking to so many that Passwater has gone to great trouble to document some facts that ought to be obvious by this time: that low-cholesterol diets do not prevent heart disease; that the cholesterol levels of the blood are related only vaguely and distantly to dietary intake of cholesterol; and that we will have to look in other directions for the causes of and preventatives to heart disease.

With the air thus cleared, Passwater is in a position to examine with new interest a multitude of biochemical studies—some of them as much as thirty, forty, or even fifty years old—that have been generally ignored by medical science because the facts they brought to light were not in agreement with the prevailing cholesterol theory of heart disease. Research on the effects of alpha tocopherol (vitamin E), for example, was for the most part abandoned twenty years ago. Passwater has rescued from obscurity a study made at Johns Hopkins and reported in the *American Journal of Physiology* in 1948 showing that this essential nutrient possesses a strong antithrombic activity. This study was followed up by others in 1949 and 1950, and a variety of supportive peripheral studies were made at the same time.

But the medical profession, infatuated with cholesterol, has lost all interest in vitamin E and has completely forgotten what this vitamin can do. One famed surgeon, Dr. Alton Ochsner, has a remarkable postsurgical recovery rate among his patients, which he attributes, at least in part, to his use of vitamin E to prevent thrombosis. Yet his lead has not been followed because younger surgeons are unaware of all the vitamin E research that has gone on and do not understand how the vitamin can have this particular effect. I do not think that anyone, not even the knowledgeable and scholarly Dr. Evan Shute of London, Ontario, has organized so thoroughly the totality of research on vitamin E and put it all together as well as Passwater has done, so as to create a complete and intelligible picture of how and why it is that insufficient vitamin E will not only fail to prevent internal blood clots but will actually cause them.

By the time Passwater has reviewed all the evidence, there can be little doubt in a reader's mind that an increase in vitamin E intake is going to help substantially with the problem of heart disease. Yet this book does not ride any particular hobbyhorse and does not maintain that vitamin E alone is the answer. Passwater has noted so many nutrients that have significant effects on the circulatory system and the health of the heart that he finally leads us to conclude that there is no such thing as a magic formula for the prevention of heart disease. Rather, what seems to be involved is the general condition of the body, the effects on that condition of a host of nutrients, and proper exercise.

Another way to state this would be: in order to have the best chance of avoiding a heart attack, keep yourself in overall excellent health internally as well as externally. By the time you have finished reading *Supernutrition,* you will know—as well as anybody does today—just how to do that.

In fact, a complete reading of *Supernutrition* will leave you convinced that you have learned not only how to improve your chance of avoiding heart attack, cancer, high blood pressure, and osteoarthritis, but also of avoiding the most widespread and deadly of all the diseases that afflict us today—premature old age.

Even though the emphasis is necessarily on what is *not* going to happen to you if you provide yourself with good nutrition, what is most important is what *is* going to happen. That is, you will experience a sense of overall wellbeing; a possession of vast stores of energy, mental as well as physical; a general capacity for enjoyment and an optimistic outlook that most of us are aware of only as the envied possession of somebody else. This is super-health, and it is quite likely that you will discover the highroad to it in *Supernutrition*.

Harald J. Taub
Associate Publisher and Editor
Let's LIVE magazine
Los Angeles, California
(former Executive Editor,
Prevention magazine)

Contents

SUPER-NUTRITION

America Needs Supernutrition

Supernutrition is a program for good health based on good foods supplemented by vitamins. The plan is designed so that a person following this regimen can reach his point of optimum health generally within two or three months, and, as long as he continues with the plan, remain at his peak of health. The program recognizes that while many people seriously try to eat a nutritionally balanced diet they are unknowingly denied the food value they seek because today's foods are usually so heavily refined and processed that vast quantities of the nutrients essential to general good health have been removed. The lack of these nutrients is so severe that the body is all too frequently unable to resist the onslaught of heart disease and cancer, even though a person may still be in his thirties, forties, or fifties. **Extensive research evidence leads me to conclude that millions of Americans each year suffer from diseases that Supernutrition could prevent.** Unfortunately, great numbers of people are misled by the Food and Drug Administration (FDA), the American Medical Association (AMA), and their personal physicians into believing that, as long as they receive the United States Department of Agriculture's (USDA) recommended daily allowance (RDA) or minimum daily requirements (MDR), they need no vitamin supplementation.

Millions of Americans, many of them believing that they are eating balanced diets, are consuming foods whose nutritional value does not come up even to the inadequate levels of the RDA. In 1971, Dr. Edith Weir of the USDA reported that if the public adhered to a diet which achieved the RDA levels, 300,000 deaths could be prevented each year from heart disease and stroke and another 150,000 deaths could be prevented each year from cancer. Improved nutrition, she further reported, would create substantial reduction in the incidence of arthritis, muscular disorders, and kidney disease. The details of her report are in Chapter 15; for the moment, it is startling enough to realize that she estimated that if all diets were improved to RDA levels, there would be dramatic improvements in at least nineteen major health problems and that half a million lives could be saved yearly.

The Supernutrition program, which supplies nutrients beyond the level and scope suggested by the USDA, can do even more. It can, according to my research and the research of many other biochemists and nutritionists, prevent 500,000 to 1,000,000 premature deaths each year!

The research that has forced me to conclude that more than half a million Americans die prematurely each year because of insufficient nutrition is carefully detailed in subsequent chapters. Chapters 10 and 11 explain the highly beneficial effects of vitamins E, C, and B-complex in combating heart disease. Chapter 13 reveals why supplements of vitamins E and C in amounts beyond those suggested by the RDA can reduce deaths due to cancer by at least one-third. The fact that large doses of the B-complex vitamin have resulted in the astonishingly successful treatment of mental and emotional disorders is discussed in Chapter 7, while Chapter 14 examines the factors that account for premature aging and the ways in which vitamins E and C can bring about an encouraging reversal of the unnecessary signs of aging.

A major aim of this book, a criticism of the nutritional myths fostered by the FDA, the AMA, the USDA, and many commercial suppliers of food, is found in Chapter 15, as well as in Chapters 8 and 9. These latter chapters present a wealth of material that exposes the commercially manipulated cholesterol scare, bares the role of the FDA in perpetuating the cholesterol controversy, and demonstrates that low-cholesterol diets do not prevent heart disease and that high-cholesterol diets do not cause heart disease. Indeed, **many Americans are doing themselves far more harm than good by drastically cutting down on their intake of butter, whole milk, and eggs.**

Projections based on the research detailed in all the above mentioned chapters lead me to believe that if people followed the Supernutrition program:

1. Heart disease would be reduced by 60–80 percent.

2. Cancer would be reduced by 30–40 percent.

3. Air pollution damage to the human body would be reduced by 95 percent.

4. The cure rate for schizophrenia would be increased by 500 percent.

5. Arthritis and other crippling diseases would be reduced by 40 percent.

6. The incidence and severity of all types of diseases would be reduced by 40 percent.

Startling as it may seem, the standard American diet is, in fact, dangerously deficient in the nutrients essential to good health; and, as a result, millions of Americans are consigned to years of struggle with debilitating diseases and victimized by fatal ailments that rob them of decades of disease-free life. In 1955, the USDA discovered that 40 percent of the diets surveyed failed to meet the RDA of nutrients necessary to prevent the onset of a host of diseases. In 1965 and 1966, an extensive USDA survey revealed that the quality of our diets was declining from the low levels of the 1950s; only 50 percent of American households surveyed in 1965 had diets that could be classified as "good" by USDA standards (that is, up to RDA levels), and 20 percent had diets considered "poor" because they provided less than two-thirds of the RDA.

But an even more shocking report was released in 1969, when the United States Public Health Service published the results of a ten-state study that evaluated the presence of essential nutrients in the diets of 12,000 persons. Gross vitamin deficiencies were confirmed by pathological examinations: 20 percent of those surveyed had one or more essential nutrients below the minimum acceptable level, 19 percent were deficient in vitamin B_2, 15 percent had sup-par vitamin C levels, 13 percent had unacceptably low levels of vitamin A, and one of every three children under six years old had iron-deficiency anemia!

In summing up our nutritional status, Dr. Jean Meyer of Harvard's Department of Nutrition and Chairman of the 1969 White House Conference on Food, Nutrition and Health reported in *Science* (April 21, 1972): "Malnutrition, whether caused by poverty or improper diet, contributes to the alarming health situation in the United States today. . . . Indeed—in almost thirty nations, life expectancies for adult males [have since 1950 been] greater than they were in the United States."

It must be seriously noted that the USDA's judgments about our diets rely on MDR and RDA levels as acceptable standards. Yet the MDR and RDA are highly inadequate guides for essential nutrition in American diets—

diets which in the last few decades have been inundated with refined foods, processed foods (canned and frozen), food additives, and food preservatives—since as much as 98 percent of a food's critical nutrients may have been destroyed by the time the food reaches the table. Additionally, air and water pollution tax the body severely by consuming essential nutrients, as do smoking and the strains of many contemporary life-styles. For all these reasons, the MDA and the RDA have become increasingly poor nutritional guides.

Yet the most important reason why the MDR and RDA are such poor guides to optimum health is that the suggested quantities represent only the levels of vitamins required to prevent immediate, recognizable deficiencies in the average person or animal. In Chapter 15 the fallacies of the MDR and RDA are examined in detail; for the time being, consider the words of Senator William Proxmire of Wisconsin who, in a 1974 issue of *Let's LIVE*, summed up the RDA very accurately: "At best the RDAs are only a 'recommended' allowance at antediluvian levels designed to prevent some terrible disease. At worst they are based on conflicts of interest and self-serving views of certain portions of the food industry. Almost never are they provided at levels to provide for optimum health and nutrition."

Why are we not better protected by the FDA? Why are we not better counseled about the dangers of inadequate nutrition and the benefits of vitamin supplements by the AMA? Both questions are answered in Chapter 4; for now, suffice it to say that the judgments of both organizations are seriously outdated, and designed to protect their previous evaluations.

Family physicians often tell you that taking vitamins is a needless expense because, sadly, few doctors are nutrition experts and most physicians are well beyond their area of expertise when they attempt to advise you about nutrition. The 1969 White House Conference on Food, Nutrition and Health concluded, "At the present time, nutrition teaching in medical schools and in teaching hospitals is woefully inadequate. Alarming as the problem is [and it is dealt with more fully in Chapter 4], the facts are that medical schools with nutrition departments are rare, and not one medical school can claim to teach nutrition seriously."

If you've read nutrition articles or books, perhaps you're not sure about the unfamiliar health foods their authors recommend or whether their claims have scientific support. You may think their diets sound better than your present one, but if you could eat that way, you would already be doing it. You may wonder, "Is there any hope for me even if I don't eat the way most nutritionists say I should? Do I have to eat yogurt, sprouts, fertile eggs, whole-wheat bread, black-strap molasses, brewer's yeast, bone meal, lecithin, and the like?"

You need a sensible program that is compatible with your present life-style. Supernutrition is your program. If there are limitations that you have to live with, Supernutrition will do the best for you under those conditions. If you cannot eat properly, give up smoking, or bear exercising, Supernutrition will do wonders for you. There is no reason to throw yourself to the dogs because you cannot obey all the rules for good health. Few can. The Supernutrition program is tailored to those who cannot.

You may have been taught a number of false ideas about nutrition that are doing you more harm than good; you will have to unlearn these fallacies. For example, if you think that preventing heart disease has something to do with eating polyunsaturated fats and avoiding cholesterol, you have been misled by a popular misconception. Despite the acceptance of this idea, the heart disease rate has skyrocketed.

Antioxidant therapy and free-radical pathology may be new terms to you, but you will learn how a simple, easy-to-follow plan combining vitamin C and vitamin E (anti-

oxidant therapy) can prevent or reduce in severity many of
our most feared diseases.

Figure 1.1

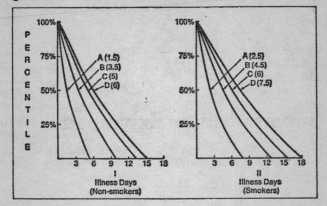

Antioxidant therapy, which combats free-radical pathology, will probably add nine or ten healthy years to your
life.

No matter how far anyone is from being in optimum
health, the road is easy because the Supernutrition program
goes one step at a time. It is up to you to take the first
step. In fact, the worse your health is, the sooner you will
notice marked improvement.

Chapter 2 outlines the Supernutrition program and
Chapter 16 contains the details of the Supernutrition plan,
but you will have greater success if you read the book
through. You should know the factual data behind this
program; they will provide the encouragement to institute
your Supernutrition program today.

2

Supernutrition Explained

The Supernutrition Plan

The Supernutrition program integrates the concepts of orthomolecular medicine, megavitamin therapy, antioxidant therapy, and other scientific applications of nutritional optimization.

The term orthomolecular medicine was coined by Dr. Linus Pauling. The prefix *ortho* means right or proper, as in *orthodox* (right beliefs); thus orthomolecular means having the right molecules in your body *in the right amounts*. The right molecules are the ones naturally used (vitamins, minerals, amino acids, proteins, fats, carbohydrates), and the right amounts are the ones that give *you* the best health. Orthomolecular medicine is the prevention of disease through the preservation of good health, and the treatment of disease by varying the concentrations in the human body of the molecules that are normally present.

Megavitamin therapy, which gets its name from *mega,* meaning "great," implies large doses of certain vitamins. In the more than twenty years since megavitamin therapy

8

was initiated, primarily by Drs. Abram Hoffer and Humphrey Osmond (in 1952), an estimated thirty thousand patients have been cured of mental and emotional problems with the aid of megavitamins. Even specific genetic defects that lead to mental or emotional illness can be partially overcome with large doses of vitamins.

Supernutrition is more than orthomolecular medicine or megavitamin therapy—and it consists of more than vitamins. Supernutrition is a program that finds the optimum level of each nutrient for each individual and tells you how to ascertain when you have reached *your* point of optimum health. The plan also encourages you to work closely with your physician, who can help by monitoring various health indicators. The Supernutrition plan will show you how to apply scientifically, to a detailed, customized program for yourself, the knowledge gained from this book.

The Skeptics Are Learning

Each of the concepts to which I have just referred is denounced as a fad of the "health nuts" by the archaic spokesmen of the AMA. The evidence is clear, however; the AMA opinion will have to change as the old guard fades away. Consider how the AMA and FDA attacked Dr. Linus Pauling, winner of two Nobel prizes. He was called senile and out of his area of knowledge when he astutely pointed out the evidence demonstrating the benefits of vitamin C—evidence already in the scientific literature but generally ignored by the medical profession.

Skepticism in science is not only healthy, but essential, for it insures an examination of the facts. Fortunately Pauling was challenged properly, rather than merely denounced by "know-it-all" authorities. Dr. Beaton, head of the Department of Nutrition of the University of Toronto and chairman of the United Nations Committee on Vitamins, took issue with Pauling in a scientific manner. He set out to prove Pauling wrong with a proper double-blind test, carrying out a study which involved 818 people. One group took 1 gram of vitamin C a day, the other group ingested a placebo. Beaton found that the duration and severity of illness due to the common cold was 30 percent less for the vitamin C group. Additionally, he found that the duration and severity of illness from other diseases was 40 percent less, and total time lost from work due to illness was 67 percent less.

Many other studies have shown that vitamin C has a general antiviral activity against a whole array of viruses, as well as a general antibacterial activity. Pauling has recently stated that optimum vitamin C intake would cut down the amount of illness from all causes by 50 percent. **The vitamin C skeptics have based their opinion either on inaccurate interpretations of old tests or on tests involving too little vitamin C for too short a period.** More than four large-scale tests confirmed Pauling's claims of vitamin C's effectiveness against colds, but the "authorities" of the FDA, the AMA, and the food-industry-supported nutritionists did not apologize for their assaults—they only muted their denouncements, probably because they could no longer find audiences that would listen. Pauling could have kept his findings to himself without going out on a limb and risking his reputation. His decision to endanger his reputation was an act of conviction such as is witnessed all too seldom.

As soon as Pauling had received scientific vindication in the vitamin C-against-the-common-cold issue, he entered into the megavitamin therapy issue by formulating the basic concepts behind orthomolecular psychiatry. This therapy has helped many mentally disturbed individuals return to and function better in society—not through vitamins alone, but through standard treatment plus orthomolecular psychiatry. These encouraging stories are examined in Chapter 7.

A Doctor Should Monitor Your Progress

You should have a complete physical examination by your physician before you start your Supernutrition program.

Explain the program to your doctor and ask him or her to help monitor your progress and to tell you if there are any reasons why you should not participate in the Supernutrition program.

While Supernutrition works better with medical supervision, you should not make radical changes in your diet and vitamin supplementation even under a physician's guidance. Move slowly, but surely, to better health. Not everyone's stomach can tolerate a sudden diet change to concentrated vitamins and other nutrients, but almost everyone can tolerate them if the change is made gradually.

Do not attempt to self-treat diseases with Supernutrition. Your problem may be different from your diagnosis, and you may waste valuable time needed to fight the disease.

The Danger of Excess Vitamins

A number of people, unfortunately, believe that the more vitamin pills they stuff themselves with, the better off they are. This is just not so, and there are several reasons why. First of all, **everything ingested in excess is toxic**—even good drinking water or table salt. If we drink too much water for a very prolonged period, our kidneys overwork, too many minerals—especially potassium—are washed out, and several fatal diseases can develop. True, the chance of anyone taking a toxic amount of water is extremely remote, but it *is* possible.

Similarly, we don't think of table salt as poisonous; but in excess, it can cause hypertension (high blood pressure), which can lead to heart disease. Excess salt can disturb our electrolyte (cell water-regulator) balance and increase water retention. Though there is no poison label on salt, many nutritionists feel we use too much of it for our own good, and they attribute part of the increase in hypertension to the increased consumption of salty snack foods. Still, all in all, we don't have to monitor our daily salt intake for fear of poisoning.

Some of our most valuable nutrients can be poisonous,

but, fortunately, most toxic nutrients have a wide margin of safety between the optimum nutrient level and the beginning level of toxicity.

Don't Take Vitamins at Random

Since all nutrients can be toxic, you must know the limits of each. To use the Supernutrition plan you must learn your individual limits. Most minerals and some vitamins, if taken for prolonged periods, can be toxic in amounts easily put into one or two capsules. For example, vitamin A can be toxic either in pill form or as it occurs in natural food. Vitamin A is stored in the livers of animals; marine animals store large amounts of vitamin A because they eat great numbers of smaller fish that have ample supplies of vitamin A. Eating polar-bear liver, seal liver, or large amounts of fish-liver oils can be poisonous. Reports of poisoning from hypervitaminosis A (overdose) incurred by explorers eating the livers of polar bears and certain seals date back to Willem Barents in the late sixteenth century. Polar-bear liver is said to contain about 500,000 USP (a standard unit of measure as defined by the U.S. Pharmacopeia) units of vitamin A *per gram*. (A normal serving by our standards [3″ by 6″ by ½″] would contain 100 times that amount.) Explorers eating only a quarter pound of polar-bear liver could become seriously ill on 50 million USP units of vitamin A.

Dr. Basil Brown, a forty-eight-year-old chemist in Croydon, England, died in 1974 of hypervitaminosis A. He regularly drank a gallon of carrot juice daily, and whenever he didn't, Dr. Brown would take excessive amounts of vitamin A capsules—he once took over 70 million USP units in ten days. Dr. D. L. McRae, radiologist-in-chief of the Sunnybrook Medical Center of the University of Toronto, described to me two cases of death in children following the accidental administration by ignorant parents of large quantities of halibut-liver oil. Both children suffered extensive degeneration and calcification in many of their organs, particularly the kidneys, and both children died from kidney failure. Dr. McRae did not know how much vitamin A had been taken, but other infant deaths have occurred from 75,000 USP units daily given over six months.

Fortunately, toxic effects can be reversed if caught in time merely by withdrawing the vitamin. Early signs of toxicity are dry, rough skin, yellowing of the skin and whites of the eyes, swelling in the joints, and pain.

Since hypervitaminosis (overdose) is possible with vitamins A and D, the Food and Drug Administration has limited the per pill allowance to 10,000 USP units for vitamin A and 400 USP units for vitamin D. Pills containing greater amounts are available only by prescription. This strategy reduces the chance of overdosage among people unaware of the potential danger. However, Senator Proxmire pointed out in a Senate speech that, through 1971, there were no known deaths from swallowing vitamin A pills. Natural foods (besides polar-bear liver) can contain larger amounts of vitamin A than the 10,000 USP limit for a pill. A 3″×6″×½″ serving (100 grams) of liver contains 20,000 USP units of vitamin A. A 3.3-ounce carrot has 11,000 USP units of vitamin A, and just two-thirds of a cup of dehydrated carrots has 117,000 USP units.

Safe Dosages

Clearly, Supernutrition calls for safe amounts of vitamins A and D, but far more than the FDA per-pill limit.

For Supernutrition, I report (not prescribe) that the optimum level of vitamin A is 35,000 USP units daily. There are of course individual variations, so the normal range would be 25,000 to 35,000 USP units. Some people, such as professional athletes, might require 75,000 to 100,000 USP units, but that is far too much for the average person. The last chapter tells how you can find *your* Supernutrition amount for all vitamins.

Absorption Rate Is Your Guide

Besides putting a limit on vitamin intake because of possible toxicity considerations, you have to consider the amounts that your body can use at one time. Our digestive tract can absorb only so much of a given nutrient in a given time and the leftover is eliminated through the bowel. What is not used is wasted. Taking excess vitamins is not only needlessly expensive but misleads us into thinking that we have taken the proper amount—a false security. Hopefully, you realize that you just don't stuff yourself with pills without understanding the consequences.

In subsequent chapters I will explain in detail the optimum amounts and normal ranges of variances for each nutrient.

3

America's Diet
Is Dangerously Deficient

America, once the "land of plenty," provides a wide assortment of foodstuffs on the market. Do people choose nutritious foods from this great variety?

Dr. Roger Williams commented on the problem in his article "Nutrition for Chemists," which appeared in *American Laboratory* (April 1974):

"How do people get perfect nutrition—every item in just the right amount?" The answer is, "They don't." People get along on imperfect nutrition just as corn plants growing in a field and producing 10 bushels per acre instead of 200 bushels, which is possible. A perfect food environment is as rare as a perfect climatic environment. In a perfect climatic environment, the temperature day and night, the humidity, the rainfall, the wind and the sunshine would always be right.

One of the reasons why we need good nutrition is to feed our brains. The brain is a "hot-spot" of chemical activity. An adult brain weighs only 3 to 4 percent of the whole body weight, but the chemical burning which takes place in the brain may be 25 percent of the [body's] total. Fuel has to be supplied to the brain every minute, but the brain cells also need to be maintained so they can carry on this active burning. How do our brain cells get perfect nutrition? They don't. They have to get along; often they limp along with whatever they can get.

It is estimated that on the average 1,000 brain cells die off every hour in an adult. They are not replaced. Why do they die off? The answer must be poor nutrition. Some people's brain cells die off much more rapidly than others. It has been found recently that the brains of alcoholics after death are useless for dissection by medical students. They tend to become structureless "mush."

When we consume the refined storage materials of plants and animals (sugars, starches and fats) instead of the cellular tissues of plants and animals, we get mostly fuel and very little of the building blocks we need to build and maintain our metabolic machinery.

How can we get the very best food possible? How can we get into our bodies and into the internal environment where our living cells subsist, the best assortment of raw materials? These are worthy questions to think about.

To answer Dr. Williams's questions, we must first consider what *not* to eat. Junk foods should be expelled from a Supernutrition diet. They are not necessarily harmful, but they waste calories and space. We need highly nutritious foods—as much as we can eat without ingesting too many calories; concentrate as much nutrition as possible for each calorie. It is not as wise to add good foods to your present inadequate diet as it is to start with good foods and then let a few treats sneak in. The Supernutrition program will help you to some degree, whichever way you choose. You can be half-alive or supercharged; the decision is yours!

Undernutrition Is the Rule, Not the Exception

What do I have against the average diet? Well, let's look at some surveys in detail. Malnutrition is widespread and has been with us for some time. A six-year Pennsylvania State University survey released in 1942 showed only one person in a thousand escaped malnutrition of some form (*The Pennsylvania State College Bulletin* 36, No. 52 [1942]). Most people, the survey revealed, were deficient in several nutrients, especially vitamins A and D, calcium, and phosphorus. Several nutrients were not studied in the survey, so deficiencies could not be found for them.

In 1955 the USDA found that only 6 percent of American diets could be classified as "good," based on USDA recommended standards (RDA). In 1959, Dr. Agnes F. Morgan of the USDA showed that three-fourths of American women had less than two-thirds of the calcium RDA, and 40 percent were low in vitamins B and C. In 1965 and 1966 an extremely extensive survey made by the USDA discovered the quality of diets declining from that of the 1950s. In 1965, only 50 percent of American households had diets that were rated "good" based on USDA standards; 20 percent had diets rated "poor" because they had less than two-thirds of the RDA. The survey did not measure the blood or tissue levels of the nutrients, but instead evaluated the diet only on the basis of weekly records of food purchases. The amounts of protein, calcium, iron, and vitamins B_1, B_2 and C were calculated from food tables, and the survey considered only these six nutrients. Foodtable values, almost always, are higher than after-preparation losses; thus, the percentage of "poor" diets was probably higher than 20 percent. The 1965 survey showed that 30 percent of the diets were low in calcium and vitamins A and C. The survey did not look into overeating.

The real shocker came in 1969, when the U.S. Public Health Service released figures from a 12,000-person, 10-state study of people from all walks of life. More nutrients were evaluated by the survey, and blood and urine samples were taken. Gross vitamin deficiencies were confirmed by pathological examinations. Here are some of the results that had wide political and social repercussions: 20 percent of those surveyed had one or more essential nutrients below the minimum acceptable level; 19 percent were deficient in Vitamin B_2; 15 percent had subpar vitamin C levels; 13 percent were deficient in vitamin A; and 9 percent were deficient in vitamin B. One out of three children under six years of age had iron-deficiency anemia, and 4 percent of the same group of children were deficient in vitamin D. Nearly 5 percent of the total group had protein or calorie shortages and showed pot-belly and winged scapula. Five percent were also lacking in iodine and had enlarged thyroids. This survey was headed by Dr. Arnold Schaefer.

In December 1969 President Nixon convened the White House Conference on Food, Nutrition and Health. Programs for the poor and elderly were discussed; but nothing was offered to correct our foods, our soils, or the FDA's concept that the average diet is adequate.

Helping the poor eat better is a fine "moral" act, but few paid attention to that part of the survey showing nutritional problems among the affluent. Vitamin B_2 levels among people living below the poverty level ranged from 5.3 to 31.6 percent deficient in some states, but those above the poverty line averaged a deficiency of 23 percent.

Vitamin A levels in one state were similarly distributed; below the poverty line, 3.8 percent deficient; above the poverty line, 5.8 percent deficient. The moderately affluent and affluent averaged an 11 percent deficiency of vitamin C.

Larger government funded surveys are scheduled to be taken. The 1975 figures will be worse when the effects of greater processing and prolonged storage of foods are considered: processed foods accounted for 50 percent of our diet in 1970; they were only 10 percent in 1940.

In summing up our nutritional status, Dr. Jean Meyer of Harvard's Department of Nutrition and Chairman of the 1969 White House Conference reported in *Science* (April 21, 1972): "Malnutrition, whether caused by poverty or improper diet, contributes to the alarming health situation in the United States today. Since 1950, that portion of the Nation's income devoted to health services [has] risen from $12 billion to $70 billion. Yet, during the same period, there [has] been absolutely no increase in the life expectancy of males at age ten, and a very insignificant increase for women. Indeed—in almost thirty nations, life expectancies for adult males during this period were greater than they were in the United States."

Life span is not the preferred unit of measure, however. The number of years we live is not too important if they are miserable years; our goal is to live better longer. Yet 10 percent of us are anemic and 25 percent are overweight. More than half of the population doesn't eat well enough to be half-alive. Essentially the same is true in England, according to Dr. Geoffry Taylor of the Royal College of Physicians. Those of us who have experienced Supernutrition don't understand why people still condemn vitamin pills. What are they afraid of? Better health?

Now, to answer the question of what the average diet has done, consider the 1971 report by Dr. Edith Weir of the USDA. Dr. Weir estimated that if all American diets were improved to the RDA level (substantially deficient compared with the Supernutrition level), there would be dramatic improvements in at least nineteen major health problems and a half-million lives saved yearly.

Among the benefits forecast by Dr. Weir are the following estimates: 25 percent reduction in heart disease incidence and deaths, 20 percent reduction in cancer incidence and death, 10 million more elderly without health impairments, 15 to 20 percent fewer days per person lost from work due to respiratory infections, slashed arthritis incidence, diabetes and infant mortality reduced by half, and 3 million fewer children born with defects (see Table 16.1,

Chapter 16). The forecast is dramatic—but it is mild when compared to what Supernutrition can do. (See pages 190 and 191.)

Food Quality Does Depend on Soil Quality

Many people refuse to believe that soil quality affects food quality; they believe that a plant will extract what it needs from the soil. If the nutrient isn't there, then the plant won't grow as big. To them, a carrot is a carrot. This contention can be refuted by modern analytical chemistry, and many people have recently changed their minds. Even the FDA is in the process of moderating its views, but it seems to have two faces and a forked tongue on the issue.

In a June 1968 news release, the FDA quoted Dr. Fredrick J. Stare, once the chairman of the Department of Nutrition at Harvard University, as saying, "Fertilizers, regardless of the type, do not influence the nutrient composition of the plant in regard to its content of protein, fat, carbohydrate, or the various vitamins. These nutrients are influenced primarily by the genetic composition of the seed and the maturity of the plant at harvest."

Fertilizers *do,* however, influence the mineral composition of plants. The iodine content of the plant will vary with the iodine content of the soil; the same is also true of the essential trace elements, zinc, cobalt, and selenium. In an April 27, 1973, news release on selenium, the FDA stated that "levels naturally found in animal feed vary widely depending on the soil in which the feed crops were grown." The FDA news release went on to estimate that about 70 percent of the domestic corn and soybeans do not contain adequate selenium. (Soil quality is a factor that I consider very important; I have already discussed it in Chapter 2 and do again in Chapter 10 on heart disease and Chapter 13 on cancer.) The FDA release further pointed out that "such a deficiency can lead to decreased growth, disease and death of animals feeding on such crops." How about humans? (See Chapter 15.)

At one time there were selenium problems in Australia and New Zealand, but thanks to new fertilizers containing the element selenium, the problems are disappearing. There was also a problem in these countries in the past with a lack of cobalt. The cobalt deficiency resulted in reduced vitamin B_{12} (which has cobalt in its molecule) in grazing animals; of course, this led to diseased animals. In Australia and New Zealand this problem was eliminated when this essential micronutrient was added to fertilizers. Dr. Homer Hopkins of the USDA says, "The statement that the nutritional values of our crops are not significantly affected by either the soil or the kind of fertilizers used cannot be defended." Dr. Hopkins made that statement in a special FDA hearing known as the "Vitamin Hearings" during the late 1960s.

The FDA claims that it is not saying that the soil cannot cause variation in the nutritional value of food—or that there is no nutrient loss from cooking, storing, or transporting foods. The agency *is,* however, prohibiting unsupported generalizations about foods that may frighten or deceive consumers into buying dietary supplements. Thus, no claim can be made that an inadequate or deficient diet is due to the soil in which a food is grown.

Foods Rapidly Lose Nutrients

As other food-quality factors decrease with time, foods also lose nutrients during storage and shipping. Exposure to light and heat breaks up the sensitive vitamin molecules; they are destroyed and cannot be regenerated. The antioxidant vitamins, especially vitamin E, are destroyed by oxygen in the air. Some nutrients are volatile and evaporate during normal drying. The calculated intake of vitamins based on standard nutritional tables is inaccurate. Nutritionists normally take the values for raw foods and reduce them by 25 percent. This is not a true representation of the nutrient loss. As an example, peas cooked garden-fresh lose 56 percent of their vitamins by the time they are served; but canned peas lose 94 percent, and frozen peas lose 83 percent. The losses in each process are as follows:

Cooked fresh	56 percent in cooking
Canned	30 percent in the scalding process
	25 percent in the sterilization process
	27 percent in the liquor diffusion
	12 percent in reheating
Frozen	25 percent in the scalding process
	19 percent in the freezing process
	15 percent in the thawing process
	24 percent in cooking

Other inaccuracies in calculated vitamin intake result because food tables are rough averages at best, and they do not consider how much of a nutrient is available for absorption by the body. For example, the vitamin C content of potatoes fluctuates between 4 and 26 mg per 100 grams of potatoes. Nutritionists generally use the figure of 15 mg per 100 grams, which must be wrong one-half of the time, even for the raw potato. Another example of an inaccurate estimate of ingested nutrients may be found in the supposed vitamin C content of prepared cabbage. This vitamin C is not available to the body since it is chemically tied up in the form of ascorbinogen.

Fresh foods lose their nutrients rapidly because of enzymatic decomposition. Green vegetables lose nearly all their vitamin C in a few days when kept at room temperature. When buying foods at a market, especially a health-food store where trade may be slower, be sure the food is local-grown and fresh. Vegetables must be blanched (or scalded) before canning or freezing to destroy partially the enzymes that would otherwise decompose the vegetables; this scalding process also, however, destroys nutrients. The surviving enzymes must be deactivated by freezing or sterilization.

Even frozen foods continue to lose nutrients. At zero degrees F. more than 50 percent of the vitamin C can be lost from some frozen vegetables in slightly more than six months. Even at –5 degrees F., 20 percent of the vitamin C can be lost over the same period of time.

Food Processing Destroys Nutrients

Nearly everyone realizes that nutrients are lost during cooking, but how many realize that vitamins are lost during processing? Milling wheat into white flour removes vitamin E and most trace minerals. Nutrients are destroyed because of sensitivity to acid (pH), oxygen, light, heat, or a combination of these factors. Trace elements and enzymes speed this deterioration. A considerable part of the nutrient level can be lost, according to Dr. Frederic R. Senti of the USDA:

"Forty percent of the vitamin A, 100 percent of the vitamin C, 80 percent of the B complex, and 55 percent of the vitamin E can be lost during the processing of TV dinners."

Many feel that bread and cereals have been enriched by the return of three B vitamins (B_1, B_2, and niacin) to the white flour. But what about the more recently discovered B_{15} and B_{17} vitamins, and the seven other B vitamins (choline, inositol, paba, biotin, folic acid, B_{12}, and pantothenic acid)? Many people don't even know about them, so they are not aware that they may be missing from a processed-food diet.

Garden-fresh vegetables contain nearly twice the vitamin C of market-fresh vegetables, according to Agriculture Handbook No. 8.

There is an art to preparing foods in order to conserve nutrients:

Use little water, or add it back to the meal to keep water-soluble vitamins.

Don't destroy protein by needless frying.

FOOD AND NUTRITION BOARD,
NATIONAL ACADEMY OF SCIENCES-NATIONAL RESEARCH COUNCIL
RECOMMENDED DAILY DIETARY ALLOWANCES, Revised 1974

Designed for the maintenance of good nutrition of practically all healthy people in the U.S.A.

	Age (years)	Weight (kg)	Weight (lbs)	Height (cm)	Height (in)	Energy (kcal)	Protein (g)	Vitamin A Activity (IU)	Vitamin D (IU)	Vitamin E Activity (IU)
								Fat-Soluble Vitamins		
Infants	0.0-0.5	6	14	60	24	kg × 117	kg × 2.2	1,400	400	4
	0.5-1.0	9	20	71	28	kg × 108	kg × 2.0	2,000	400	5
Children	1-3	13	28	86	34	1300	23	2,000	400	7
	4-6	20	44	110	44	1800	30	2,500	400	9
	7-10	30	66	135	54	2400	36	3,300	400	10
Males	11-14	44	97	158	63	2800	44	5,000	400	12
	15-18	61	134	172	69	3000	54	5,000	400	15

	19-22	67	147	172	69	3000	54	5,000	400	15
	23-50	70	154	172	69	2700	56	5,000		15
	51 +	70	154	172	69	2400	56	5,000		15
Females	11-14	44	97	155	62	2400	44	4,000	400	12
	15-18	54	119	162	65	2100	48	4,000	400	12
	19-22	58	128	162	65	2100	46	4,000	400	12
	23-50	58	128	162	65	2000	46	4,000		12
	51 +	58	128	162	65	1800	46	4,000		12
Pregnant						+300	+30	5,000	400	15
Lactating						+500	+20	6,000	400	15

FOOD AND NUTRITION BOARD, NATIONAL ACADEMY OF SCIENCES-NATIONAL RESEARCH COUNCIL RECOMMENDED DAILY DIETARY ALLOWANCES, Revised 1974 (CONTINUED)

Designed for the maintenance of good nutrition of practically all healthy people in the U.S.A.

| | Water-Soluble Vitamins | | | | | | | Minerals | | | | | |
	Ascorbic Acid (mg)	Folacin (µg)	Niacin (mg)	Riboflavin (B₂) (mg)	Thiamin (B₁) (mg)	Vitamin B₆ (mg)	Vitamin B₁₂ (µg)	Calcium (mg)	Phosphorus (mg)	Iodine (µg)	Iron (mg)	Magnesium (mg)	Zinc (mg)
Infants	35	50	5	0.4	0.3	0.3	0.3	360	240	35	10	60	3
	35	50	8	0.6	0.5	0.4	0.3	540	400	45	15	70	5
Children	40	100	9	0.8	0.7	0.6	1.0	800	800	60	15	150	10
	40	200	12	1.1	0.9	0.9	1.5	800	800	80	10	200	10
	40	300	16	1.2	1.2	1.2	2.0	800	800	110	10	250	10
Males	45	400	18	1.5	1.4	1.6	3.0	1200	1200	130	18	350	15
	45	400	20	1.8	1.5	2.0	3.0	1200	1200	150	18	400	15

	45	400	20	1.8	1.5	2.0	3.0	800	800	140	10	350	15
	45	400	18	1.6	1.4	2.0	3.0	800	800	130	10	350	15
	45	400	16	1.5	1.2	2.0	3.0	800	800	110	10	350	15
Females	45	400	16	1.3	1.2	1.6	3.0	1200	1200	115	18	300	15
	45	400	14	1.4	1.1	2.0	3.0	1200	1200	115	18	300	15
	45	400	14	1.4	1.1	2.0	3.0	800	800	100	18	300	15
	45	400	13	1.2	1.0	2.0	3.0	800	800	100	18	300	15
	45	400	12	1.1	1.0	2.0	3.0	800	800	80	10	300	15
Pregnant	60	800	+2	+0.3	+0.3	2.5	4.0	1200	1200	125	18+	450	20
Lactating	80	600	+4	+0.5	+0.3	2.5	4.0	1200	1200	150	18	450	25

Table 3.1 Adapted from FOOD AND NUTRITION BOARD, NATIONAL ACADEMY OF SCIENCES-NATIONAL RESEARCH COUNCIL RECOMMENDED DAILY DIETARY ALLOWANCES, Revised 1974

Cook slowly and use low temperatures.

Keep food as cold as possible while storing.

Eat raw foods as much as possible.

Cook potatoes in their skins, leave beans and peas in their pods till cooking time.

Buy small quantities to avoid storage losses.

What Is a Balanced Diet?

Debate continues on what constitutes a balanced diet. My own conclusion is that a varied diet ensures that you will get the greatest number of nutrients and reduces the concentration of any one particular poison, i.e., food coloring, food preservatives, insecticides, etc. Try to eat from each of the *seven* (not *four*) major food groups each day. Each day's menu should include something from each of the following groups:

1. green and yellow vegetables
2. citrus fruits and tomatoes
3. potatoes, rice, and fruits
4. milk and milk products
5. meat, poultry, fish, and eggs
6. bread, flour, and cereals
7. butter

Try to eat an unprocessed, natural diet of the same foods that your ancestors ate. Your body has similar chemistry to your greatgrandparents', so you can probably do well on what they did well on.

How Often Should You Eat?

As to how often to eat—that is still a question. The best evidence, based on experience with my laboratory animals, is to eat *ab libitum* or "as you wish." Eat small meals 5 or 6 times daily. This prevents overloading or overworking your complicated digestion and transport system. It seems to put less stress on the organ reserves and your heart. It produces fewer harmful by-products. Using this system, each meal need not be a balanced meal, but each day should include a diverse and balanced diet.

Some argue that three square meals are best, and some even argue for one large meal. Many animals feast on a large kill and then don't eat again for days, but I don't think that this is best for modern man. Perhaps each of us does better with a schedule for eating that "feels" best for us, regardless of what the "experts" say. Most of us probably do better on at least three meals, including a good breakfast and dinner, with a small lunch and a snack or two. Some people cannot seem to tolerate a hearty breakfast, but this is an important meal because of the lack of nutrients ingested while you sleep. Try good breakfasts for a while and see if you can learn to tolerate better food than coffee, cigarettes, and white toast, pastry or doughnuts. The recommendations for calories, protein, and some vitamins and minerals of the National Research Council are given on the preceding page for reference only.

Good Nutrition Is Preventive Medicine

Perhaps people haven't been alarmed by our country's relatively poor health and nutrition because they feel that what exists is normal and good. It is not. Sickness is not normal. Many physicians think preventive medicine means frequent examinations to detect diseases in their early stages. It does not. Prevention means not getting to the first stages at all.

4

Controversies in Nutrition

The Supernutrition program is new. Although taking large amounts of vitamins is not new, an easy-to-follow plan for finding the optimum amount for each individual is. Because Supernutrition is new, you can expect rousing criticism of it—especially from those who have not read the program but respond to the concept alone.

The Supernutrition program charts a new path between two extremes—one, the archaic segment of the medical establishment, and the other those who believe that superhealth requires exotic foods. Because its concepts are between those of the two extreme groups, the Supernutrition program may be attacked by each extreme. Do not let their criticism discourage you; follow the plan and watch it produce indisputable results; ask the critics to explain your improved health and vitality; ask why *their* health is not as good.

Controversy can serve many useful purposes. It can call attention to an area that needs discussion; it can inspire others to do further research in the area; it can encourage government and private funding to underwrite further research and speed implementation of current findings. Controversies are commonplace in science, and some of them are about subjects critical to your health. Anything that affects your health is important to the Supernutrition plan, and in this chapter we will examine some of the more important controversies.

Theory and Fact

The scientific method is based on exacting logic that requires challenges and skepticism; progress requires fresh thinking and new evidence that answer all the questions that can be asked about the subject. Theories or data that cannot explain all observations or answer all questions cannot be accepted unequivocally; and even when such proof is presented, widespread acceptance lags considerably.

During the period of controversy many questions arise, and progress would be impossible without the freedom to challenge. Not too long ago, doctors were afraid of the consequences of speaking out against AMA policy. There are certainly as many controversies in medicine and science as there are in politics, art, or religion, all popular subjects for debate; but for some reason, people feel that although architects and economists may disagree scientists and physicians should not.

Controversy Precedes Change

The history of science is a chronicle of controversies. Claudius Galenus of Pergamus (A.D. 130–200) was harassed throughout his life for his anatomical findings and for his concept that blood, not spirits, was contained in the arteries. Vesalius (1514–1564) was removed from the faculty of the University of Padua when he published his *De Humani Corporis Fabrica* showing two hundred errors in the classic anatomical charts. William Harvey was ostracized in the 1600s when he described the circulation of blood. G. A. Borelli had to leave Messina in 1674 as he prepared his *De Motu Animalium* explaining body motion in terms of mechanical principles. Contemporaries were greatly angered by Albert von Haller who, in 1759, disproved the old concept that nerves were tubes that pumped "nerve fluid" into the muscles, causing them to bulge. For years no one took Anthony van Leeuwenhoek (1632–1723), a lens maker, seriously when he described what he saw with his invention, the microscope; his observations of life cycles did not end the popular spontaneous-generation theory. Louis Pasteur in 1862 and Robert Koch in 1875 were laughed at for talking of germs, bacteria, and disease. Austrian physician Ignaz Philipp Semmelweis was attacked in 1861 by his colleagues for suggesting that physicians should wash their hands before attending women giving birth. Dr. Zabdiel Boylston was almost hanged in Boston in 1721 as he attempted to thwart a smallpox epidemic by giving vaccinations of pox from infected cows. Although physicians in Europe were reporting success, American physicians were helping to pass laws that would imprison both the doctor administering and the patients submitting to vaccinations. The skeptics then, as now, are mostly from the medical establishment, a very conservative group when it comes to new ideas.

Today, the medical profession is busy fueling the controversies pertaining to diet and obesity, cholesterol and heart disease, vitamins and health. The AMA and the FDA feel that they must speak out on all controversies to protect the public, although sometimes their stand seems more protective of themselves.

A researcher who dares speak out against orthodoxy has much to lose, especially future funds, for funding committees hesitate to allot research grants to controversial scientists. When you examine the merits of a scientific debate, be sure to consider the source of each side's funds, the newness of the idea, the challenge to the established authorities, and other emotional issues besides the data selected for publication. **Don't count on scientists or physicians being open-minded.** They, like everyone else, have their prejudices. They find it difficult, if not impossible, to discard or change prevailing concepts.

Doctors Are Not Nutrition Experts

Many people think that physicians are experts in nutrition because they seem to know about everything affecting human health. Well, physicians are great for saving lives and relieving pain, but very few are taught to *prevent* illness. They are body repairmen: hard-working and dedicated, they are highly trained to diagnose illness, administer drugs, and perform surgical procedures. Their schooling demands so much time for learning about drugs and the complications of drug interactions, however, that they have little time for studying nutrition. What scant information they do receive is usually outdated and less detailed than that which nurses receive in their training. I realize this may be hard to believe, but in 1970 when Professor Richard Ahrens of the University of Maryland School of Nutrition proposed more nutrition courses for the School of Medicine, he was turned down on the grounds that the medical students needed to devote still more time in their crowded schedules to learn the latest information about more and more drugs. I do not mean to belittle the medical profession. When you are sick, see a doctor—at once; don't try to treat an illness with nutrition first and go to a doctor after you have discovered that nutrition doesn't work. Proper nutrition will help any treatment prescribed by the physician, but good nutrition alone will not prevent all diseases. Supernutrition will reduce the *incidence* of all diseases, but it cannot prevent all diseases all the time in all people. You should see a physician regularly, even when you are super-healthy.

A barrage of sex-advice books written in the late 1960s and early 1970s pointed out that while most people had heard that they should consult a doctor about sexual problems, few doctors had had formal training in advising people in all areas of sexual dysfunction. Some of my physician friends are exceptions, but others know less about sex than today's partially informed teen-agers. A similar situation prevails in nutrition. If physicians don't receive extensive training in medical school, how can they be qualified to speak out so emphatically on nutrition? A very small percentage specialize in preventive medicine, but most better fit the description given by Dr. Julian B. Schorr of the New York Blood Center, in a January 1971 *Wall Street Journal* article by Mary Bralove: **"Often doctors are trained in nutrition by doctors who heard it from another doctor who made it up."** Yet they believe what they say is true and get upset when they are contradicted.

The average physician is not a nutrition imbecile; he can recognize overweight, gross malnutrition, and other nutritional problems. But physicians usually get out of their area of expertise when they talk about dietary cholesterol, subclinical scurvy, and long-term dietary studies. *Time* (December 18, 1972, p. 75) quoted Dr. Michael Latham of Cornell University's Graduate School of Nutrition: "Nine out of ten doctors in New York City would give wrong answers to dietary questions." Senator Richard S. Schweiker of Pennsylvania, a member of the Senate Committee on Nutrition and Human Needs, said (in *Prevention,* October 1972), "I am particularly concerned about the need for better practical nutrition education for our doctors." It was Senator Schweiker who introduced Senate bill S.3696, Nutritional Medical Education Act of 1972, which would authorize federal grants from the Department of Health, Education and Welfare to medical schools to permit them to plan, develop, and implement programs of nutrition education within their curricula.

Senator Schweiker wrote in the same *Prevention* article: "The advice of family doctors carries a great deal of weight with most people. But, unfortunately, many doctors simply do not receive sufficient training in nutrition while they are at medical school to enable them to give the sound advice on nutrition that we urgently need. . . .

"Because of the importance of sound nutritional practices to the maintenance of health and prevention of medical disorders, doctors must have enough knowledge of the relationship between nutrition and good health to advise patients how to help prevent medical problems from occurring."

The 1969 White House Conference on Food, Nutrition and Health concluded, "The effectiveness of physicians in providing optimal care for the many patients who have diseases with an important nutritional component is dependent in considerable part on the kind of nutrition teaching offered them at medical school and thereafter. *At the present time, nutrition teaching in medical schools and in teaching hospitals is woefully inadequate.*" (Italics added.)

One medical school, according to Schweiker's article, surveyed student and local physicians to determine their opinion on the inclusion of nutrition courses in the school curriculum. They found that younger doctors felt that they did not know as much about nutrition as they should and would like to learn more; in contrast, older doctors not only didn't know much about nutrition but also didn't feel that additional education was needed. Medical schools with nutrition departments are rare. Most don't even offer separate courses in nutrition but mingle what little they do offer in an elementary chemistry course. **Not one medical school can honestly say it teaches nutrition seriously.** Yet, physicians asked to comment on nutrition often speak with all the authority they can muster and utter statements like, "Forget the baloney about vitamins and worry about being fat." Half-truths can kill!

It would help reduce the confusion if physicians also knew more about chemistry and biology. If they knew more chemistry, they would worry more about the vitamin disappearance from foods because of soil depletion, and instability during shipping, storage, and preparation; certainly, we no longer eat many locally grown foods.

If physicians knew more chemistry, they would realize that cholesterol deposits on arteries are not just simple precipitates from the blood. When cholesterol plaques (patches or deposits) are formed in the arteries, cholesterol is scavenged from the blood, regardless of the blood-cholesterol level; but it is some *other* factor which makes conditions right for the plaque formation. If physicians knew more biology, they would realize that it is the redundant feedback mechanisms which control the production and removal of cholesterol, not how much cholesterol we eat. Blood-cholesterol levels increase when we eat too many calories—of any type. And when we are deficient in vitamin C, cholesterol isn't converted to bile as it normally is.

There would be less confusion, too, if vitamin C (ascorbic acid) and vitamin E (tocopherol) were not thought of as vitamins alone, but also considered in terms of the larger role that they play in the body. Ascorbic acid is a chemical needed for many purposes besides preventing scurvy; most animals manufacture this chemical in their bodies, but man does not because he has undergone a genetic mutation. Dr. Irwin Stone, author of the *Healing Factor: Vitamin C Against Disease* (Grosset and Dunlap, 1972), has traced this mutation back sixty million years to a common ancestor of man and primates who suffered the mutation that eliminated an important enzyme from its biochemical makeup. Tocopherol (vitamin E) can act as a general antioxidant in addition to any specific mechanism that classifies it a vitamin; therefore, we have need for greater quantities than are implied by the word "vitamin" and its strict definition. "Vitamin" refers to the small quantity of a compound that is needed by our body, but not manufactured within our body. Vitamins generally act as catalysts, speeding up many reactions without being consumed in the process. Ascorbic acid and tocopherol, however, do not fit this definition. Greater quantities of them are needed, for they *are* consumed.

As suggested earlier, both physicians and biochemists can reduce the confusion if they keep in mind that not everything is yet known about nutrition, and that some recent findings may alter previous concepts. An open mind is needed by all, not dogmatic opinions from out-of-date "experts."

Americans Do Not Eat Nutritiously

The controversy over food and food quality (or rather the lack of it) is one thing, but the controversy over even admitting that malnutrition exists in America is another. It is not only malnutrition that is a problem, it is also undernutrition and overweight that should concern us. People today are busy creating nutrient deficiencies that are bound to result in serious illnesses later. America's teen-agers, right now, are building future misery for themselves; an abuse of health by the young usually doesn't show up for twenty to thirty years.

According to Dr. E. Cheraskin, chief of the Department of Oral Medicine of the University of Alabama in a July 1974 letter to me, "At the present rate of increase in sickness in this country, one may expect all persons now 17–24-years-old to be ill by 1997. I would suspect that this would be largely a function of dietary intake."

The Supernutrition program takes such previous abuse into account and helps repair the damage done through years of undernutrition by utilizing the proper levels of nutrients as restoratives. Some damage, however, cannot be repaired.

5

Recent Discoveries in Nutrition

Even relatively simple discoveries about nutrition are still being made. There is a high probability that several vitamins remain to be isolated. Vitamin Q, which aids in blood clotting, was discovered as recently as 1972; and who knows what will be discovered this year or next? Will new discoveries change present concepts in nutrition? Will they solve present problems? Even with major problems to solve, a great deal *is* known for certain about nutrition; but getting the correct answers is difficult with so much misinformation circulating. To what source do you turn for the correct answers?

A most significant discovery has recently been made by three researchers independently of each other; its importance has been overlooked by many scientists, and the physicians haven't even heard of it yet. The discovery concerns the value of large doses of vitamins, not because of what the vitamins do through their chemical reactions, but because of what the vitamins do just by being in the body. Everyone has been looking at how vitamins work in "doing their specific job"; but until recently, no one has investigated what the vitamins do when "not working." It has always been assumed that vitamins not in "use" were just passively stored; it turns out that while these vitamins are "just" being stored, they are performing extremely valuable functions.

Vitamins Protect Cell Membranes Against Cancer-Causing Chemicals

Dr. Lionel Leong of the University of Minnesota and Dr. Dan Nebert of the National Institutes of Health, while studying the activation of cancer by chemicals in 1968, discovered that vitamins protect cells by coating the cell-membrane receptors. The cancer-causing chemical (carcinogen) is activated by an enzyme called Aryl Hydrocarbon Hydroxylase (AHH). Enzymes work only on chemicals having structures that three-dimensionally "fit" or "match" the enzyme shape—in a lock-and-key fashion. Some vitamins have structures that can either tie up enzymes that activate carcinogens or coat the receptor portion of the cell membrane where the activated carcinogen normally does its damage. Therefore, the more "excess" vitamins available to interfere with this cancer-activation process, the less chance there is of getting cancer. This is recent research that has been confirmed in but three or four labs, and it is still too new to be accepted as fact. It is, however, healthy speculation.

Equally important is the conclusion that Dr. Clive Bradbeer and his colleagues at the University of Virginia School of Medicine reached in 1973: "excess" vitamins can prevent viruses from invading living cells. They have found that viruses and other destructive substances gain entrance to cells by adapting themselves in such a manner as to be able to use the vitamin B_{12} receptor site. If these receptor sites are saturated with vitamin B_{12}, the cell is protected against the onslaught of harmful substances. **Dr. Bradbeer speculated in** *Laboratory Management* **(November 1973) that "human disease exists where viruses** use the same transport system as nutrients to gain access to a cell. Claims of protection against cold viruses with large doses of vitamin C may be an example of this phenomenon in humans."

This type of passive protection cannot be predicted by the "active" role of the vitamin. It may be "cute" for some nutritionists to say that Americans have the most expensive urine in the world because "excess" vitamins are eliminated in urine, but they have missed a very important point. "Excess" vitamins do more than enrich the sewers.

Vitamins Deactivate Cancer-Causing Chemicals

Besides the passive protection of vitamins against cancer, some vitamins, especially vitamins C and E, may play an *active* role against cancer. Chapter 13 discusses several of these active roles—including membrane protection, free-radical scavenging, chromosome protection, and the prevention of carcinogen formation.

Evidence of Yet Undiscovered Vitamins

Laboratory experiments with animals give evidence that certain factors present in liver possess vitamin activity. Experiments have been conducted in which animals given all the known vitamins do not survive long. Other animals, similarly treated, but also given liver or various liver extracts, live normally. Unknown agents, vital to health, must exist, and are stored in the liver.

Two classic experiments have made this point. In 1970 Dr. Roger Williams of the University of Texas Clayton Research Foundation found that returning the few known B vitamins to white-flour bread ("enriching" it) did not suffice for good nutrition. Laboratory animals (sixty-four weanling rats) fed "enriched" bread died or 'had severely stunted growth because of malnutrition. Forty were dead within ninety days; the rest had stunted growth. Similar

animals fed whole-grain bread were normal. All but three
thrived. Stripping vitamins away when de-germing the
grain to increase shelf life removes vitamins unknown or
unrecognized by the creators of "enriched" bread.

In the *Proceedings of the Society of Experimental Biology and Medicine,* July 1951, a second experiment, conducted by Dr. B. H. Ershoff, was described. He divided
laboratory animals into three groups; the first group received an ordinary diet, the second group received additional B vitamins from brewer's yeast, and the third group
received the conventional diet plus desiccated liver. The
experiment was divided into two parts, growth and endurance. The second group grew a little faster than the first
group, but the third group grew significantly (15 percent)
faster. To test the endurance or fatigue rate, the animals
were placed in a water tank to swim until exhausted. The
first group lasted an average of 13 minutes and the second
group a tenth of a second longer. The third group, twelve
rats, had three that swam for 63, 83, and 87 minutes.
The remaining nine rats were still swimming vigorously
after two hours, but were removed because Dr. Ershoff
had to close up the lab for the day. Liver must contain unknown factors needed for both growth and endurance.

Vitamin B$_{15}$ Wrongly Excluded from U.S. Vitamin Formulations

Vitamin B$_{15}$ is a vitamin researched widely in the USSR; it
is rarely listed in American texts. Why is it that the Russian
literature contains reports of many double-blind tests showing
that vitamin B$_{15}$, in the form of pangamic acid or calcium
pangamate, is extremely effective in treating circulatory disorders, premature aging, heart disease, emphysema, and liver
diseases, while it is not allowed in vitamin formulations in the
United States? It is not a problem of toxicity; the FDA does
not believe it is effective.

Vitamin B_{15} is involved in oxygen transport and helps nourish all cells with oxygen. Russian athletes have found that 300 mg of calcium pangamate daily has helped heal many muscle injuries, especially injuries to the legs. One popular vitamin preparation for athletes in Russia is AEVIT, which contains vitamins A, E, and B_{15}. Vitamin B_{15} was isolated by an American physician and biochemist, E. T. Krebs, but probably the only way that you will get it in the United States is in your diet. You can buy several brands of vitamin B_{15} in Russia, Germany, Mexico, and elsewhere; but in the United States you had better include whole-grain cereals, liver, or brewer's yeast in your diet to get this vitamin. Of course, that's a good idea anyway.

Vitamin U Prevents Ulcers

The Russians have isolated a new vitamin (metioninic acid) called vitamin U (for ulcers). It will cure and prevent ulcers and many other gastric disorders. Its discoverer, Dr. Vasily Bukin, isolated the vitamin from dairy curds. Vitamin U normalizes the mucous membrane of the stomach and intestine and has cured small ulcers in thirty to forty days. Preliminary results indicate a positive effect on heart disease and some skin problems.

Vitamin Q Essential to Clotting

Vitamin Q was isolated from a soybean extract in 1972 by Dr. Armand J. Quick of the Medical College of Wisconsin. Vitamin Q, somewhat like vitamin K, is essential to the blood's clotting mechanism. It is still so new that its exact chemical structure isn't known. Dr. Quick has had good results using vitamin Q with twenty-five patients who had clotting or bleeding disorders. He has found the vitamin to be especially effective against hereditary hemorrhagic telangiectasia, a condition characterized by bleeding from capillary lesions. Unfortunately, the classic hemophilias have not responded to vitamin Q.

Vitamin Supplements a Must for Dieters

Because of difficult schedules and other strains on the body, many people have "special" needs that require better diets than the ones they eat.

Dieting places a stress on the body. People diet, not because they are overnourished, but because they are over-fed and overweight. They are not active enough to burn off the calories they consume. Many of their foods are high in calories but are incomplete as far as other nutrients go. When they reduce their calories to reduce their weight, the nutrients *already* lacking are virtually eliminated. **Vitamin and other nutrient supplementation is a must for dieters.**

"The Pill" Requires a Companion Vitamin

Another large group having needs not supplied by the "standard" diet are women regularly taking birth-control pills. According to a 1972 Knight News Service article, one of the effects of taking the pill, reported by Dr. Daphne A. Roe, head of Cornell University's School of Nutrition, is a reduction of folic acid, a member of the B-complex, in the blood. Decreased tissue levels of vitamin C have also been reported in women on the pill. Dr. Roe claims, "The theoretical danger is frightening because folic acid deficiencies in laboratory animals result in many types of malformation."

Recently several physicians (including Dr. John Linden-baum of Harlem Hospital, Nancy Whitehead of New York University, and Franklin Reyner of Valley Stream, N.Y.) have detected an increasing presence of enlarged, mal-formed cells in the cervix of one-fifth of the women taking the pill, and occasionally the abnormal cells have been mistaken for cancerous cells in procedures such as the Pap smear (*Journal of American Medical Association*, 1973). Researchers are finding other nutrient abnormalities allegedly caused by the pill; vitamins B_6 and B_{12} are also depleted in the blood, often resulting in premenstrual depression. In my opinion, women taking contraceptive pills should also be taking high-potency B-complex plus vitamin C pills, liver, and lots of leafy green vegetables. If a woman is on the pill *and* dieting, her nutritional need is urgent. (Adding celery and leafy green vegetables helps conquer hunger and adds more folic acid to the diet.)

Pregnancy Creates Additional Demands for Vitamins

Pregnant women need at least 10 percent more vitamins and minerals, according to Dr. William McGanity, head of the Department of Obstetrics and Gynecology at the University of Texas. Since the most important period of fetal development comes during the first weeks after conception, women should not wait until they are well along in their pregnancy to improve their nutrition. Most gynecologists immediately prescribe a vitamin-mineral supplement for their patients. The dosages are generally considered high by physicians, but they are only medium by Supernutrition standards. As a rule, most formulations for pregnant women approximate the guidelines given in the RDA for pregnant or lactating women in Table 3.1. If you are already taking higher amounts of vitamins when you become pregnant, there is no logical reason to lower your intake. You should, of course, be more conscientious about your selection of foods during pregnancy; however, pregnancy is no time to experiment with vitamins. Don't try to find your Supernutrition point or suddenly raise your vitamin intake dramatically unless you have been undernourished. In review, the best logic suggests that pregnant women previously undernourished would do well to take the vitamins suggested by the Supernutrition program. Pregnant women taking vitamins in moderation should check with their physicians to see which is the better for them: their standard program or the Supernutrition program. Those that *normally* take vitamins approaching the Supernutrition level should continue to do so. Avoid radical changes in vitamin intake and avoid all medication that you safely can.

Pregnancy or lactation creates a greater demand for all nutrients. Nature tries to feed the baby first, often at the expense of the mother; for instance, calcium used for the baby's bones may create a drain on the calcium that otherwise would go into the mother's teeth. If you are trying to keep your weight down during pregnancy, do not do it at the expense of good nutrition. The vital link between vitamins and intelligence and personality is, of course, established during pregnancy.

Women Need Additional Iron
Prior to Menopause

Of course, all women not past menopause need more iron to build blood. As a rule, most of these women get only one half of the iron they need to replace and build blood. Perhaps this is the reason that many women complain of tiredness and nervousness. Because of the hidden shortcomings of modern foods, women not past menopause need to fortify their diets with additional iron, extra vitamin C to help absorb the iron, and the B-complex vitamins to help build the blood. These vitamin supplements will return many women to their vigorous and vivacious "normal" selves, so that they can say good-bye to tranquilizers and amphetamines. Preferred forms are ferrous gluconate, ferrous lactate, and ferrous peptonate; a form less preferred is ferrous sulfate. Another problem of today's diet is hypoglycemia. Check Chapter 12 to see if hypoglycemia is the hidden culprit that is causing you to be tired and jittery.

Modern Life-Styles Require
Vitamin Supplements

More women are entering the labor force and have dual roles as worker and housekeeper. Their schedules are often too hectic to plan and cook good meals. People living by themselves tend to skip or skimp on meals; they have toast and coffee or tea rather than a good breakfast; they eat TV dinners rather than dirty a lot of pans and dishes. Older people have limited funds and eat less and less as prices go up.

Smoking destroys many vitamins in the body. Smokers' lungs use up vitamins A and E when filled with smoke, and the blood and tissue levels of vitamin C decrease. Each cigarette smoked destroys an estimated 25 mg of vitamin C; this may be as much as many people obtain in their diet. The RDA is only 45 mg.

People with prolonged illnesses or those taking medication for long periods increase their needs for vitamins and minerals. Those with heart disorders requiring nitroglycerin, diabetics requiring insulin, epileptics requiring dilantin, and reformed addicts on methadone maintenance are a few such examples. Drugs can decrease the appetite, impair the absorption and deplete the blood of nutrients, or interfere with the body's mechanism for using vitamins and minerals. **Temporary problems such as fever, infection, and surgery require extra vitamins.**

Children and teen-agers, even though growing rapidly, do not need extra nutrients if they eat well. But how many do? Candy cereals, sweet snacks, and carbonated, flavored-sugar-water drinks spoil their appetites for fresh fruits and vegetables. Athletes and hard workers need extra nutrition; so do formula-fed infants. Congressmen and businessmen are often more concerned with economics than gastronomics. Rush, rush, rush! A fast breakfast, a business luncheon, and a late warmed-over dinner is the usual diet regimen. The poor cannot afford to eat properly; the rich often eat the wrong foods or overeat, and then they become dieters.

Even those who eat the proper number of calories for their activity level may be in trouble if they are sedentary. The human body is designed to function on a higher activity level than modern man does. Thus, historically, humans have consumed more calories and more nutrients along with the calories. Now that we are less active and eat less food to maintain proper weight, we miss the extra nutrients we received before. Of course, all those nutrients aren't needed; some of them were consumed because of the greater activity of our ancestors. But some *are* needed and are now missed. As we lower our activity, we concentrate our food volume and need to supplement some nutrients. Also, we eat more processed foods and foods that are stored longer, so that we lack those nutrients destroyed or removed in processing or deteriorated during shipping and storage. Even fiber can be removed; although it is not a nutrient, fiber is needed to maintain regularity, to remove cholesterol from the body, and even perhaps to prevent cancer of the colon. Even our "fresh" foods are grown in soils increasingly depleted of minerals, force-grown with high-nitrogen fertilizers, and sprayed with poisonous chemicals. As a result, our foods are becoming deficient in selenium and zinc; and our bodies consume vitamins fighting off the effects of pesticides that have been used.

Who is there left that eats nutritiously?

Vitamin C
and the Common Cold

Verification of the value of the Supernutrition program is easily demonstrated with vitamin C; perhaps this is primarily because vitamin C is more than a vitamin; it is actually a liver metabolite (a product normally formed in metabolism) that is absent in man. Most animals manufacture their own vitamin C. Humans, along with a few other animals, are exceptions. We cannot manufacture ascorbic acid (the chemical name for vitamin C) out of glucose (stored sugar), which is abundant in our bodies. Most animals, under comfortable, nonstress conditions, make ascorbic acid out of glucose, in a human equivalent of between 2 and 10 grams normally, and over 20 grams when under stress. We cannot because, some 60 million years ago, our ancestors experienced a genetic mutation that eliminated an enzyme, L-gulonolactone oxidase, which is required to produce ascorbic acid out of glucose. Fortunately, our ancestors had a ready supply of ascorbic acid because of the abundance of berries and fruits in their diet. In those days, more calories were needed to support their vigorous activity; thus they consumed copious amounts of foods and received ample ascorbic acid.

Pioneers of Vitamin C Therapy

I am indebted to those who brought the idea of larger doses of vitamin C to my attention. Dr. Pauling brought "respectability" to modern, large-scale tests of vitamin C. But he was not the pioneer in this area. Credit should also go to Dr. Irwin Stone and to Dr. Fred R. Klenner. Dr. Stone has researched vitamin C since before 1940 and spent ten years compiling an excellent book, *The Healing Factor: Vitamin C Against Disease.* Dr. Stone has done a commendable job of explaining the genetic mutation that occurred in our prehistoric ancestors and of clarifying the relationship of vitamin C to a wide variety of human ills, showing that vitamin C is an important part of the body's defense mechanism.

Dr. Klenner, a North Carolina physician, has been since the 1950s a pioneer in using massive injections of vitamin C to detoxify poisons and drug overdoses as well as cure bacterial infections. Since 1960, several hundred of his patients have regularly taken 10 grams or more of vitamin C daily for periods of between three and fifteen years, without side effects. He finds that 90 percent of these patients are free from colds and feels that the others simply need more vitamin C. Dr. Klenner may be right about the latter, but it might also be that they are deficient in vitamin A or other nutrients. In any case, the Supernutrition program is designed to find which deficiency, if any, you have and to compensate for it.

Linus Pauling and the Common Cold

I respect Dr. Pauling's intellect, nerve, and his dedication to people. I do not want to imply that winning awards makes a person's arguments sounder, because awards can be given for political reasons rather than for merit. It is, however, important to tell you a little about Dr. Pauling. He was awarded a Nobel prize in chemistry in 1954 for his contributions to the theory of chemical bonding and the elucidation of complex structures. His book, *The Nature of the Chemical Bond and the Structure of Molecules and Crystals: An Introduction to Modern Structural Chemistry,* was a milestone in chemistry and still is a "chemist's Bible."

To realize the impact of that single book, consider that it was the most cited book in the literature of physics and chemistry between the years 1961 and 1972, receiving 1,514 citations, 50 percent more than the next most cited book.

In his book *Vitamin C and the Common Cold,* Dr. Pauling recommended from 1 to 5 grams, or more, of vitamin C daily, depending on how the dose is divided and on the person's individual needs. If signs of an oncoming cold appear, such as sniffles or scratchy throat, he suggested one should take ½ to 1 gram immediately and repeat that amount each hour until the impending cold was thwarted. If the cold was not thwarted by bedtime, he suggested 2 grams one half hour before and another 2 grams just prior to retiring.

Dr. Pauling's advice was derived from his study of the scientific literature, his own personal experience, and that of his colleagues. He admitted that he had not performed large-scale studies because of insufficient facilities, but called on other researchers to do so. He did not, however, rely on brief abstracts of these published reports, as so many "busy" researchers do, but studied all the details. He extracted information sometimes overlooked by the abstractors, and he sometimes interpreted the data better than the original investigator had.

Studies Confirming Pauling

Although many simply criticized Dr. Pauling's assertions, others scurried to their labs to refute or confirm his findings scientifically. The main thrust of the research for biochemists was to examine the need for vitamin C in animal and man, while physicians examined the possible effect of vitamin C on colds.

Some researchers, such as Drs. Irving Stone and Man-Li S. Yew of the University of Texas, were curious about the inconsistencies in the recommendations of different groups within the National Research Council. The Committee on Animal Nutrition, in their *Nutrient Requirements for Laboratory Animals* (Pub. No. 990, National Academy of Science), recommends 3,850 mg of vitamin C for every 154 pounds of body weight for monkeys, our closest mammalian relative, who also cannot make their own vitamin C. A gorilla in the wild eats 5 grams of vitamin C daily. Yet the Human Nutrition group in 1974 dropped the recommended daily allowance from 60 to 45 mg for adults.

Dr. Stone's search of the literature revealed the following amounts of vitamin C synthesized, on a daily basis, in animals: rat (unstressed), 1.8 grams; rat (another study), 4.9 grams; rat (stressed), 15.2 grams; mouse, 19.3 grams; rabbit, 15.8 grams; goat, 13.3 grams; dog, 2.8 grams; cat, 2.8 grams. Have you ever noticed that your cat or dog gets a cold only every other year or so, while the total family colds may average five or six a year?

Dr. Yew tested guinea pigs, who, like humans, do not synthesize their own vitamin C. He studied the requirements of vitamin C in terms of growth, wound healing, and surgical stress. The results indicate that 5 mg of vitamin C per 100 grams of guinea pig (equivalent to 1.5 grams per 66-pound human youngster) were necessary for the animals to grow well, heal quickly, and recover from stress. Dr. Yew concluded at the National Academy of Sciences October 1972 meeting, "The enormous discrepancy, nearly forty-fold, between this amount [see above] and that recommended by the Food and Nutrition Board calls attention to an important public health problem related to the best development of young people."

One more point to consider before examining the ultimate proof—recent large-scale double-blind tests—is that **there have been no papers published in scientific literature** refuting or taking issue with the scientific validity of Dr. Pauling's conclusions concerning vitamin C.

The first favorable report (June 1972) did not come from Dr. Pauling's American colleagues but from the University of Strathclyde in Glasgow, Scotland. Since this report was favorable but not based on large-scale tests, it may have been a major influence on others to test the hypothesis.

Drs. Mary Clegg and Sheila Charleston conducted a test (in 1972) with 90 volunteers, 47 of whom received a gram of vitamin C daily and 43 of whom received a placebo. Those receiving the vitamin C daily had nearly 50 percent fewer colds than the control group. The test was conducted over fifteen weeks during the winter months with the control group getting 80 colds and the vitamin C group 44 colds (and even these colds were milder). The cold-duration differences were dramatic. For example, the control group had 38 colds lasting four days (compared to twelve in the vitamin C group), and 26 colds persisting for five days (as opposed to only five in the vitamin C group). Other colds (27 in the control group versus 16 in the vitamin C group) were of lesser duration. The researchers suggested that their findings are so conclusive that they need perform no further testing. As far as they are concerned, large dosages of vitamin C help prevent the common cold.

Three months later, the *Journal of the Canadian Medical Association* published the confirming results of a large-scale double-blind study specifically designed to test Dr. Pauling's claims. The researchers, Drs. T. W. Anderson, D. B. W. Reid, and G. H. Beaton of the University of Toronto, found to their surprise that there was a statistically significant difference between the two groups in the number of subjects who remained free of illness throughout the study period. Furthermore, the subjects receiving 1 gram of vitamin C experienced approximately 30 percent fewer total days lost from work than those receiving the placebo, and this difference was statistically highly significant. (Refer to Figure 1.1 to visualize the impact of vitamin C on your total health.) The investigators were honest sci-

entists and admitted their scientific skepticism. Dr. Beaton
had already published a review, in the same journal, highly
critical of Dr. Pauling's book. However, the researchers
reported, "Our finding that [non-working days of] disability
was substantially less in the vitamin C group was entirely
unexpected and may have important theoretical and prac-
-tical implications." The diverse group of 818 subjects in
the study were told to take four tablets when they felt a
cold coming on, and otherwise one a day. The subjects
were divided into two groups: one group received 1 gram
of vitamin C, the other group received a placebo; neither
they nor the researchers knew at the time which group
received which tablets. The vitamin C group had fewer
colds, as well as reduced severity; but the conservative
researchers felt that the statistical difference wasn't large
enough to make conclusive claims about the number of
colds—only the severity of the colds and work time lost.
The facts remain that the symptoms are less severe, so
much so that fewer people "have colds."

In March 1973, in Dublin, Ireland, a study was published on the effect of smaller doses of vitamin C on colds
over a very long period. A team of researchers, led by
Dr. Cedric W. M. Wilson of Dublin University's Department of Pharmacology, conducted an eight-year study at
four Dublin boarding schools. With a low level of 200 to
500 mg of vitamin C daily, the severity of colds was significantly reduced (a 50 percent reduction), although the
incidence of colds was not reduced significantly. Dr. Wilson stated, "When maintained at high enough levels, there
is no doubt in my mind that vitamin C has a prophylactic
effect against colds."

The fourth published test of Dr. Pauling's claims was
conducted by Drs. J. L. Coulehan, K. S. Reisinger, K. D.
Rogers, and D. W. Bradley and was described in the
January 3, 1973 issue of the *New England Journal of
Medicine*. The study was a double-blind test of 641 children at a Navajo boarding school conducted over a four-
teen-week period. Those given 1 or 2 grams of vitamin C
had fewer days of illness—34 percent in an older-child
group and 28 percent in a younger-child group. The study

concluded, "Significantly more [of those] children on vitamin C had no sick days observed. In addition, children [treated] with higher blood vitamin C levels had fewer symptomatic days noted than those with lower levels." The results might have been even more impressive if it were not for the fact that for some reason the blood content of vitamin C in a placebo group of older boys also increased —during one month (March) of the study when many viruses are common. This may have reflected dietary improvements or the boys may have been switching some tablets around. Also of interest is the fact that when those in a vitamin C group did get colds, they had fewer symptoms; 40 percent had fewer days of two or more symptoms. In March of the study period, those children with higher levels of vitamin C in their blood had 46 percent fewer sick days than those children with lower blood levels of vitamin C. Twice as many children on vitamin C had no cold symptoms at all (a 100% improvement).

In a formal presentation at an August 1973 symposium at Stanford University by Dr. R. H. Colby of Stockton State College in Pomona, New Jersey, he stated that those taking a gram of vitamin C daily had only half as many colds as the control group. His double-blind study had involved 107 adults, but because of the smaller number of subjects it is not viewed as highly significant by statisticians.

"There is no doubt that vitamin C is a great help in reducing the risk of catching a cold," according to Dr. Brian Sabiston, who conducted a test for the Canadian Defense Research Board. The test conditions involved the dual stresses of eating only army rations while living in tents in subzero Arctic weather for two weeks. Fifty-six soldiers received vitamin C in two daily doses of 500 mg; another 56 received placebos. Vitamin C reduced the cold incidence to half. Twenty-five percent of the control group caught colds; less than 11 percent of the vitamin C group did. Of those catching colds, those taking vitamin C had 50 percent less nausea and fever.

Several other studies have been reported at scientific meetings, but they have not been published at the time of this writing; they correlated well with the published tests reported here. There are no contradicting reports. **It no longer is a question as to whether vitamin C prevents or reduces cold symptoms, but how it does so.** Scientists still may debate the semantics as to whether only the cold symptoms or the cold itself is prevented. Evidence at this time points to prevention and cure of the cold itself.

7

Megavitamin Therapy Cures Mental and Emotional Disorders

The amazing success in curing the mentally confused by using large doses of vitamins is another example of the Supernutrition principle. Megavitamin therapy, the popular name given to the technique of Dr. Abram Hoffer (former director of psychiatric research, University Hospital, Saskatoon, Saskatchewan) and Dr. Humphrey Osmond (New Jersey Neuro-Psychiatric Institute, Princeton, New Jersey), preceded Dr. Pauling's orthomolecular medicine. In 1968 Dr. Pauling published his initial article on orthomolecular psychiatry in *Science* magazine. Megavitamin therapy had suffered from great criticism and skepticism from its start in Canada in 1952, but when Dr. Pauling championed the concept, it received more respectful attention. Yet today, after more than twenty years' success with more than thirty thousand schizophrenics, alcoholics, addicts, and autistics, there are still those who denounce the concept.

Megavitamin therapy derives its name from *mega,* meaning great (as in huge or "great" doses). Typical programs include 1 to 8 grams of niacinamide, 1 to 3 grams of vitamin C, 200 mg of pantothenic acid, and 150 to 450 mg of vitamin B_6. How can these large doses of vitamins relieve mental and emotional disturbances, especially those caused, at least in part, by inherited chemical imbalance? To hear some psychiatrists talk, you have to be nuts to take large doses of vitamins in the first place.

Mental Disorientation and the B-Complex Vitamins

Let's begin by examining the problems of mental disorientation and then look at the mode of action of the B-complex vitamins. Mental disorientation arises when an individual misinterprets the signals from his senses; the chemical reactions and electrical impulses produced by the senses go awry on the way to the brain or in the brain. People with healthy body chemistry interpret the senses correctly, but the mentally confused often see a distorted world with weird sounds. They have difficulty with time perception and logical thought processes; they may see others as having piercing eyes, strange pulsating faces, or glowing halos around them; when they close their eyes, they may continue to see strange things and hear sounds that aren't there; their minds occasionally go blank.

These events can all be explained chemically. The mentally confused usually have either been born deficient in some enzyme needed to carry out the proper chemical reaction, or have had poor nutrition and as a result cannot provide the chemicals to produce the necessary quantity of the required enzymes and hormones. A smaller number of mental illnesses are caused by physical injuries, tumors, emotional shock, syphilis, or poisons.

About two out of every one hundred people have some schizophrenic reactions. Schizophrenia and depression, the two most prevalent mental disorders, affect more than 10 million Americans each year. In the past, schizophrenics constituted 20 percent of first admissions to public mental hospitals and 60 percent of their permanent residents. The condition usually develops in adolescence or early adult life, but onset can range from childhood to late middle life. Symptoms are often precipitated by a traumatic experience; the traumatic experience is not the cause of schizophrenia, only the last "straw." Previously the disorder had been wholly blamed on personality stresses, lack of adaptability, or failure of the parents. Today, the biochemical basis is well documented.

Paranoia differs from schizophrenia in that the confusion is characterized by a persistent delusion of persecution or grandeur. Normally there are no hallucinations in paranoia. Manic-depressives alternate between two phases—overactivity and depression. Infantile autism is a condition best described as the presence of unusual learning difficulties unaccompanied by mental retardation. All these personality disorders can be appreciably helped by megavitamin therapy.

If you were born deficient in a critical enzyme, how can taking extra vitamins overcome your enzyme deficiency? The answer is in two parts: the first deals with the nature of the B-complex vitamins, and the second involves basic chemistry.

The Nature of the Vitamin B Complex

The B vitamins appear together in nature as a family and have similar chemical properties. They are water-soluble and act as catalysts. The B-complex family consists of thiamine (B_1), riboflavin (B_2), niacin (B_3, also called niacinamide or nicotinic acid), pantothenic acid (B_5), pyridoxine (B_6), cyanocobalamin (B_{12}), pangamic acid (B_{15}), amygdalin (B_{17}), lipoic acid (or thioctic acid), biotin (H), folic acid (B_c or M), inositol, p-aminobenzoic acid (PABA), choline, and other, still unisolated vitamins. With the exception of choline, all function as coenzymes.

A coenzyme is a part of an enzyme, a large molecule that is a body-chemistry catalyst. Without enzymes, the chemical reactions that occur in the body would proceed too slowly to sustain life; enzymes speed these reactions and control their rate. Enzymes have two major portions, the coenzyme and the apoenzyme: the apoenzyme is the protein portion and the coenzyme is the nonprotein portion. The B-complex vitamins form major portions of many coenzymes. Without enough B-complex vitamins, sufficient enzymes cannot be formed to carry out many vital body reactions.

Niacinamide (B_3) is usually given in large doses in megavitamin therapy. It forms two important coenzymes, nicotinamide adenine dinucleotide (NAD) and nicotinamide adenine dinucleotide phosphate (NADP). More than fifty enzymes have NAD or NADP coenzymes in them. They metabolize carbohydrates (especially sugars), fats, and proteins. Without adequate NAD or NADP, these normal nutrients—especially the amino acid tryptophan—end up as poisons in the blood because they are improperly metabolized. The resulting poisons are believed to be the cause of hallucinations. The amino acid tryptophan can form serotonin, a mental stimulant similar to LSD. A similar chemical normally found in the brain, tryptamine, can be converted into a well-known hallucinogen called dimethyl-tryptamine, if the brain chemistry is abnormal.

Catecholamines (hormones affecting nerve-impulse transmissions) are also abnormal in cases of schizophrenia, resulting in improper transmission of nerve impulses. They, too, are affected by enzyme levels. Sugar-restricted diets are used in megavitamin therapy for schizophrenia because sucrose unnecessarily consumes valuable nicotinamide during its metabolism. A subclinical deficiency (one having no apparent clinical symptoms) of niacinamide produces depression; and a niacinamide-deficiency disease, pellagra, produces hallucinations and behavioral changes similar to schizophrenia; in fact, some physicians prefer to classify schizophrenia as subclinical pellagra. Similar chemical alterations of normal nutrients can cause depression, and destruction of chemicals called monoamines can also cause depression. Pyridoxine (B_6) is also involved in tryptophan metabolism. One study showed that nine of sixteen patients had improper tryptophan metabolism and were helped by extra vitamin B_6. (The investigators were Drs. A. S. Heely and G. E. Roberta; the study was published in *Developmental Medicine of Child Neurology,* 1966.)

Pantothenic acid (B_5) is also used in megavitamin therapy. It is a constituent of coenzyme A, which is involved in a great many reactions, including sugar metabolism and hormone production. A pantothenic acid deficiency causes nerve degeneration and depression.

Thiamine (B_1) forms the coenzyme thiamine pyrophosphate, which in turn forms many different enzymes. A thiamine deficiency causes degeneration of peripheral nerves, deterioration in the hypothalamus, loss of appetite, mental depression, irritability, confusion, memory loss, and inability to concentrate. Thiamine supplementation restores normality.

Biotin deficiency produces hallucinations, depression, panic, and lassitude. Other vitamins aid circulation of blood in the brain, balance coenzyme formation, and balance the B-complex to avoid a deficiency.

Vitamins Can Correct Enzyme Deficiencies

A person producing only half of the apoenzymes he needs can still have a normal level of active enzymes by doubling his coenzyme production. A person ordinarily producing only 1 percent of a required enzyme might be normalized with a hundredfold increase in B vitamins in the blood.

The same equilibrium principle holds true in coenzyme production. Taking more vitamins shifts the equilibrium toward the synthesis of more coenzyme. Therefore, taking large doses of the B-complex vitamins can restore proper enzyme activity and health, mental and physical. The old medical-school adage that says taking extra vitamins is like trying to pour more coffee into a full cup is wrong. In the body, the cup is never full; although some spills over, more is used.

Body Chemistry Influences Mental Attitude

The idea that mental attitude can influence the production of chemicals in the brain and that chemicals produced in the brain can influence mental attitude is relatively new. Scientists have learned more in the last twenty-five years about the chemistry of the brain and human behavior than in all the rest of history. I do not mean to suggest psychiatrists and psychotherapists cannot cure emotional illness. These specialists have cured many, but not, I believe, as many as they *could* cure with psychotherapy or drug therapy and megavitamin therapy combined. All too often the psychiatrists or psychotherapists in mental institutions prefer electric shock, insulin shock, Metrazol shock, or lobotomies. Much evidence indicates that mental and emotional disorders are nutritional problems, triggered by a stress or shock that requires more than the body's reserves can handle. The stress or shock precipitates the mental illness; but teaching the patient to cope with the stress or shock or attempting to cure him by means of the above therapies will not alleviate the underlying problem of undernutrition or genetic defect. **Those treating emotional disturbance must also diagnose and treat the nutritional or genetic deficiency.**

With the evidence mounting on biochemical causes of mental disturbances, additional clinical tests can be added to the arsenal of the scientific psychiatrist. A simple urine test detects "mauve substance," which is present in high concentrations in 75 percent of acute and 50 percent of chronic schizophrenics. It is also high in 50 percent of the mentally retarded, 40 percent of alcoholics, 20 percent of neurotics, and 10 percent of other physically sick persons. Rarely is it detected in mentally and physically healthy people. If the psychiatrist does not employ clinical tests and relies solely on the old teachings, he is practicing only the art, not the science of psychiatry.

If you want to learn more about the biochemical basis for emotional disturbance, read:

Mark Bricklin's article "Psychiatry Is a Sick Science" in the July 1973 *Prevention* magazine;

Orthomolecular Psychiatry by David R. Hawkins and Linus Pauling;

The article by Drs. William Philpott and Marshall Mandell in the February 1972 *Roche Image of Medicine and Research;*

Dr. D. Vann in *Medical Journal of Australia* (November 11, 1972);

The June 27, 1959, issue of the *Journal of the American Medical Association;*

Shrinks, Etc. (Dial, 1974), which reveals more about the problems of psychotherapy.

My point is that science must be added to psychiatric treatment.

Psychiatrists and Megavitamin Therapy

One proof that mental illness has a biochemical basis can be seen in the fact that symptoms can be switched off and on at will by adding or withdrawing megavitamin therapy —even when the patient is not aware of the change in treatment. Most of the mentally and emotionally ill are deficient in one or more of the B-complex vitamins or vitamin C. Stable people may have vitamin C deficiencies, but their bodies may have sufficient enzyme or catecholamine production to compensate. When catecholamine or enzyme production is meager, a vitamin C deficiency may trigger abnormality. British physician Dr. R. Shulman reported in 1967 in *the British Journal of Psychiatry* that 48 of 59 psychiatric cases had folic acid deficiencies. German psychiatrist Dr. F. Lucksch reported in *Wien Klin Wochenschr,* 1940, that 75 percent of his patients had vitamin C deficiencies; administering large doses of vitamin C improved two-thirds of them. Other evidence that mental illness has a biochemical basis: (1) the symptoms of mental disturbance can be mimicked in healthy people by the use of chemicals; (2) the presence of abnormal chemicals in mental patients' urine; (3) the hereditary nature of mental disorders and (4) physical changes brought about by the disease. All four indicate chemical reactions rather than purely "psychological" factors.

Still further evidence is to be seen in the fact that normal people become depressed and experience other early symptoms of emotional disturbance when made niacin or folic-acid deficient. People born in the first three months of the year, when fresh vegetables are scarce, have nearly a 10 percent greater incidence of mental disturbances. Drs. Edward Hare, John Price, and Eliot Slater examined the records of all patients admitted to psychiatric units in England and Wales during 1970 and 1971. They noted that the birth rate of schizophrenics and manic depressives was 7 to 9 percent above normal during the first quarter of the year. No other mental disorders showed an abnormal relation to birth date. The researchers concluded in the *British Journal of Psychiatry* (Vol. 124) that "winter-born children are prone to nutritional deficiencies or infections which may damage the constitution and so facilitate the manifestation of a functional psychosis in those generally at risk."

The question arises then: Why don't more psychiatrists use megavitamin therapy? Is it because you can't teach old dogs new tricks? Is it because they would rather earn more money from long periods of treatment, sometimes including expensive shock treatments? Is it because general physicians can use the technique successfully? I don't believe any of these is the answer. What is probably true is that megavitamin therapy is so opposed to what they have been taught that they refuse to consider seriously the possibility that it could work. This is mega-ignorance!

Since my studies have led me to chastise old-line, straight-Freudian psychiatrists, let me also chastise any readers who would recommend to someone in need of psychiatric care that he try megavitamin therapy without proper treatment by a scientific psychiatrist. The dangers are great. Dual treatment is required—learning to cope with the triggering problem and correcting the body chemistry. Delaying professional treatment could cause the disease to progress to the point that hospitalization is required or the patient commits suicide. Why gamble? Have the person contact a local schizophrenia society, the Huxley Institute for Biosocial Research (formerly the American Schizophrenia Association), 1114 First Avenue, New York, N.Y. 10021, or Schizophrenics Anonymous International, Box 913, Saskatoon, Saskatchewan, Canada, for the name of a local psychiatrist, physician, or institute practicing megavitamin therapy.

The Advantages of Megavitamin Therapy

The vitamins used in megavitamin therapy are relatively inexpensive; furthermore, they reduce the need for expensive drugs. Soon after megavitamin therapy is added to a drug regimen, the tranquilizer need is often cut in half. With continued megavitamin therapy over several months, tranquilizers can be reduced gradually until they can be eliminated.

The drugs used to treat schizophrenia, chlorpromazine and haloperidol, are effective; but excesses produce symptoms similar to those of Parkinson's disease, including lack of coordination and uncontrollable tremors. Megavitamin therapy reduces the need for these drugs and protects against harmful side effects as well. An additional saving comes about because the psychiatrist or physician can treat more patients with megavitamin therapy added to his protocol than with drug therapy alone. The patient is spared much of the expense and trouble of visits to the office of the psychiatrist or physician. The reduced number of visits per patient allow a psychiatrist or physician to treat more patients. Dr. David R. Hawkins, Medical Director of North Nassau Mental Health Center (New York), reported in a book he wrote with Linus Pauling, *Orthomolecular Psychiatry*, 1972, that the number of yearly visits required per patient dropped from 150 to 15 with the combined therapy. Hospitalization can be avoided, too.

Dr. Hawkins cites a case reported in the *Philadelphia Inquirer* (December 10, 1972) in which a patient suffering from malnutrition resulting from a reducing diet was in and out of seven mental institutions over a period of five years before being cured, at a cost of $230,000.

Even when a patient is first treated in a hospital, the avoidance of rehospitalization is significant to the patient or taxpayers who support state hospitals. Megavitamin therapy in the North Nassau Mental Health Center in New York reduced the rehospitalization rate by 50 percent and saved the hospital $100,000 per year; rehospitalization stays were reduced to one or two weeks rather than months (*Orthomolecular Psychiatry,* 1972).

Cost is only a minor concern; the effect on human life is much greater. How well does it work? Generally speaking, when megavitamin therapy is combined with conventional drug treatment, it is twice as effective as drug treatment alone. The suicide rate, which in schizophrenics is twenty-two times the normal rate, drops to almost zero (*Orthomolecular Psychiatry,* 1972).

Clinical Confirmation

Dr. Hoffer, one of the original developers of megavitamin therapy, has reported a 93 percent cure rate for patients in combined therapy ill less than two years (thus not chronic).

Although psychiatrists and physicians treating emotional and mental problems with megavitamin therapy have files bulging with thousands of individual case histories, large-scale double-blind tests are not plentiful. Drs. George Watson and W. D. Currier reported a single-blind test (the patients didn't know what medicines they were getting, but the physicians did) in the *Journal of Psychology* (March 1960). Thirty patients given inert placebos were observed and rated according to a standard personality survey (MMPI). Of the thirty patients, seventeen remained the same during the first phase of the survey, seven improved, and six became worse. The personality survey score for the group improved on the average only an insignificant 4 units out of 220 units. When megavitamin therapy was substituted for the placebos over an equal period of time, twenty-two improved, six remained the same, and two became worse. (It is suspected that adding magnesium to the formula would have prevented the two from becoming worse.) The improvement in the personality test was a significant 17 points. When the megavitamin therapy was continued even longer, twenty-four improved, five remained unchanged, and only one was worse. The test score improved by an average of a highly significant 27 (out of 220) units.

Drs. Hoffer and Osmond compared two large groups of schizophrenics under long-term observation in institutions in Canada and New Jersey. The 350 patients who received standard treatment (drugs and counseling) combined with megavitamin therapy were contrasted with 450 patients receiving standard treatment alone. The ten-year cure rate of those receiving megavitamin therapy was over 75 percent, while the standard-treatment patients showed only a 30 percent cure rate without relapse after ten years.

Dr. Hawkins reported a 70 per cent recovery rate in 2,000 seriously ill schizophrenics at the North Nassau Mental Health Center with megavitamin therapy. (*Orthomolecular Psychiatry*, 1972.)

His study was published in 1971 by the American Schizophrenia Association. In his private practice he has treated over 4,000 schizophrenic patients (including 600 alcoholics); the vast majority showed marked improvement or fully recovered. Dr. Hawkins reported in *Psychosomatics* (November 1970) that in a test situation, eighty schizophrenic patients receiving megavitamin therapy had only half the relapse rate of a control group of eighty schizophrenic patients receiving standard treatment.

Dr. Bernard Rimland of the Institute for Child Behavior Research, San Diego, enrolled 300 autistic children in nationwide, volunteer, megavitamin therapy in 1966. All enrolled children were under the medical care of their local physician throughout the study, and were placed on megavitamins for three months. After that time, they were asked to abstain from the vitamins for one month. Letters from parents to Dr. Rimland told of children returning to normal activity, talking and playing—instead of being withdrawn and virtually vegetables. Many parents refused to adhere to the abstinence portion of the experiment, as their children began to deteriorate again. During the course of the test 3 percent of the children (nine cases) became more irritable and difficult to manage. At Adelle Davis's suggestion, magnesium was added to the regimen, and the undesirable side effects disappeared overnight (from a paper delivered to the Canadian Schizophrenia Foundation, Toronto, 1973).

In 1963 Dr. G. Milner reported in the *British Journal of Psychiatry* a true double-blind study showing significant improvement on the part of twenty vitamin C-treated schizophrenic patients over a placebo group of the same number.

Dr. Hoffer reported in 1964 a ten-year follow-up of the treatment of schizophrenia with nicotinic acid in the *Acta Psychiatrica Scandinavia;* and, also in 1964, reported a controlled study on the effect of nicotinic acid on the frequency and duration of rehospitalization of schizophrenia patients in the *International Journal of Neuropsychiatry.* He commented in the first-quarter 1972 issue of *Orthomolecular Psychiatry* on the two studies just mentioned:

It turned out that of the ten or so patients receiving nicotinic acid seven had remained well over that year. Of the ten or so nicotinamide patients, seven or eight had remained well, while of the ten placebo patients only three had remained well. Around 75 percent of the patients receiving vitamins had remained well, whereas only one-third of the patients receiving placebo had remained well. It is important to remember that about two-thirds of all the patients had also received shock treatments so that this was a study of the combination of shock treatments plus megavitamins.

The results of the study were relatively clear cut, but it seemed very important to us not to report this until we repeated the study on a larger scale, to make sure there had been no hidden errors. We, therefore, started the second double-blind clinical experiment using the same design except that this time we did use nicotinic acid and placebo while informing the staff that we were going to follow the previous design. With our second study, we were able to treat 82 patients. The results were very similar.

Megavitamin Treatment for Emotional Disorders

In treating emotional and mental disorders, the following dosages of vitamins are generally given along with a low-sugar, high-protein, balanced diet.

Niacinamide (Vitamin B_3 or niacin) is given in high dosage as the keystone of megavitamin therapy. The dosage for adults ranges from 3 to 30 grams per day, although some use as little as 1 gram daily. Typical initial doses seem to be 6 to 8 grams daily. Children receive 1 gram of niacinamide for each 50 pounds of body weight.

Thiamine (Vitamin B_1) is given in 1 or 2 gram doses, although some prefer to use 0.1 gram (100 mgs) of thiamine for each gram of niacinamide (1:10 ratio).

Pyridoxine (Vitamin B_6) is included in the 100- to 500-mg level with 100 to 300 mg being typical.

Pantothenic acid is used at the 200- to 300-mg level. Vitamin B_{12} (1 mg) is generally given by injection in addition to another 50 to 100 micrograms orally.

Vitamin C is used on almost an equal weight basis as niacinamide. Dosage ranges from 3 to 20 grams daily, with an average of 6 grams.

The alpha tocopherol (vitamin E) dosage is 400 to 800 mg.

A high-potency multiple vitamin and mineral formulation, liver tablets, and a B-complex formulation are generally included. Minerals, including zinc and magnesium, are important in megavitamin therapy. Lithium has been successfully used to treat manic-depressives.

Megavitamin therapy normally takes two to three months to produce dramatic results, although fatigue and depression are reduced very quickly. Some patients experience excellent results in a few days. Megavitamin therapy is typically given for a year; during this period, other medication is eliminated gradually. Most patients continue to take large maintenance amounts of the vitamins, but not at the initial treatment rate. When the deficiency has been extensive and prolonged, some irreparable damage occurs and complete cure cannot be obtained.

Megavitamin therapy produces dramatic results, but more fatal diseases as well can be prevented or cured by Supernutrition. Chapters 8 to 11 explain how Supernutrition can prevent heart disease.

Cholesterol Doesn't Count

Early indicators of the mortality rate have predicted that the American median life span, which has been on a plateau for some twenty years, will be decreasing between 1975 and 1985. This projected decrease has been blamed primarily on inactivity, smoking, suboptimal nutrition, and pollution of air and water.

Many are concerned about nutrition and make serious efforts to be properly nourished, but what happens when they are misled? A case in point is the concern about heart disease.

The unexpected heart attack of consulting chemist Dr. Jacobus Rinse in 1951 was baffling. None of the so-called high-risk factors applied to his life-style. He watched his cholesterol and fat intake, was not overweight, did not smoke, had no special tensions, had sufficient physical exercise, and did not have a family history of heart disease.

71

He had always treated his health with concern and intelligence, followed the popular concepts for preventing heart disease; and then, at the age of fifty-one, he was suffering from angina pectoris. Where had he gone wrong? He could only speculate that something was *missing* from his diet rather than that there was too much of a particular nutrient such as cholesterol or saturated fat.

Dr. Wilfrid E. Shute, former chief cardiologist of the Shute Foundation for Medical Research, Ontario, Canada, reported in his book *Vitamin E for Ailing and Healthy Hearts* of another case where all the accepted guides for the prevention of heart disease had been followed, but heart disease struck anyway:

Let us consider the chairman of the Diet-Heart Committee of the American Medical Association, who was scheduled to present to the annual AMA meeting in June 1967 his recommendation for a very expensive long-term evaluation of the restriction of animal fats in the diet. He, himself, had followed his own recommended low fat regimen for years, had kept slim and exercised frequently, and in all ways followed his own authoritative advice on how to prevent heart attacks. He was unable to attend that June 1967 meeting because he was in a hospital recovering from a coronary thrombosis!

Dr. Albert Starr, a forty-seven-year-old world-famous heart surgeon at the University of Oregon Medical School in Portland was thin, lean, a nonsmoker, physically active, and a careful eater. Yet in January 1974 he suffered a major heart attack requiring open-heart surgery such as he himself had performed 3,000 times.

A reporter for the Washington bureau of *Newsweek,* Stephen Lesher, suffered a heart attack in 1973 at the age of thirty-eight. His blood pressure was normal, he was trim and fit, exercised regularly, had a normal cholesterol level, and felt that he experienced little stress or strain in handling his personal problems or his office workload.

Apollo 15 astronaut James B. Irwin suffered a heart attack at age forty-three while playing handball. Our space technology helped him walk on the moon, but our health technology could not prevent him from developing heart disease.

At forty-four years of age, a well-known Toronto science writer, Robert F. Legge, experienced a massive heart attack in spite of having taken all orthodox precautions. He had no family history of early heart disease. He used polyunsaturates to excess and, as he admitted in his later testimonials to vitamin E, followed a vitamin E-deficient diet. (The role vitamin E played in his survival is told in the September/October 1971 *Canadian R & D* [research and development]).

Nutritionist Dr. Carlton Fredericks reported in the January 1975 issue of *Prevention* about a well-known (but in the article unnamed) proponent of low-cholesterol diets and jogging who also fit this pattern. The expert had written an article for a national magazine entitled "You Can Prevent Heart Attacks." His article heavily stressed the evils of cholesterol, eggs, and animal fats, while highly recommending jogging. When the issue was published, the expert was in the hospital with a coronary thrombosis. Dr. Fredericks also commented that the expert was quoted later in a medical journal as being very disillusioned.

A thirty-four-year-old football coach at the University of Maryland, Ron Rice, died of a coronary attack while on a recruiting trip. His regular exercise had not provided enough protection.

Chemist Dr. D. Wood also followed the accepted anti-coronary guides but suffered a cerebral thrombosis (stroke) and a heart infarct (damage to the heart) at the age of fifty-three.

The list goes on, and I am sure that you could add to it. Even though doctors have been warning us for fifty years that cholesterol—a chemical of the alcohol* family—is the cause of atherosclerosis (deposits in the arteries), heart disease is striking increasingly larger portions of our population—and striking at progressively earlier ages. If choles-

---

* Cholesterol is not a fat or a fatty acid, although writers nearly always call it a fat. It is a solid alcohol present in some animal fats and edible oils.

terol reduction were effective, better results would have
been apparent long ago.

Cholesterol and Heart Disease

True, cholesterol is the major compound found in the fatty
deposits *in* the walls of diseased arteries (see figure 8.1).
Various forms of heart diseases, including each of the following, are related to cholesterol deposits. *Atherosclerosis*
is the heart disease that progressively narrows blood vessels. Narrowing of the coronary arteries, which link the
aorta with the heart, is called *angina pectoris*. When the
coronary arteries are blocked by a clot (coronary thrombosis), the heart is damaged and death of portions of the
muscle tissue, *myocardial infarct,* occurs. When the arteries are completely blocked by a blood clot, the condition
is termed a thrombosis. If the carotid artery leading to the
brain is blocked, a stroke—*cerebral thrombosis*—occurs.

The arteries gradually clog, but the final blockage is
usually caused by a blood clot (thrombus) formed from
red blood cells damaged as they are forced through the
narrowed arteries. After the initial cholesterol-rich deposits
(plaques) form in the arteries, they begin to attract calcium and harden. This is hardening of the arteries, *arteriosclerosis,* that we once associated with growing old.
Actually, any type of hardening of the arteries is called
arteriosclerosis. The arteries have three layers: intima,
media, and adventitia. When plaques form and harden in
the inner lining, the condition is called intima atherosclerosis, and this condition is more serious than when
the plaques are formed in the outer layers. Lesions form in
the intima and are composed of varying proportions of
fibrous tissue, cholesterol, cholesterol ester, phospholipid,
neutral fat, carotene, protein, and calcium. When fat and
cholesterol predominate, the plaques are soft and yellow.
When the "streaky yellow" plaques become pronounced,
they raise the intima wall and appear as a pearly plaque.
Fibrin (a protein formed by thrombin that is the bulk of a

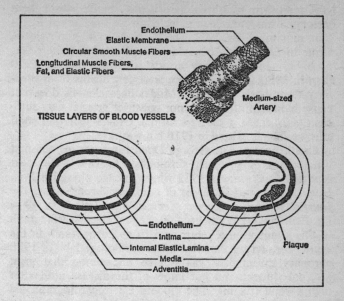

Figure 8.1 Atherosclerosis—The plaque (or deposit) that forms in the arteries does not form on the inner surface as is the general belief, but *within* the intima (or inner layer).

clot) can be deposited on these plaques, causing thrombosis and further narrowing of the passageway.

Heart Disease Has Reached Epidemic Levels

There were no cardiologists in the early twentieth century. Heart disease was rare. When cholesterol was identified as the culprit in atherosclerosis in 1911 by the Russian researcher Dr. Nikolai Anitschkov, it may have seemed logical for one to be wary of an excessive intake of cholesterol. Many physicians made the assumption that a high cholesterol intake would raise the blood level of cholesterol which would, in turn, cause cholesterol deposits.

A mild form of atherosclerosis has occurred throughout history; it has even been detected in well-preserved Egyptian mummies. In 1951 Dr. J. N Morris, a physician, wrote in *Lancet* that his evidence indicated that there was probably more coronary artery atherosclerosis in 1910 than in 1950. However, there were few deaths from coronary thrombosis in 1910. (Mild atherosclerosis does not cause blockage of arteries nor constrict arterial flow sufficiently to cause a clot to form.) Others feel that mild atherosclerosis existed in 1910 but was rare.

Credit goes to Dr. George Dock for reporting the first three cases of coronary thrombosis in 1896. The next reported cases were in 1912 when Chicago physician J. B. Herrick discussed six cases of coronary thrombosis in the *Journal of the American Medical Association*. In 1914 Dr. Paul Dudley White brought the first electrocardiograph to this country on a return trip from Europe and, in the same year, set up America's first cardiology lab. In 1920 coronary thrombosis was still so uncommon that most medical students did not know of the disease until after their formal training. The modern electrocardiograph did not appear until 1944, and physicians began monitoring serum (blood) cholesterol in the 1950s.

In 1900 all forms of heart diseases and strokes were responsible for only one death in seven in the United States. In 1963 these same diseases accounted for more than one of every two deaths, claiming 546,813 lives— including my father's. In comparison, 291,557 Americans were killed in World War II. In 1971 heart disease and stroke killed 1,021,630 Americans, including 675,580 with heart attacks and 207,920 with a stroke. That year all forms of heart disease combined were responsible for 53 percent of all deaths in this country. In 1973 more than 176,000 of the heart-attack deaths—including my father-in-law's—were of people under sixty-five years.

The coronary epidemic, which had been gradually mounting since the early 1900s, began to explode in 1946. Don't fall into the trap of thinking that the heart-disease epidemic resulted only because we had wiped out other diseases, such as tuberculosis. It is foolish to believe that people in the 1900s would have had coronaries if they hadn't died of pneumonia or TB. **Today people are dying of heart attacks at ages earlier than most people died of TB in 1900.** The death rate from heart attack among young men between twenty-five and forty-four years of age rose 14 percent from 1950 to 1970, while the death rate for older men (forty-five to sixty-four) rose only 4 percent over the same period. Some of our greatest surgeons and skilled students of anatomy would have discovered coronary thrombosis and infarcts, if they had existed in the early 1900s.

A little over fifty years later, atherosclerosis was detected in 72 percent of the soldiers autopsied in the Korean War. These soldiers had an average age of twenty-two, did not eat much fat or cholesterol, did not eat too many calories, were active, exercised, and had no more stress or tensions than soldiers in other wars. Yet during World Wars I and II, before foods became too highly processed, autopsies of young soldiers showed little or no signs of atherosclerosis.

Heart disease is showing up at earlier and earlier ages. This again disputes the claim that more heart disease has resulted only because people have not died earlier from contagious diseases. Nonsense. People did survive to advanced ages a hundred years ago and they didn't have thrombosis.

A study by Dr. Samuel A. Levine of twenty fathers and twenty-one sons, reported in the *Atlantic Monthly*, July 1963, showed a trend to earlier onset of and death from heart disease. The age at onset averaged 13.1 years sooner (48.1 years of age for the sons as opposed to 61.2 years for the fathers), and the deaths averaged at 54.8 years of age for the sons against 68.7 years for their fathers.

Is it a coincidence that the epidemic of coronary thrombosis lags just a few years behind corresponding decreases in our dietary vitamins B_6 and E together with decreased activity? Vitamins B_6 and E were first removed from our breads and cereals through the de-germing of wheat to increase its shelf life in the late nineteenth century, and this practice became widespread in the early twentieth century.

Today more and more people are walking or jogging, the bicycle has taken on new life, and people are supplementing their diets with vitamin E pills. It was estimated by a leading vitamin E manufacturer that between 10 and 20 million Americans took some form of vitamin E supplement in 1974. Maybe we will see some slowing of the coronary thrombosis epidemic soon.

Some Popular Risk Factors Debunked

Heart studies in the 1950s and early 1960s statistically linked various factors with the risk of developing heart disease. In 1964 the major risk factors were typically described as high blood pressure, physical inactivity, cigarette smoking, obesity, diabetes, a family history of heart diseases, and an elevated level of blood cholesterol. Research was aimed at discovering ways to control cholesterol, blood pressure, and obesity. In 1974 blood triglyceride (fatty materials) levels were added to the list of risk factors. Also, lung vital capacity (amount of air expelled by the lungs in a single breath) was used more as a measure related to physical activity, and the electrocardiogram was relied on increasingly.

Attempts to control the heart-disease risk factors, however, have not reduced the incidence of heart disease. Controlling diabetes, for example, does not lower the risk of heart disease, but it does reduce the probability of dying from other causes. Study after study has shown that lowering the blood pressure does not lower the heart-disease *incidence,* but it does reduce the risk of *dying* from heart disease or stroke.

Reducing cholesterol intake or reducing serum cholesterol levels has not been proved to reduce heart-disease incidence.

Reducing severe obesity does not lower the risk of heart attack unless other concomitant factors, such as blood pressure, serum cholesterol, etc., are also reduced. Smoking has received widespread agreement concerning its role in heart disease, although findings are not conclusive. According to a twenty-five-year study beginning in 1950 in Framingham, Massachusetts, those who smoke more than a pack of cigarettes a day have a larger than three times as great a chance of dying of a heart attack as a non-smoker. Heavy smokers who quit smoking experience declining risk until after ten years of nonsmoking when their risk becomes only slightly higher than a nonsmoker's risk.

The degree of risk of incurring heart disease was determined primarily from a mathematical equation derived in the Framingham study. The Framingham study is an "untouchable deity" to most physicians, but recently it has come under attack. The twenty-five-year study, directed by the Boston University Medical Center, of 5,000 residents of Framingham, Massachusetts, may have been a multimillion-dollar waste because of a wrongly applied equation. Using the equation, however, the above risk factors were postulated.

Serum cholesterol above 240 mg % (milligrams of cholesterol per 100 milliliters of blood) was said to be three times worse than below 200; a level above 260 was considered six times worse. Systolic blood pressure over 160 was four to eight times worse than below 120. Cigarette smoking, varying according to contributing factors, was two to six times worse than not smoking. Men smoking more than one pack of cigarettes a day were said to be six times as likely to have a stroke as non-smokers. Electrocardiogram abnormality increased the risk by a factor of two. The sedentary man, according to the study, had twice the risk of the active man. Having high serum cholesterol, high blood pressure, and an electrocardiogram abnormality, it was claimed by the Framingham study, gave you twenty-three times the probability of dying of a heart attack. Later we will look at errors in the Framingham study that may invalidate these factors.

Many physicians treating heart disease will concentrate on reducing serum cholesterol and dietary cholesterol, because they believe the alleged link of higher blood cholesterol with greater risk. **Is there direct evidence linking heart disease to the dietary intake of cholesterol, or even to blood cholesterol levels? NO! There is none.**

My thesis is that neither coronary thrombosis nor atherosclerosis will occur in genetically normal people, provided they have *complete* Supernutrition and engage in moderate activity. **Any vitamin or mineral deficiency may directly or indirectly lead to heart disease. The most important vitamin for lowering the incidence of heart disease is vitamin E; it is, unfortunately, the most deficient in our diet. Vitamin C is next in importance with vitamin B_6 third. The minerals selenium, magnesium, and zinc are the key minerals in warding off heart disease.**

Failure to stimulate the body naturally with motion and activity will cause poor circulation, hormone imbalances, and atrophy of organs needed for health. Personality patterns such as "personality type A" may be influenced and protected by Supernutrition. Personality type A characteristics have been defined as a high drive toward poorly defined goals, persistence of work for recognition and advancement, eagerness to compete, and heightened mental and physical stresses and drives which consume more B and C vitamins than they ingest. Smoking also destroys vitamins, especially vitamin C; this may explain the link between smoking and heart disease.

Evidence That Proves the Cholesterol Theory Wrong

In order for my thesis to gain support, I must prove that the popularly accepted belief that cholesterol and saturated fats are the villains is incorrect. I will show this through three main points: (1) low-cholesterol diets do not lower the incidence of heart disease; (2) high-cholesterol diets do not increase the incidence of heart disease; and (3) dietary cholesterol is not related to blood cholesterol.

I will further show that low-cholesterol diets can *increase* the incidence of heart disease and possibly increase the incidence of cancer, that heart disease can be brought on by increasing other dietary factors, including proteins and carbohydrates, and that decreasing vital nutrients will cause heart disease.

Later, I will discuss the errors in the experiments that have misled so many. Most previous experiments have either used vegetarian animals such as rabbits which handle cholesterol differently from humans, or haven't balanced the test case diets with nutrients required for the higher-fat or higher-calorie diet.

What the Cholesterol Scare Has Done

First, let's consider what the current beliefs concerning cholesterol have done. The cholesterol fear is a part of America—you might even feel I am being irreverent by attacking the current belief unless you realize the seriousness of what is happening. Without supporting evidence, many doctors recommend that cholesterol and fats be reduced in the diet. After all, they reason, no harm can come from such a dietary restriction. It can even be a method of getting their patients on a weight-reducing regimen. This advice appears to follow the physicians' maxim, "Guard against doing more harm than good." But do they?

Over the last twenty years, people have trimmed fats from their meat, eaten less fried foods, and consumed more polyunsaturated fats than ever. Dietary fats has been reduced by nearly one-third of what it was. Our intake of polyunsaturated fat is at an all-time high. Therefore, our ratio of polyunsaturated fats to saturated fats has changed drastically, by 37 percent between 1909 and 1961. In the same period, total calories consumed per day have been decreased from 3,570 to 3,180 (Dr. B. Friend, *American Journal of Clinical Nutrition,* 1967).

Dr. Harold Kahn of the National Heart and Lung Institute has shown that there has been no change in the proportion of cholesterol consumed over the last sixty years and, further, that polyunsaturated fats were 6 percent of our diet in 1970 as compared with only 2 percent in 1950. Yet, heart disease increases, in epidemic proportions. (*American Journal of Clinical Nutrition,* 1970.) **The generations that ate gravies, fatback, whole grains, and fresh vegetables did not experience coronary thrombosis.**

It appears that although the first attempts to reduce the consumption of high-cholesterol foods did not reduce heart disease and, in fact, the atherosclerosis rate continued to increase, all too many people—with the blessings of their physicians—have become fanatical about the avoidance of cholesterol-containing foods. There is evidence that "cholesterolphobia," the unwarranted fear of consuming cholesterol, has caused unbalanced diets and subsequent disease, even caused or contributed to the heart disease that these diets were, hopefully, to have prevented. People in many cultures eat low-fat diets and still have heart disease, while in other cultures those who eat high-cholesterol diets are relatively free of heart disease. Our forefathers had little heart disease, yet their healthy diets have been changed radically. Cholesterolphobia is very much in evidence. Mothers serve with their peanut butter sandwiches water or sodas to their children instead of milk; only one-third of American families use butter; cholesterol-free egg substitutes and polyunsaturated meats have been developed; for many families bacon-and-egg breakfasts are a thing of the past.

Milk and eggs are two of our best foods. They are nearly complete foods that help balance and help utilize the other foods in our diet. Even low-cholesterol diets recommended by most doctors contain one egg daily or three eggs weekly. But the cholesterolphobic tends to remove *all* eggs from his diet. Although egg protein can be replaced by other food proteins, where will the other trace nutrients (minerals, B-complex, sulfur and selenium compounds) come from in our modern, highly processed food diets?

Physicians, especially cardiologists, feel that, at least, low-cholesterol diets "don't hurt anyone." When I asked a number of physicians why they recommend skim milk, they replied, in effect: "It can't hurt, it's lower in calories, and it's cheaper." Not one of the ten that I asked knew that the fat and cholesterol in whole (cow's) milk and mother's (human) milk is essential for the formation of myelin sheaths of nerve fibers. What happens to infants getting low-fat formulas when it comes to preventing future heart disease? Sub-optimal nutrition is not healthy; but, equally important, recent research warns us to go slow on high-polyunsaturated-fat diets for still other reasons.

The incidence of cancer and other diseases appears to increase in laboratory mice on high-polyunsaturated-fat diets. (See Chapter 13.) This is not to suggest that poly-unsaturated fatty acids cause cancer, as this is not the case. A certain level of polyunsaturated fats is required for proper nutrition; but if we distort the standard diet radically, we may be more subject to a variety of diseases. Again, there is no evidence that the mice studies apply to humans; but it is a caution sign that suggests we should not experiment with human lives unless we have conclusive proof that the change is for the better. The standard American diet of the 1850s or 1920s, high in saturated fats, is still today consumed in many countries where the heart disease incidence is low. The point here is that there is reason to question the low-cholesterol diet. OK, you're still somewhat skeptical; so let's look at the newer facts.

Low-Cholesterol Diets Do Not Prevent
Heart Disease

It is not accurate to describe diets solely as "low-cholesterol" or "high-cholesterol"; the description is too broad. Total nutrition must be considered and described. Is it a low-cholesterol balanced diet or a low-cholesterol unbalanced diet? **Unfortunately, it is difficult to balance a low-cholesterol diet.**

Many comparisons have been made between the diets of various cultures. One study that you don't hear much about is the study of the dietary differences between northern and southern India. Northern Indians eat a high-cholesterol, high-saturated-fat diet. Of all the fats eaten by northern Indians, only 2 percent are unsaturated, giving a polyunsaturated-fat-to-saturated fat (P/S) ratio of 0.02, far lower than the 1.2 or 2 P/S ratio recommended by the American Heart Association. Northern Indians eat mainly meat and dairy products, lots of animal fats, butterfat, and milk. They eat ten times the amount of total fat of their southern neighbors, who consume mainly polyunsaturated fats and virtually no cholesterol. Of the small amount of fats eaten by southern Indians, 44 percent of the total is polyunsaturated (P/S-0.8).

You may be surprised to learn that the study revealed both groups had normal blood-cholesterol levels. But are you prepared to learn that the southern Indians (low-cholesterol diet) have fifteen times the heart disease incidence of the northern Indians (high-cholesterol diet)? You cannot explain the difference by referring to activity, genetics, or culture. The water is the same. Certainly the dietary cholesterol theory won't explain the difference. Better nutrition *does* explain the difference. The high-cholesterol diet of the northern Indians contains better-quality foods. The milk and butter promotes synthesis of vitamin B_6 in the intestines, vital to a healthy heart and to the prevention of cholesterol deposits. Southern Indians may have deficiencies of the B-complex vitamins because they lack the portion normally made in our intestines if we eat dairy products.

It is not surprising that these findings are not widely publicized; two independent researchers have commented on the dietary relationship to disease in these groups and been published. One report is by Dr. S. L. Malhotra in the *American Journal of Nutrition* (1967) and the other by Dr. G. V. Mann in the *Journal of Atherosclerosis Research* (1964). But you have to search hard to find these studies quoted by heart researchers.

The Gujeratis tribe of Kenya are vegetarians, eating a low-cholesterol diet; their heart disease incidence and mortality rate are the same as Kenya's general population. (Charters & Arya, *Lancet*, 1960.)

Prisoners, especially prisoners of war, eat mostly scraps or rice and get very little meat, eggs, or milk. Yet their low-cholesterol diets produce cholesterol deposits and heart disease. Every one of the 10,000 autopsies performed at the Nazi concentration camp at Dachau in World War II revealed some degree of atherosclerosis. The prisoners had eaten only soup and bread diets, averaging about 1,000 calories a day. They worked at hard physical labor every day. Such a high incidence of heart disease was unheard of in the early 1940s, although it is not so surprising today. Most likely, prisoner-of-war diets are low in vitamin C, which is a critical factor in the prevention of heart disease, as we will see. Dr. W. Koch and Dr. M. Lamy, et al., have discussed the cardiovascular diseases of prisoners at length in the medical research literature.

Drs. Cuyler Hammond and Lawrence Garfinkel of the American Cancer Society conducted a study on the dietary habits of 804,409 persons who had no previous history of heart disease or stroke. After a six-year period, 14,819 of these had died of heart disease and 4,099 had died of stroke. The subjects were divided into two groups at the inception of the study. The first group consisted of those who ate whole eggs five or more times a week in addition to the eggs consumed in the preparation of other foods. The second group ate fewer than four eggs per week or no eggs at all. Those in the second group who ate practically no eggs had more deaths from heart attacks and stroke than those who ate all the eggs they wanted.

Placid Trappist monks are strict vegetarians. They do get about 35 grams of butterfat daily from milk and cheese, but this is lower than the American average. Yet in 1963 nearly 60 percent had some form of cardiovascular disease and nearly 50 percent had high blood pressure. The Benedictine order of monks eats eggs, meat, and butter. Yet they have no higher an incidence of heart disease than the low-cholesterol vegetarian monks (*Nutrition Reviews,* 1963.)

If lowering dietary cholesterol worked, heart disease would have drastically decreased by now. The cardiovascular death rate is increasing yearly, with one million cardiovascular deaths a year, exceeding all other causes of death combined (U.S. Bureau of Census, Vital Statistics and Life Tables). **One new factor to deal with is that the heart-disease rate of women under age forty-five increased 11 percent during a recent seven-year period (1961–1968).** For 1971 the heart-disease rate of women was reported up 14 percent over the same base period, according to Dr. David Spain of the Brookdale Hospital Medical Center in Brooklyn. Dr. Spain also reported for a 1973 *Science News* article that in 1955, men under fifty-one were twelve times more vulnerable than women of the same age, but for the 1967 to 1971 period the ratio narrowed to four times as vulnerable.

At an AHA conference in 1972 Dr. Theodore Cooper, director of the National Heart and Lung Institute, cited the increase in recorded heart-attack deaths (coronary thrombosis) for men (238,962) and women (135,339) according to the 1968 statistics. Other physicians continued their twenty-year-old cholesterol scare with comments such as "the holy value of milk should be de-emphasized."

The National Heart and Lung Institute of NIH tested a drug for five years that lowered blood-cholesterol levels. A report published in the *Journal of the American Medical Asso-*

ciation (1972) tells of the disastrous results of that drug-induced blood-cholesterol reduction of 10 percent. The Framingham risk factors predicted that this 10 percent reduction in blood cholesterol would concomitantly reduce the heart disease incidence by 24.4 percent. The tragic result obtained, however, was an 18.4 percent *increase* in cardiac death! The drug used in the study was dextrothyroxine, a form of thyroid hormone, thought to lower cholesterol by speeding its metabolism.

The hormone estrogen was given to men who had suffered heart attack. The five-year study by Dr. J. Marmorston showed a significant reduction in blood cholesterol in the estrogen group (198 vs. 236), but there was no significant difference between the two groups in the incidence of heart attacks (*Proceedings of the Society of Experimental Biology and Medicine,* 1962).

Another anticholesterol drug, MER/29, was used on 400,000 patients by physicians before the FDA banned its use because it caused blindness, loss of hair, skin disease, and loss of sexual desire (*Circulation,* 1961).

One low-cholesterol diet does seem to work well, because it is a low-calorie but highly nutritious diet. The Prudent Diet recommended by the Bureau of Nutrition of the New York City Health Department (Dr. N. Jolliffe and associates) has been shown in a ten-year study to reduce the heart-disease incidence from 10.3 per 1,000 man-years to 4.3 per 1,000 man-years. (Projects are measured in man-years; one man working for 2 years is 2 man-years. Also, two men working for 1 year is 2 man-years. Therefore, a project said to take 5 man-years can be done in 5 years by assigning one man or in just 1 year by assigning five men.) The Prudent Diet is based on good basic foods; the fact that it is a low-cholesterol diet is incidental to the lower incidence of heart disease.

High-Cholesterol Diets Do Not Cause Heart Disease

Maybe eating low-cholesterol diets doesn't lower heart-disease incidence, but eating too much cholesterol is different. Hasn't research shown a strong link between eating high-cholesterol foods and heart disease?

Definitely not! Earlier research confused the issue by not considering diets in terms of caloric value or total nutrition. The high-cholesterol diets or high-fat diets were often very high-calorie diets. These diets affect blood cholesterol levels and, in some cases, heart disease, but no more than a low-fat or high-protein diet of the same calorie content. **The bigger error was not to consider the difference in nutrient balance that high-fat and high-protein diets require. To increase one nutrient, such as a fat, without increasing its required companion nutrients, such as vitamin B_6 and magnesium, is exactly the same as creating a deficiency of these companion nutrients.** It is more correct to consider such an unbalanced high-saturated-fat diet as containing a deficiency in Vitamin B_6 and magnesium. The trouble is that this is a deficiency diet, not one with too many fats.

Drs. L. D. Greenberg and J. F. Rinehart have found that rhesus monkeys (which have, essentially, identical body chemistries as humans) on a standard diet required 1 mg of vitamin B_6 daily to prevent xanthurenic acid excretion, an indicator of vitamin B_6 deficiency. The same monkeys on a high-fat, high-cholesterol diet required 5 mg of vitamin B_6 for the same protection. (*Proceedings of the Society of Experimental Biology and Medicine,* 1951.) This extrapolates to 25 mg of vitamin B_6 daily for humans. Cardiac patients have often been found to have xanthurenic acid in their urine. Most likely they have not been getting vitamin B_6 adequate to their fat intake.

You can feed laboratory rats a normal diet with large amounts of pure fat added and produce atherosclerotic rats; you can also feed them the same percentage of fat

(62 percent) but select a diet that contains high-quality protein and adequate vitamins and minerals and get rats free of atherosclerosis. You get fat rats all right, but no heart disease. Dr. J. Barboriak and his Yale colleagues published a report in the *Journal of Nutrition* (1958) of a test in which rats were fed 62 percent of their diet as animal fat (saturated fat) one time and 62 percent of their total diet as vegetable fat (polyunsaturated) another time. Each time they got healthy, but very fat rats, up to four times their normal weight. The tests were with 600 rats for each test and lasted nearly two years. There were no abnormalities in the hearts or arteries of the experimental animals that were protected by balanced nutrition.

These experiments were verified by Dr. S. Naimi and his associates at Tufts University School of Medicine. Their study in the 1965 *Journal of Nutrition* involved a high-butter diet, in which 65 percent of the total diet calories were from butter. Again, fat rats, but no increase in blood cholesterol or atherosclerosis. This experimental diet contained twice the vitamin content of the Yale study in order to balance the dietary cholesterol and saturated fat intake.

In 1941 Drs. R. Steiner and Domanski fed dogs 100 grams of egg-yolk powder daily for fifty-six weeks (equivalent to approximately 15 to 20 eggs daily). Their article in the *American Journal of Medical Science* (1941) reported no heart changes or cholesterol deposits from this diet. In 1955 Dr. G. Sperling reported a similar experiment with rats. He found that rats fed dried whole eggs (10 percent of total diet) not only had normal hearts, but also lived longer than control animals not receiving daily eggs (*Journal of Nutrition*, 1955).

Just as you hear little about studies of Indian dietary habits, you don't hear much about studies of the Masai in Tanganyika. The Masai eat little other than meat and milk; they average more than two gallons of milk a day, with 60 percent of their diet being of animal fat. Their blood-cholesterol levels are low by our standards, and they show no evidence of coronary thrombosis or atherosclerosis. Their diet is high in cholesterol and also high in balanced nutrition—they eat fresh food and are very active people.

Dr. F. W. Lowenstein reported on the Somalis and the Samburus of East Africa in the *American Journal of Clinical Nutrition* (1964). Both groups are sheep- and goat-herders, eating mostly milk, blood, and meat, with their diet consisting of 60 to 65 percent animal fat (saturated); both are clinically free of detectable signs of atherosclerosis and heart attacks. Drs. A. Shapers and T. Jones reported similar findings among the Somalis and Samburus in *Lancet* in 1962.

Drs. D. Gsell and J. Mayer tell of the Swiss of the Loetschental Valley. They eat a high-cholesterol, high-saturated-fat, high-calorie diet, but have low blood-cholesterol levels and little heart disease (*American Journal of Clinical Nutrition,* 1962). Milk and cheese provide good nutrition for climbing the Alps and fighting the cold.

People in the United States, the United Kingdom, and Sweden consume essentially the same percentages of total fats and polyunsaturated-to-saturated ratios. Yet, as Table 8.1 shows, the heart-disease death rate in the United States is nearly three times greater than in Sweden and nearly twice that of the United Kingdom.

Dr. A. M. Cohen reported in the *American Heart Journal* in 1963 that Jews living in Yemen eat very high-fat diets yet have little heart disease. Those that migrate to Israel, however, eat a less primitive diet and have higher heart disease rates, approaching those of the United States. Russian researcher Dr. A. S. Loginov reported in *Kardiologiya* in 1962 that whether the blood cholesterol levels are high or low, there is practically no heart disease in Ethiopia. The French, who are great cheese eaters, rank almost at the bottom of the heart disease mortality table.

Table 8.1 Atherosclerosis Death Rate and Fluid Milk Consumption

Country	Death Rate per 100,000 (1967)	Milk Intake (pounds per person)	Homogenized	Pre-boiled
Finland	244.7	593	about 33%	no
United States	211.8	273	almost all	no
Australia	204.6	304	15%	no
Canada	187.4	288	partly	no
United Kingdom	140.9	350	about 7.5%	no
The Netherlands	106.9	337	infrequently	—
West Germany	102.3	213	partly	—
Austria	88.6	327	occasionally	—
Italy	78.9	137	12.5%	yes
Switzerland	75.9	370	small quantity	yes
Sweden	74.7	374	—	yes
France	41.7	230	negligible	yes
Japan	39.1	48	occasionally	—

Source: Dr. Kurt Oster, in Medical World News, Feb. 18, 1972.

Yogurt-and-buttermilk-consuming Albanians are also relatively free of heart disease.

Dr. R. Stout and his associates reported on an Italian colony in Roseto, Pennsylvania, which eats a diet rich in cholesterol and saturated fats—peppers fried in lard (fat), bread dipped in lard, ham ringed with fat, and dairy products. They had less than one-half the general-population incidence of heart disease in the 1950s and 1960s (*Journal of the American Medical Association,* 1964). A nearby town, Stroudsburg, had more than twice the normal incidence of heart disease. The figures for the early 1960s were: Roseto, 157 deaths per 100,000 due to heart disease; Stroudsburg, 671 deaths per 100,000. Ten years later, in 1974, Roseto had lost the advantage and assumed the national standard rate of heart-disease incidence (360 deaths per 100,000). The younger generation in Roseto didn't grow their own vegetables or make their own bread; they did buy mass-produced fowl, meats, and sugar-rich foods; they walked less. Typical Americana, delayed a few years.

Drs. A. D. Charters and B. P. Arya report that the Punjabis in Kenya eat a high-cholesterol, high-saturated-fat diet and yet have the same heart-disease incidence and mortality as the general population and as the vegetarian Gujeratis who eat no cholesterol (*Lancet*, 1960).

Other studies, including the ones done on the Atiu and Mitiaro natives of Polynesia and the primitive Eskimo, showed no relationship between high-fat or high-cholesterol diets and heart disease. **Japan has had a 14 percent** *decrease* **in heart disease since 1955, while their diet has** *increased* **in dairy products, eggs, and saturated fats.**

Let's look at one more detailed study closer to home—the Irish-Boston Heart Study. "It's not the cholesterol intake that hurts the heart. It is letting the cholesterol build up. Physical activity burns it up," summarized Dr. Frederick J. Stare, former head of Harvard's Nutrition Department, referring to the Irish-Boston study. This study, jointly led by Dr. Stare and Dr. W. J. E. Jessop, Trinity's dean of the School of Medicine, helps dispel the dietary cholesterol fear. A team of nineteen researchers, including cardiologists and nutritionists, studied 575 pairs of brothers between the ages of thirty and sixty-five. Both brothers in each pair had been born and subsequently raised for at least twenty years in Ireland. One of each pair of brothers had emigrated to the Boston area and lived there at least ten years. Controls included another 312 urban and 152 native rural Irishmen still living in Ireland but not related to the 575 paired brothers, as well as 375 first-generation Americans whose parents had been born in Ireland.

Both dietary and serum cholesterol were measured in addition to physical activity and body fat (skin fold). Their hearts were studied in detail and their diets thoroughly evaluated. It was found that the hearts of the Irishmen were healthier and their blood-pressure and serum-cholesterol levels were lower, even though their dietary cholesterol was higher and calorie intake averaged 400 to 500 calories higher. Their rich diets—lots of butter, milk, cream, bacon, potatoes, mutton, and brown bread—produced less heart disease than was found in their Boston brothers. Autopsies from accidental deaths or noncardio-vascular disease deaths revealed that the hearts of the Irish brothers averaged fifteen to thirty years younger than the American brothers. The primary conclusion that can be drawn is that activity—regular physical activity—is the main reason for the better heart health of the Irish. Sec-ondary factors may be increased dietary magnesium and vitamin E, not discounting their optimistic attitude.

Calories Are More Important Than Cholesterol

Dr. Sam Berman, a Boston physician, put more than four hundred Boston policemen on a weight-reducing diet that included several eggs each day. These men were all obese and mostly middle-aged. After eight years, there have been no heart attacks reported among the men on the diet. Don't forget, our ancestors' diet was a high-cholesterol diet, and they had little heart disease even in old age.

In 1955, Harvard University studied the effect of exer-cise on blood-cholesterol levels. Dr. G. V. Mann and his Harvard colleagues found that the blood-cholesterol levels did not rise in healthy young medical students placed on extremely high-calorie diets with large amounts of sat-urated fats when the students increased their physical activity enough to maintain their body weight. When they did not exercise, their blood-cholesterol levels rose with their body weights.

Dr. J. N. Morris found in 1953 that bus drivers have more heart attacks than train conductors, and postal clerks more than mail carriers. (*British Medical Journal,* 1963.)

You may rightfully ask, "If there is so much evidence sug-gesting that dietary cholesterol is not involved in heart disease, why do so many believe that cholesterol is dangerous?" The answer is that many of the cholesterol tests are misleading. Rabbits have been widely used in heart research for two rea-sons: (1) their aortas and hearts are large enough to examine readily; and (2) it is more difficult to produce heart disease in mice, rats, and dogs. Unfortunately, rabbits are natural vegetarians. Their bodies are not equipped to handle dietary cholesterol, and they have no ways of converting cholesterol to bile as humans do. Thus they handle dietary cholesterol completely differently from humans; any cholesterol tests based on rabbit studies are invalid.

A second experimental flaw exists when humans or experimental animals are fed large amounts of purified cholesterol crystals, rather than natural foods containing cholesterol. This is similar to feeding crystalline sugar. Blood levels go up for a while but gradually return to their normal levels; the time element has not been considered in these tests. Another point is that wherever nature puts cholesterol, lecithin is there to keep it soluble in the blood. An unnatural condition is created when purified cholesterol is administered. Other experimental flaws, such as not considering total calories and overall nutrition, have already been discussed. The Framingham study which developed the popularly accepted heart attack Risk Factors used a statistical formula that was later shown by Dr. Kurt Oster to be invalid for interpreting cholesterol data.

The process of how cholesterol is captured from the bloodstream by the artery is the important factor in atherosclerosis, not the amount of cholesterol available to be removed. Many people with high blood-cholesterol levels have no signs of atherosclerosis. The plaque-formation mechanism is one of my areas of research, and other biochemists are also researching this area. What causes the change in the artery wall so that it extracts cholesterol from the bloodstream and causes it to strongly adhere to the wall? My research has centered around damage to the artery wall caused by free radicals (highly reactive compounds formed in the blood) when certain antioxidant nutrient deficiencies exist. Other researchers are concerned with the lubrication of the artery walls, chronic inflammation, tumors, or the structural flexibility of the artery.

Dietary Cholesterol Does Not Increase Blood Cholesterol

Why isn't the amount of cholesterol eaten of importance in heart disease? First, there is a feedback mechanism that adjusts the total body cholesterol amount to the amount we get from our food. When we eat more cholesterol, we make less in our bodies. Cholesterol is produced primarily in the liver but also in the adrenal cortex, skin, intestines, testes, and aorta in varying amounts according to the individual. Cholesterol is synthesized from simple two-carbon fragments that can arise from the metabolism of carbohydrate and protein as well as from fat. Acetyl-Co A is the source of all carbon atoms in cholesterol; thus, cholesterol can be made from fats, protein, or carbohydrates.

A typical adult male synthesizes about 1 gram of cholesterol daily, although the actual amount synthesized varies widely from individual to individual and normally depends upon demand and supply as governed by the individual's biofeedback system. Average American diets contain about one-third the amount of cholesterol synthesized daily. Within limits, if more cholesterol is assimilated from the diet, less can be made in the body. There is an abnormality that occurs in about one out of every thousand people, called type IV hyperlipidemia, in which dietary cholesterol intake influences blood-cholesterol levels.

Cholesterol has important functions in the body. It is made into various hormones, including the sex hormones. It is also made into bile, has an important role in the brain, and is incorporated into cellular membranes. The incorporation of serum cholesterol into steroids or bile may vary with age due to a decrease in activity of the endocrine glands (hypophysis, thyroidea, pancreas).

"Normal" cholesterol values vary between 150–300, 150–250, or 150–280 mg% (mg of cholesterol per 100 mls of blood), depending upon the textbook or institution. People under stress have shown normal variances in their cholesterol of 10 to 20 percent. A normal "average"

male may have a serum cholesterol of 200 mg% one day
and 240 mg% the next. The 40-point difference would
not reflect a worsening condition, simply the average normal
range for that individual during stress. **One is just as likely
to have heart disease without high serum cholesterol as
with it.** Drs. Ray Rosenman and Meyer Friedman of the
Mount Zion Hospital in San Francisco stated that 62 percent of their heart disease patients had serum cholesterol
levels less than 260 mg% (*Nutrition News,* 1971). **Only
20 percent of heart-disease patients have serum-cholesterol
levels above 222 mg%** (*Journal of the American Medical
Association,* 1964). Just a few of the many tests showing
no relationship between dietary cholesterol and blood
cholesterol levels are given here.

Dr. S. D. Splitter and colleagues reported in *Metabolism*
(1968) a study done at Highland Hospital, Oakland, California. The investigators fed the equivalent of at least nine
eggs per day (50 to 110 grams of egg-yolk lipids) to
thirteen people. Six of the subjects were bedridden, seven
were healthy. Of the thirteen, only two showed a marked
blood-cholesterol elevation; both were in the bedridden
group and had histories of difficulty in the cholesterol-
cardiovascular area. The seven healthy, ambulatory subjects had an average serum-cholesterol level slightly lower
at the end of the study than at the beginning.

Serum Cholesterol Can Be Increased by Noncholesterol Factors

Drs. Meyer Friedman and Ray Rosenman point out in
their book *Type A: Behavior and Your Heart* (Knopf,
1974) that dietary cholesterol is not the controlling factor
for blood cholesterol. They checked the blood-cholesterol
level of a group of accountants over a six-month period,
from January to June. When the April 15 tax deadline
approached and their subjects' sense of time urgency (personality type A behavior) intensified, their blood-cho-

lesterol levels rose sharply as well. There were no basic changes in their diets or weights.

Serum Cholesterol Levels Can Be Lowered While on High-Cholesterol Diets

In Washington, D.C., a Howard University School of Medicine group headed by Drs. H. Wing and A. D. Fletcher reported that exercise lowers serum cholesterol and atherogenesis in cholesterol-fed cockerels (Federation of American Societies for Experimental Biology, 1972). In the case of humans, the Irish-Boston Heart Study showed the same relationship. Later, we look at vitamins and minerals, such as vitamins B_6, C, E, and the mineral magnesium, among other nutrients that lower blood cholesterol.

Dr. Robert C. Atkins pointed out in his book *Dr. Atkins' Diet Revolution* (McKay, 1972) that "Not long ago, the big villain here [in coronary heart disease] was thought to be cholesterol. But, it now appears that the correlation with heart attacks may be even higher with elevated triglycerides [fatty materials in the blood] than with high cholesterol levels." Dr. Atkins recommended low-carbohydrate diets high in protein, fats, and cholesterol. In his book he cited several examples of patients having significant reduction in blood-cholesterol levels while on his diet.

Dietary Cholesterol Does Not Produce Heart Disease

Guinea pigs with normal serum-cholesterol levels develop arteriosclerosis when they are made deficient in vitamin C. Dietary cholesterol and other fats in their diet do not play a role. The formation of the fatty deposits on the inside of arteries can be reversed by restoring vitamin C to their diet. The arteries can be made to lose their "hardness" within three days, according to a 1970 article in the *Journal of Clinical Nutrition* by Dr. Carl F. Schaffer; the deposits continue to disappear until finally eliminated as long as excess vitamin C is given. Baboons have also developed atherosclerosis and coronary disease on diets *low* in cholesterol.

The American Heart Association's Stand

The greatest proponent of reducing dietary cholesterol is the American Heart Association (AHA). Recently (in May 1972), they slightly modified their position. Their new stance is improved, but they should also modify their public-service advertisements to reduce cholesterolphobia and the poor nutrition resulting from the public's trend toward fanaticism in its avoidance of cholesterol. The AHA's medical director, Dr. Campbell Moses, admits to the confusion and misunderstanding about the role of dietary fat and cholesterol in the development of atherosclerosis.

"Data from many sources indicate that lowering the cholesterol level will lower the recurrence rate of heart attack. There is as yet no absolute proof that a low-cholesterol, low-fat diet followed from early adult life will reduce the primary occurrence of heart attack in Americans." (*Clinical Chemistry,* 1972.)

Many Researchers Discover No Correlation Between Dietary Cholesterol and Heart Disease

Many researchers have doubted the alleged causal relationship of dietary cholesterol to heart disease. Recently, increasing evidence that they are right has encouraged them to speak out.

Dr. Teh C. Huang, president of the AHA's East Central Ohio section and a heart researcher, laments the cholesterol scare trend of recent years and sees no harm in eating eggs. He believes the recently published AHA cookbook is a mistake. He says, "It's a cookbook without any mention in the index of eggs. I think that's overdoing it." Dr. Huang also said at the August 1973 American Chemical Society meeting in Chicago that "people avoiding butter, eggs, milk, and cheese in hope of avoiding heart attacks may have been misled." He added, "Propaganda against cholesterol and saturated fat has been going on and been well accepted, while for centuries millions of human lives have been saved by milk and eggs." Dr. Huang advises, "Don't cut out cholesterol and saturated fats from your diet. Warnings that they lead to heart disease are 'scare-tactics' by big business." He is referring to the high-profit sales of low-cholesterol foods, such as margarine, by the big processed-food companies.

At the Lilly lecture addressed to the American College of Physicians in April 1970, Swedish researcher Dr. Lars Werko said, "Despite considerable effort, nobody has been able to demonstrate that it is possible to reduce the incidence of . . . heart disease by lowering serum cholesterol."

In the January 1975 issue of *Prevention,* nutritionist Dr. Carlton Fredericks commented, "Despite all the hue and cry, the case against eggs—which is the case against cholesterol—is in no way proved." Dr. Fredericks asks, "Why are there cities in the United States where dietary habits are in no way different from those of cities with high heart attack rates, [but] where the risk of heart disease is lower by almost 50 percent?" (He feels that soft drinking water, deficient in essential minerals, is far more a factor in heart disease than the consumption of eggs.)

Dr. Michael De Bakey, who has performed some of the most successful heart transplants, sees little relationship between diet, cholesterol level, and heart disease. Quoted in the *Washington Star,* June 15, 1972, he said: "Much to the chagrin of many of my colleagues who believe in this polyunsaturated fat and cholesterol business, we have put our patients on no dietary program and no anticholesterol medications. About 80% of my 1,700 patients with severe atherosclerosis requiring surgery have cholesterol levels of normal people."

Dr. Joseph D. Wassersug, a cardiologist, stated: "It is almost impossible to regulate the amount of cholesterol in the blood by manipulating the diet. The body has its own regulatory mechanisms, curbs and controls. Factors that control blood cholesterol include total calories in the diet and the normally functioning circulation of bile acids through the liver and intestine. Keep the diet low in calories. Keep your weight at average or below average figure." (*Chemical and Engineering News,* 1972.)

Dr. Edmund S. Nasset, professor of physiology, School of Medicine and Dentistry, University of Rochester, remarked, "The elimination of eggs or butter from the diet of a healthy person, merely because they contain cholesterol, is an extreme measure which can scarcely be justified on the basis of present knowledge." *(Chemical and Engineering News,* 1972.)

Dr. James M. Iacono, chief of lipid research, USDA, said in a March 1973 letter to me, "A change in diet is not what is needed, only a moderate decrease in total diet fat. Fats are needed for fat-soluble vitamin transport, for essential fatty acids, and flavor to encourage total nutrition. **At best, the most that man can reduce blood cholesterol by the high intake of polyunsaturated fatty acids is 10%.** The best solution is to idealize the body weight, neither be obese or skin and bones."

Dr. C. W. Carlson, professor of animal science at South Dakota State University, commented on the subject of eggs and serum cholesterol in a February 1972 letter to *Chemical and Engineering News:* "There is no evidence that the inclusion of one egg a day will contribute materially to the blood cholesterol level. We recognize that eggs are the best known natural source of cholesterol, both in amounts (250-300 mg) and availability. However, aside from genetic and stress effects, the most important factor in altering blood cholesterol levels is total caloric intake. A person in caloric equilibrium synthesizes approximately 800 mg of cholesterol per day if none is consumed in the diet. Dietary intakes are compensated for by reduced synthesis. With increased caloric intake, the blood cholesterol levels immediately rise.

"The egg contains many beneficial and essential nutrients—protein (globulins), lecithins, polyunsaturated fatty acids, vitamins, and minerals (iron as well as sulfur, and many others). It is a great disservice to the consuming public to deprive them of these plus nutritive factors for no substantiated reason. Incidentally, **many physicians recommend an egg a day in a cholesterol reducing diet.**"

Dr. Richard C. Bozian, professor of medicine at the University of Cincinnati College of Medicine stated: "Neither proven causal relationship for dietary cholesterol-heart disease, nor altered prognosis following hypocholesterolemic (blood-cholesterol lowering) regimens have been established." (*Medical Tribune,* 1970.)

Dr. Roger J. Williams, director of the Clayton Foundation Biochemical Institute of the University of Texas, commented in his 1971 book *Nutrition Against Disease:* "The cholesterol-rich foods that many people are trying to avoid also contain lecithin, which tends to dissolve dangerous cholesterol deposits. The lecithin helps the body to handle cholesterol and prevent it from accumulating in arteries."

Dr. Linus Pauling (see Chapter 6) suggested in his 1970 book *Vitamin C and the Common Cold:* "We must educate people away from the dangerous idea that you can control heart disease by not eating foods such as eggs, butter and milk. This oversimplified idea is totally wrong."

Dr. Carl F. Schaffer commented in the January 1970 issue of the *Journal of Clinical Nutrition,* "The cholesterol deposits induced in most laboratory animals by feeding them high-fat, high-cholesterol diets is morphologically unlike human atherosclerosis. The apparent atherosclerosis so induced is accompanied by extreme lipid (fat) deposits throughout the body, particularly in the reticuloendothelial system (cells throughout the body that have the ability to ingest particulate matter). Such a state of lipid saturation [extreme accumulation of fat deposits throughout the body] has no counterpart in human atherosclerosis."

Dr. Kurt A. Oster, chief cardiologist at Park City Hospital, Bridgeport, Connecticut, said: "The recommended dietary changes deriving their rationale from the hypercholesterolemia concept are largely uninspiring, unrealistic and impractical for the population at large. An increasing need is felt for new ideas to elucidate the origin of the chemical processes leading to both atherosclerosis and heart disease, since present theories are disappointingly unproductive."

Dr. Oster, at The Annual Meeting of the International Study Group for Research in Cardiac Metabolism in 1970, additionally stated: "The hyperlipidemia theory of atherosclerosis has been in existence for more than fifty years. Because it attributed the origin of atherosclerosis to an increase of various fatty substances in the plasma, it has proposed prevention of the condition by such dietary changes as low cholesterol and normal fat, low fat, normal cholesterol and lower saturated fats, and increase in polyunsaturated fats. This has spawned a deluge of animal experiments designed to mimic human pathology; and much of the work has caused confusion by creating conditions of unreality and by producing strange diseases which do not fully simulate human atherosclerosis."

Dr. Edward R. Pinckney, a California physician and the subject of discussion in the next chapter, wrote in the May 1971 issue of *Medical Counterpoint:* "Thanks almost solely to 'Madison Avenue's' promotion by certain commercial food producers and the American Heart Association, a great many people imagine that if they lower their blood cholesterol—assuming it is elevated—they will prevent heart disease, heart attacks, and even treat any heart trouble they may now have.

"At the same time, most people do not know the whole truth about cholesterol testing, what cholesterol really is, or the importance of cholesterol to body function. **Few people realize that there has never been a proven, scientific relationship between lowering blood cholesterol levels and**

preventing heart disease. Even if you could lower the amount of cholesterol that can be measured in your blood, there is no proof that you will, in any way, reduce your chances for a heart attack."

9

Exposé of the Cholesterol Controversy

An article that appeared in the May 1971 *Medical Counterpoint* by a well-known physician and former associate editor of the *Journal of the American Medical Association*, Dr. Edward R. Pinckney, brought out another aspect of the heart disease problem that I hadn't considered. The article, "Is Commercialism Controlling the Controversy Over Cholesterol?", examined the motives and interrelationships of the American Heart Association (AHA) and the commercial interests whose profits center around food products incorporating polyunsaturated fats and oils. These manufacturers actively promote the polyunsaturated-fat diet as a means of preventing heart attacks, as well as a treatment for existing heart disease. According to the National Association of Margarine Manufacturers, sales of margarine surpassed butter for the first time in 1957, with the average American consuming 8.6 pounds of margarine and 8.3 pounds of butter per year. By 1973 the figures were 11.3 pounds of margarine consumed compared with only 4.8 pounds of butter per person per year. We have been misled not only by improperly designed laboratory experiments, but also by special interest groups promoting their products under the guise of innocuous sounding psuedo-scientific committees. In their book, *The Cholesterol Controversy* (Sherbourne Press, 1973), Dr. and Mrs. Pinckney cite the following examples: In November 1971, the American Health Foundation appealed to Congress to make extensive changes in the "average American Diet"—including greater reliance on polyunsaturated fats—a matter of "national policy," in order to reduce coronary heart disease. The chairman of the foundation, David J. Mahoney, is president of Norton Simon, Inc., maker of polyunsaturated Wesson Oil. The foundation made grateful acknowledgement in developing its "position paper" to Dr. Dorothy Rathmann, director of research of CPC International, maker of polyunsaturated Mazola Oil. She is a member of the foundation's Committee on Food and Nutrition, as are others from CPC, Norton Simon and other affected interests, along with, it should be emphasized, unaffiliated scientists.

Dr. George V. Mann of Vanderbilt University's School of Medicine told the fourth annual Food Writers' Conference (Chicago, 1974), **"The evidence that our high-fat diet causes coronary heart disease is trivial despite the whooping of the American Heart Association. They have committed the nutritional disaster of the century by confusing association with causation, to the endless delight and profit of food companies that employ cholesterol-scare tactics in their advertising."** (Morton Mintz, *Washington Post*, 1971.)

To pursue the deception fostered by the special interest group and its involvement in the AHA and to thoroughly investigate the cholesterol myth, read *The Cholesterol Controversy*. Let the Pinckneys set you straight about the facts. Read how margarine manufacturers get away with making ridiculous drug claims for their product. If margarine did work as claimed, you would have to eat about three-quarters of a pound of 100 percent polyunsaturated margarine to protect against an eight-ounce steak—if steak were bad for you. That's a lot to spread on your toast. Cooking with margarine cannot help either; it loses most

of its alleged polyunsaturated activity at frying temperatures. Yet we are told by frequent ads that margarine is
good for your heart and lowers blood cholesterol.

In the October 1973 issue of *Media and Consumer*, Dr.
and Mrs. Pinckney discuss the important facts left out of
the most flagrant magazine and newspaper ad of this nature,
an ad which at this writing is still appearing: "New Promise Margarine can help lower cholesterol." The drug
claim: "When hundreds of people used Promise Margarine
instead of butter in clinical tests, the average cholesterol
level for the group went down. In just three weeks." Some
of the facts unrevealed in the ad but uncovered by the
Pinckneys include:

1. Those selected for study had very high blood-cholesterol levels, thus the greatest probability of improvement.

2. Others were rejected because of low probability of
achieving a reduction.

3. Of three experimental groups, one group that ate the
margarine had a *rise* in blood cholesterol.

4. Another group that ate butter had a reduction in blood
cholesterol.

5. The group that did get lower blood-cholesterol levels
while using the margarine was also reducing its calorie
intake by 12 percent. This alone would explain the cholesterol reduction. Members of the group also admitted they
voluntarily exercised more and smoked less.

I will add to the Pinckneys' comments. The magazine
and newspaper advertisements show a bar graph which at
first looks like it indicates that people eating butter have
blood-cholesterol levels twice as high as those eating
Promise. At closer inspection one can see that the bar
graph does not start at zero, but at 190 mg%, and the
values given are butter diet, 218 mg%; margarine diet,
208 mg%. But people normally show variances of 10 to
20 percent; thus the values are in the normal variance

range and aren't very significant, even if hundreds of people were used as subjects.

Other questionable procedures used are not disclosed in the ads, but the above five points should raise your eyebrows and those of the magazine editors that allowed this fraud to be perpetuated. But then again, margarine sales are profitable.

The Promise ad is not an isolated case. What about "Saffola. The change will do your heart good" or "Should an 8 year old worry about cholesterol?" The ad answers its own question by stating that parents should worry, but they can relieve their worry by feeding the child Saffola margarine. The ad claims this "reduces one important risk of coronary disease."

"A vital message from the makers of Mazola margarine" provides a further example. The headline of its magazine advertisement implies a relationship to disease and the final paragraph states: "After all, we can't give you the willpower to lose weight, cut down smoking or take up exercise. But we can give you a good tasting margarine that can be a useful part of your overall heart attack prevention program." Then there is the Mazola ad showing a photo of a preteen-ager with the headline, *"Is* there a heart attack in his future?"

If you aren't convinced of the "druglike" nature of that ad, how about the margarine ad with the picture of a heart composed of margarine wrappers? This ad advises us to eat the margarine "for our heart's benefit." **If margarine helped prevent heart attacks, our heart-attack rate would only be one-third its present level, as two-thirds of all families regularly use margarine these days.**

Danger: Polyunsaturates at Work

I find the heavy promotion of polyunsaturates dangerous. As a gerontologist, I have long been aware of the acceleration of the aging process caused by polyunsaturated fats, and I am also suspicious of a role for polyunsaturates in cancer. Let's look at the possible harm that *excess* poly-unsaturates cause.

Dr. David Kritchevsky of the Wistar Institute was quoted by Morton Mintz of *The Washington Post* (March 1971) as saying that "heating an unsaturated fat (especially corn oil) to 200° F. for 15 minutes (far less than standard cooking conditions) actually enhanced athero-sclerosis in animals. In those instances in which it has been shown that appreciable quantities of polyunsaturates lowered blood cholesterol levels, it has been shown that the cholesterol did not leave the body but was dispatched to the tissues. This would accelerate membrane damage." In any event, **the American diet has increased its polyun-saturate content, and the heart disease incidence has paralleled it.** The relationship of excess polyunsaturates to cancer is discussed in Chapter 14.

Other dangers of excess polyunsaturates include nutri-tional muscular dystrophy, increased blood uric-acid levels (a factor in gout and possibly heart disease), increased incidence of gallstones, and under certain conditions even increased blood-cholesterol levels.

Table 9.1   Saturated and Unsaturated Content of Common Fats and Oils

Polyunsaturated	Saturated %	Unsaturated %
Safflower oil	8	72
Corn oil	10	55
Wheat germ oil	15	54
Soy bean oil	15	52
Sesame oil	14	44
Cotton seed oil	25	50
Intermediate or neutral		
Olive oil	11	7
Peanut oil	20	26
Saturated		
Egg yolk	32	7
Beef fat	48	2
Butter fat	55	3
Dairy fat	55	3
Coconut oil	86	0

Data compiled from several reference sources.

Again, I remind you, some essential polyunsaturated fats are needed in our diet; many people are deficient in essential polyunsaturated fats and need more. It is the trend toward excessive, unnatural amounts that is troublesome. Most people don't realize that our livers can convert saturated fats into polyunsaturated fats as needed, with the exception of three essential polyunsaturated fatty acids (linoleic, linolenic, and arachidonic acids). Diets that have worked for centuries are to be trusted more than the untested suggestions of the medical cholesterolophobics. Table 9.1 lists the saturated and unsaturated content of common fats and oils.

Consumption of animal fats has decreased over the years, while consumption of polyunsaturated fats has increased. In 1946, the average American consumed 22.3 pounds of animal fat (10.5 lbs. butter, 11.8 lbs. lard); in 1955, 19.1 pounds of animal fat (9.0 lbs. butter, 10.1 lbs lard); and in 1963, 13.3 pounds of animal fat (6.8 lbs. butter, 6.5 lbs. lard). The polyunsaturated oils increased from 14.4 pounds per person in 1946, to 17.7 pounds per person in 1955, to 19.0 pounds per person in 1963. Heart-disease mortality kept pace with this increase.

Vitamin E and Heart Disease

If you are one of the countless numbers misled into believing that dietary or blood cholesterol is a major factor in heart disease, you may have had mixed emotions about the preceding chapter. On the one hand, you learn that you can eat good foods again; on the other, you should be shocked out of your complacency in thinking you are safe from heart disease. Perhaps you were a little smug in your knowledge that you have been watching your weight and avoiding cholesterol, and that your blood-cholesterol level is normal.

If cholesterol doesn't count, what does? Surely, personality and smoking have an effect on heart disease, but their effect is indirect. Both stress and smoking consume nutrients, often creating deficiencies that in turn cause heart disease. "Personality Type A," in which there is a pronounced sense of time urgency, causes stress which readily consumes our normal reserves of vitamin C and the B-complex vitamins. My thesis is that heart disease is caused by undernutrition (not necessarily malnutrition) coupled with insufficient activity.

Whether or not you have a heart attack depends on many factors. Do you smoke, are you under pressure, do you overeat, are you eating lots of sugar, are you inactive? Supernutrition will improve your chances of living in good health. If you must smoke or eat poorly, it will help you considerably; if you can do away with bad habits, live moderately, become active and enjoy life, and practice good nutrition, you will most likely postpone heart disease until your eighth decade or later.

The importance of each vitamin depends on two factors: the severity of the deficiency in our diets and the severity of the effect of those deficiencies on the cardiovascular system. For this reason, I have ranked the nutrients in the following order: vitamin E first in importance, followed by selenium, vitamin C, vitamin B_6, magnesium, and others. Let's look at vitamin E first.

Vitamin E Is a Natural Antioxidant

Vitamin E (tocopherol) is a natural antioxidant and free-radical scavenger (deactivator). Its precise role in the body is still under investigation. It may act solely as a general antioxidant to protect tissue and blood components from lipid peroxidation (rancifying) or it may have additional specific roles in blood formation, electron transport (the life process itself), or other forms of energy utilization and transfer. The specific functions are more in keeping with the usual role of vitamins, whereas the general, antioxidant role is more like the role played by vitamin C. When vitamin E is functioning as a general antioxidant, it "sacrifices" itself. Even though vitamin C and some other compounds can recharge or regenerate spent vitamin E, it can be consumed rapidly and often must be replaced in quantities considered excessive in terms of normal vitamins. Ideal intake of vitamin E approaches the ideal intake level of vitamin C; both are more than just vitamins.

The relationship of vitamin E to heart disease covers many areas including preventing the formation of active sites for cholesterol plaques in arteries, influencing serum-cholesterol levels, preventing blood clots, utilizing heart energy, improving blood-circulation and blood-oxygen efficiency, and reducing scar formation in the heart due to infarcts.

Preventing the Formation of Active Sites for Plaque Deposits

Damage can occur in a blood vessel when highly reactive chemical fragments called free-radicals react with the vessel walls. Vitamin E deactivates free-radicals by sacrificing itself to the free-radical. The process of free-radical deactivation by vitamin E requires less energy than the reaction of a free-radical with a lipid (fat) in the artery wall, therefore it is a more probable reaction. If vitamin E is not present to protect the artery walls, the free-radical reaction produces an irritation or active site that starts the atherosclerotic process. Through a combination of electronic-charge attraction and further chemical reactions, cholesterol and calcium are attached to the inside layers of the artery walls.

When the active site exists, it draws cholesterol by electronic-charge attraction, removing the cholesterol as it is naturally produced within the artery for lubrication to prevent damage to the blood cells as they rush through. It is unlikely that the cholesterol in the bloodstream can be held in place sufficiently long by the electronic charge to draw the large cholesterol molecules through the inner surface of the artery wall to the active site. However, it is possible for some cholesterol to filter through the inner layer at a slow rate. Free-radicals are harmful and very reactive. They can attack the heart muscle (myocardium) to accelerate myocardial infarction.

I promised to separate speculation from known fact. Besides the old theory held by most physicians that consuming cholesterol causes heart disease, there are several other theories; we haven't conclusively proved any of them. Two or three others are equally as plausible as my theory, but

I do feel that mine best fits the observed facts concerning the atherosclerotic process itself and the effect of diet.

Polyunsaturates Promote Dangerous Free-Radicals

The danger of polyunsaturated fats began to be noticed when Dr. Fred A. Kummerow and his colleagues from the University of Illinois at Urbana reported their studies at the 1974 Federation of American Societies for Experimental Biology meeting of nutritionists and related sciences. Newspapers carried the story under such titles as "Margarine Found Health Hazard." Too bad the story didn't make the front sections. **The findings showed that a fat present in margarine may present a greater health risk than cholesterol-rich foods such as beef fat, butterfat, and powdered eggs.**

The studies involved feeding different types of diets to different groups of swine for eight months. The researchers concluded that a hydrogenated fat, which contains margarine-base stock designed to make the product more stable ("trans" fatty acids) was more atherogenic (causing atherosclerosis) than the cholesterol materials mentioned. The degree of atherosclerosis was determined by autopsies on the experimental animals. Swine were used in the tests because the aorta and heart of a pig weigh about the same as those of a human, and pigs are close to humans in their response to cholesterol. The experiments were repeated several times with identical results. The greatest degree of hardening of the arteries was in the pigs fed margarine-base stock with their diet. The group fed sugar with their diet was next. The group fed butter had almost negligible damage, and the least disease was found in the groups fed egg yolk or egg whites with their standard diet.

Polyunsaturated Fats Destroy Vitamin E

Some people have argued that polyunsaturated fats (PUFAs) contain enough vitamin E to protect against lipid peroxidation. This is wrong! If they did, we would never have to worry about rancidity.

As graphically illustrated by Dr. R. H. Hall in his book *Food for Naught* (Harper and Row, 1974), what vitamin E isn't stripped out of polyunsaturated fats is destroyed when the vegetable oils are heated to clarify the product; most of the vegetable oils are also refined, destroying the vitamin E that might remain. Any vitamin E present still in the refined oil is certainly destroyed in the bottle by light and air.

When we eat vegetable oils with their polyunsaturated fats, we need extra vitamin E to prevent lipid peroxidation. What few people realize is that we require extra vitamin E for as long as the polyunsaturated fatty acids are stored in the body; the PUFAs are readily stored at the expense of the saturated fats which are replaced. The PUFAs are retained longer than vitamin E, which is sacrificed as it protects the PUFAs from peroxidation, a continuing process.

Polyunsaturated Fats Form Harmful Dienes

The products of lipid peroxidation are fragments called dienes and free-radicals. They occur only when there is not enough vitamin E present.

Dr. Nicholas R. DiLuzio of Tulane University's School of Medicine found the harmful dienes present in the blood of 96 percent (78 out of 81) of the persons he examined at random. They definitely had a vitamin E deficiency and free-radicals and dienes were available in their blood to cause damage to artery walls and other key substances. Dr. DiLuzio measured the diene level in five volunteers, fed them vitamin E for a week, then discontinued the vitamin E supplementation. The diene level dropped during the vitamin E supplementation period, but gradually rose again after the vitamin E was stopped.

These same dienes have been directly implicated in myocardial infarction (destroyed heart muscle). Drs. K. J. Kingsbury, D. M. Morgan and R. Stovold reported in *Lancet* (December 20, 1969) that infarction was significantly associated with blood-diene concentration; they found no correlation with age, blood-cholesterol level, or two-hour blood sugar.

Chlorinated Drinking Water Consumes Vitamin E

Incidentally, another way in which vitamin E is depleted in the body besides by the increase of PUFAs is by the increase of oxidizers, such as oxygen or chlorine, in the blood. Astronauts breathe high oxygen concentrations in the atmospheres of spacecraft and spacesuits. During the Gemini space flights, astronauts were found to be suffering from hemolytic anemia, the premature breakdown of their red blood cells, caused by a vitamin E deficiency. Their diets had normal amounts of vitamin E, but they required more to handle the extra oxygen that entered their blood because of the high oxygen concentration they breathed. In 1969 NASA added vitamin E supplements to astronauts' diets and hemolytic anemia disappeared. Could this vitamin E deficiency have been what caused the heart attack of astronaut James B. Irwin at the age of forty-three?

Chlorine is an oxidant, too; most of us drink chlorinated water which consumes vitamin E in our body. We certainly drink more chlorine than did our ancestors, but we are also getting safer water. Therefore, if we take enough vitamin E, it is a good tradeoff. Complications arise, however, when pollutants react with chlorine to produce carcinogens, thus requiring still more vitamin E. (See Chapter 14.)

Vitamin E Prevents Blood Clots

Perhaps the most important property of vitamin E discussed by others is its ability to prevent or reduce blood clots. My feeling is that the antioxidant and free-radical scavenging properties are more important, but I do not mean to minimize the importance of preventing the blood clots that cause coronary thrombosis (sudden heart attack) and pulmonary embolism (in which vein thrombosis, blood clots that occasionally form in the leg after operations, break loose and lodge in the lungs, causing death).

Drs. Wilfrid E. Shute and Evan Shute, founders of the Shute Institute of London, Ontario, Canada, have often stressed the fact that vitamin E is a natural antithrombin, the only substance that prevents blood clots, and is perfectly safe because it normalizes clotting time rather than interfering with normal clotting.

The fame of the Shute Institute for Clinical and Laboratory Medicine has spread around the world since its origin in 1947. The institute has treated more than 35,000 patients, 90 percent of whom have been referred by others, after being diagnosed as having heart disease. Dr. Evan Shute admits that "some very distinguished people have come here as patients. Unfortunately, most people come after they have had an attack. They may never have had heart attacks in the first place, if they had taken vitamin E as a preventative, earlier in life."

The findings of the Drs. Shute are described in *The Summary* (Vol. 25, 1973). They explain their rationale to other physicians thus:

Alpha tocopherol has certain unique properties which no other nutritional agent possesses, forming the basis of its value in cardiovascular disease.

(a) It is both an antioxidant and improves the ability of the tissues to utilize oxygen. This latter property has been dramatically shown by Hove, Hickman and Harris, Zierler et al. and more recently in the United States Air Force, the latter study, by the way, indicating an improvement in heart reserve.

Its powers as an antioxidant are generally recognized, though Green et al. challenge this.

(b) It has a unique influence on clots, not only upon those already formed, but in preventing both embolism and extension. I need not point out how superior to the usual anticoagulants two of this trio of properties make alpha tocopherol. It is incomparably safer, too, since it is never haemorrhagic. It is a safe fibrinolysin.

(c) It is a vasodilator, at least of capillaries. Thus it opens up reserves of vascular networks which provide detours around vascular roadblocks. The best demonstrations of this have been the beautiful experiments of Enria and Ferrerro on femoral vein ligations in dogs and Dominguez and Domingiez on femoral artery ligation in rabbits. Apparently the body has large reserves of blood vessels as well as of kidney, liver or lung. Alpha tocopherol mobilizes them in need.

(d) It improves damaged capillary permeability, as many workers besides ourselves have shown.

(e) It resolves some scars, as Steinberg and others have shown.

(f) It may improve muscle power per se, as many studies on athletes, dogs and horses attest.

The observations of the Drs. Shute have been verified by others. A series of reports by Dr. J. H. Kay and his associates at the Tulane School of Medicine have shown the antithrombic effect in detail. The reports appeared in the *Proceedings of the Society for Experimental Biology and Medicine* (1950) and the *Bulletin of the Tulane Medical Faculty* (1950). The papers conclude that vitamin E quantitatively prevents the action of thrombin on fibrinogen. Vitamin E combines with fibrinogen to form a complex that is not clottable with thrombin. Previously, Dr. Alton Ochsner, one of our most famed surgeons in whose honor the Ochsner Clinic in New Orleans is named, reported the following important observations in *Surgery* (1949): "Vitamin E is an efficient anti-thrombic agent, and is probably one of the principal anti-thrombins in the blood. By supplying anti-thrombin in the form of Vitamin E, the deficiency in anti-thrombin is corrected and a clot is prevented. The great advantage of using Vitamin E is that although the thrombosing tendency is overcome, a hemorrhagic (bleeding) tendency is not produced, such as occurs when anticoagulants, for instance, heparin or dicumarol, are used."

Those drugs interfere with one factor of the clotting mechanism. This interference is continuous and is not balanced by the other factors. Patients receiving those drugs for treatment of heart disease should be constantly monitored to see that their clotting time is not unnaturally prolonged, or they may bleed to death.

Vitamin E Effective Against Acquired Hemophilia

To illustrate that vitamin E normalizes blood clotting rather than merely prolonging it—as some drugs do—consider this observation by Dr. Tropeano. He reported in the Italian medical journal *Progress In Medicine, Napoli* (1948) the case of a patient with prolonged clotting time (fibrinopenic hemophilia) was normalized with vitamin E therapy. Formerly, the patient's blood took twenty-four hours to clot, but after ten days of receiving 200 mg of vitamin E, clotting time was reduced to two hours. After twenty-five days, his blood-clotting time was further reduced to eighty minutes; finally, it was normal. (There has been to date, however, no known success with vitamin E for the normal, genetic form of hemophilia.) The list of others confirming the normalization of clotting time is long.

The clotting is important because, as pointed out in an earlier chapter, a clot in the heart produces coronary thrombosis and instant death; a clot in the coronary arteries can produce an infarct and severe heart damage or death; a clot in the cerebral arterial tree leading to the brain produces a stroke (cerebral embolism); and a clot in the lung results in the pulmonary embolism that kills approximately *one out of every 200 patients operated on.*

Faced with the facts about vitamin E and free-radicals

and blood clots, one can only conclude that not to supplement your diet with vitamin E is a form of suicide.

Vitamin E Prevents Death of Heart Tissue

Cholesterol tends to accumulate in the arteries at points having low oxygen concentrations. If arteries to the heart are blocked, the heart tissue dies because of oxygen starvation (an infarct). Vitamin E helps minimize oxygen starvation by making the red blood cells more efficient in utilizing oxygen.

In 1942 Drs. O. B. Houchin and H. A. Mattill published three studies of the effect of vitamin E on oxygen-deficient muscle tissues (two in the *Journal of Biological Chemistry* in 1942 and one in the *Proceedings of the Society for Experimental Biology and Medicine,* also in 1942). As discussed in the above-mentioned articles, muscles in vitamin-E-deficient animals have an oxygen consumption much above normal. Feeding vitamin E to animals returns the oxygen-consumption rates to normal in ten to twenty-seven hours. The vitamin E decreased the need for oxygen by 50 to 250 percent.

If your heart is being starved of oxygen, it doesn't help to have poor oxygen efficiency. Vitamin E reduces the need for oxygen and increases your chance for survival. Athletes and racehorse trainers have known of the oxygen-sparing property of vitamin E for a long time and use such supplements regularly.

You may note that vitamin E plays a role similar to exercise. By proper exercise, you increase your cardio-vascular-pulmonary efficiency. As the "training effect" takes place, you utilize oxygen more efficiently. This too helps you survive a heart attack. Vitamin E and exercise have another effect in common. They both encourage the establishment of additional blood vessels and dilate smaller blood vessels when there is an oxygen demand. This brings more blood to every part of the body and reduces the damage done by any one vessel being blocked; again, it increases survival chances.

Vitamin E Reduces Harmful Scar Tissue

Vitamin E also reduces the harmful overproduction of excessive scar tissue. Scar formation in laboratory animals has been monitored by Dr. H. Paul Ehrlich and his associates at the Department of Surgery of the University of California at San Francisco. They found that vitamin E produced a stronger covering, free of excess scar. Their work was published in 1972 in the *Annuals of Surgery*.

If a person survives a myocardial infarct, the oxygen-starved tissue dies. The dead tissue stimulates the formation of scar-tissue which acts as a patch to prevent the infarcted area from rupturing. Large scars produce deformities by their contractive force. This extra deformity in the heart tissue further weakens the heart. Drs. T. W. Gullickson and C. E. Calverley reported in *Science* (1946) that electrocardiograms obtained on vitamin-E-deficient cattle revealed definite indications of the presence of cardiac defects; atrophy and scarring of the heart tissue were found upon autopsy. Vitamin E would help recovery from an infarct by minimizing tissue death from oxygen starvation and by reducing excessive scarring.

Vitamin E Strengthens Heart Contractions

Dr. Margaret Fedelsova and her colleagues at the University of Manitoba's Faculty of Medicine have made what I feel is a very significant discovery concerning the role of vitamin E and the heart. They found marked reductions in both energy production and energy utilization by the heart when there is a vitamin E deficiency. This team of researchers observed that vitamin E deficiency decreased the levels of many enzymes and altered critical nucleotide (a basic component of DNA) ratios. Still other enzymes functioned at decreased rates; furthermore, calcium utilization, which is critical to the heartbeat, was hampered by a vitamin E deficiency. With all the decrease in energy usage and heart contractability in vitamin-E-deficient hearts, however, there was no observable physical damage. No wonder many reasearchers have been misled in studying vitamin E and the heart; often they have been looking for obvious changes in the heart, such as changes in size, color, weight, or firmness. Not finding such obvious changes, many investigators have wrongly concluded there is no relationship. Dr. Fedelsova's group was not looking for the obvious, but studying how the heart functions and which compounds affect that function. Their report was published in 1971 in the *Canadian Journal of Physiology and Pharmacology*.

Dr. K. Folkers has published a report in the *International Journal of Vitamin Research* that shows that victims of heart disease often are unable to produce enough coenzyme Q (ubiquinol) to keep their heart muscle unimpaired. Vitamin E is required to produce coenzyme Q.

Vitamin E and the Skeptics

One paper in particular should be brought to the attention of the vitamin E skeptics. Dr. E. Cheraskin, professor and chairman, Department of Oral Medicine, University of Alabama Medical Center, and Dr. W. M. Ringsdorf, Jr., associate professor at the same institution, explicitly detail evidence that the supposed inevitable increase with age of cardiovascular symptoms and signs can be thwarted by vitamin E. Their examination of the relationship between age and reported cardiovascular findings in both males and females shows that the increase in clinical symptoms paralleled age only in the subjects (80 percent of the total group) consuming less than the recommended dietary allowance (RDA) for vitamin E. They also conclude: "A review of the clinical change during the experimental year revealed that the decrease in cardiovascular findings occurred only in the group of subjects characterized by an increase in the daily intake of Vitamin E."

Further analysis of the data by Drs. Cheraskin and Ringsdorf showed that those receiving more vitamin E and better all-around nutrition had improved electrocardiograms, their blood triglyceride levels were cut in half, and the number of clinical complaints decreased from an average of seventeen to an average of twelve. Dr. Cheraskin comments, "Within the one-year period, the clinical picture of the group improved approximately 30 percent. Specifically, the average fifty-year old had become more like a forty-year old within twelve months. It is most exciting to consider the possibility of diminishing, rather than increasing, complaints as we grow older. Particularly thrilling is the potential of accomplishing this goal by relatively simple dietary means." The details are published in *Nutrition Report International* (3:107–17, 1970).

Letters have been flying back and forth in the *New England Journal of Medicine,* as physicians pass along comments about vitamin E therapy for heart disease.

Dr. W. M. Toone reported (*New England Journal of Medicine,* 1973) that 400 mg given four times daily reduced the need for nitroglycerin treatment of angina pectoris in a significant number of patients. He performed a "single-blind" test with two groups of eleven patients. Four patients in the vitamin E group were able to reduce their nitroglycerin use to two tablets or fewer per month. No patients in the placebo group reduced their use of nitroglycerin to fewer than eighty tablets per month.

A New Vitamin E Drug for Heart Disease

The drug Telsem, which consists of vitamin E and the trace element selenium, has been given a two-year clinical trial in Mexico. This combination of antioxidants was said to have demonstrated 92 percent beneficial responses in patients with recurring attacks of angina pectoris—with or without myocardial infarct. These responses involved reduction or elimination of angina attacks, increased vigor and work capacity, and improved electrocardiograms. There was no evidence of adverse side effects.

A similar drug containing vitamin E and selenium, Seletoc, was first used in 1962 on lambs and calves to combat a disease with a dominant pathology of heart-muscle degeneration. It arrested the degenerative process and restored normal heart function, and has saved the American animal industry hundreds of millions of dollars. Many veterinarians have successfully treated dogs with heart disease with this combination of vitamin E and selenium. I know of several scientists who take it, or similar products, themselves. These two antioxidants are also keystones in my formulations to slow the aging process. **Natural sources of selenium include brewer's yeast, eggs, onion, and garlic. In Europe, farmers often feed garlic and onions to their horses to cure atherosclerotic obstructions in the animals' legs.**

Other minerals are important to effective functioning of vitamin E. Dr. James P. Isaacs, a Johns Hopkins (Baltimore) surgeon, treated twenty-five patients with severe heart disease for ten years. During that period, only two of the patients died, rather than the thirteen or more who would have been expected to die in that length of time. The secret of Dr. Isaacs' fantastic success? Daily supplements of vitamin E, vitamin C, zinc, manganese, and copper, along with estrogen and thyroid hormones.

I am not at all sure that the hormones are needed; a comparison study could be made without them. Dr. Isaacs has another group of one hundred patients who will complete the ten-year period in late 1976. He hopes to have a detailed report available by 1977 and encourages physicians to write him at any time for details at Johns Hopkins, Baltimore, Maryland 21205

Almost monthly, scientific reports show vitamin E's relationship to heart disease more clearly. This vitamin has been found to regulate the penetration of magnesium and manganese into heart cells, reduce atherosclerosis in the leg (intermittent claudication), improve microcirculation where there is blue coloring of extremities (acrocyanosis), and reduce vascular permeability. In a discussion of recent research findings in *Chemical and Engineering News* (October 9, 1972), I concluded, "As vitamin E deficiency in animals leads to tissue degradation and gross changes in biochemistry, we should err on the high-intake side, rather than the low.

"**Today's typical vitamin E consumption is only a fraction of that of 50 years ago,** even when adjusted for lipid intake. Degermination, bleaching of grains, processing, and longer storage periods have depleted foods. The long-term effects of these common practices along with decreased activity may explain our worsening mortality rates from cardiovascular disease.

"In conclusion, it is difficult to assess, but borderline vitamin E deficiencies are widespread, based on both the RDA and the diene test. It is difficult to assume that the long-term consequences are not going to present a major problem."

Putting the Cause of Heart Disease in Perspective

There may be several causes of heart disease, depending upon which nutrient the body is deficient in. If vitamin E is deficient, free-radical attack may form a site for cholesterol deposition, or blood clots may form. If vitamin C is deficient, cholesterol may build up on any active site in the blood vessels; and similarly with deficiencies of magnesium, zinc, vitamin B_6, and other nutrients. Heart disease can be caused by many factors, but vitamin E can help you survive a heart attack no matter what the cause.

Although people insist on examining all the diets of the world looking for one component, such as cholesterol, to blame as a cause of heart disease, they would be doing better to look for the absence of one component, such as

vitamin E. Just as it is dangerous to worry only about cholesterol, it is dangerous to worry only about vitamin E. Total nutrition—Supernutrition—is the main concern. Without it, we are predisposed to premature heart disease.

11

Vitamin C with B Complex and Heart Disease

The relationship between vitamin C and heart disease is clear. Vitamin C is the third most significant major deficiency involved in heart disease—vitamin E is first and selenium is second. Heart-attack-prone individuals usually have extremely low serum vitamin C levels. Within six to twelve hours after heart attacks, blood vitamin C levels drop to values typical of those with scurvy. Dr. R. Hume of Southern General Hospital, Glasgow, Scotland, reported this in the *British Heart Journal* (1972) and concluded that the vitamin C goes to the heart to help repair it. Smokers have lower vitamin C levels than nonsmokers; older people have diets more deficient in vitamin C than younger people; men tend to have lower serum levels of vitamin C than women on identical diets; and people under stress have lower vitamin C levels than those not under stress. Soviet scientists have published articles on the relationship of atherosclerosis and vitamin C for years. Now they routinely prescribe vitamin C for human cases of atherosclerosis.

Dr. Ralph Mumma, a Pennsylvania State University

biologist, reported in 1971 that vitamin C and ascorbic sulfate flush cholesterol from the inner walls of arteries of rats. This was confirmed in a report by Indian researchers Drs. Bala Nambisan and P. A. Kurup, published in a 1974 issue of *Atherosclerosis*. And Dr. Boris Sokoloff found improvement ranging from moderate to impressive in fifty of sixty atherosclerotic patients treated with 1 to 3 grams of vitamin C.

Vitamin C and Smoking

Without considering the question of whether cigarette smoking is a causative factor or an associated factor in heart disease, smoking should be avoided because it speeds the aging process; causes wrinkling at earlier ages; consumes or destroys vitamins; puts carbon monoxide into your blood; constricts blood vessels, thus reducing circulation; lowers immunity to diseases (Dr. Sorrell Schwartz, *Journal of Pharmacology and Experimental Therapeutics,* 1974); causes lung, bladder, and oral cancers, as well as other lung disorders; and wastes your money.

Dr. Omer Pelletier of the Nutrition Research Division, Food and Drug Directorate, Ottawa, Canada, commented on the vitamin C status of cigarette smokers and non-smokers. His report, published in the *American Journal of Clinical Nutrition* (1970), concluded, "The differences in blood Vitamin C status were not due to different intakes. Less Vitamin C is effectively available for utilization by the smokers, or else the smokers are utilizing vitamin C differently."

It is not clear if smoking actually destroys vitamin C in the body in the same manner that it does in laboratory glassware, or if people who have a genetic difference in their vitamin C utilization tend to smoke. A test needs to be run to see what happens to vitamin C utilization after a smoker quits. In any event, smoking is harmful in many ways; and **each pack of cigarettes smoked produces a deficiency of about 500 mg vitamin C.**

The Framingham study, although flawed in its study of

cholesterol as a risk factor (Chapter 8), withstands close
scrutiny in its smoking study. The Framingham study reveals that middle-aged men who smoke more than a pack
of cigarettes a day are two to six times more likely to have
strokes than nonsmoking middle-aged men. The hardest-
hit smokers, as far as heart disease goes, are 45 to 54
years of age.

Vitamin C Detoxifies Poisons

Besides restoring vitamin C blood levels of smokers to
normal, vitamin C supplements can detoxify some of the
poisons formed in the blood of smokers. Dr. Herbert
Sprince and his associates at the Veterans Administration
Hospital in Coatesville, Pennsylvania, used a spectro-
fluorometer to determine that vitamin C protects against
acetaldehyde poisoning—acetaldehyde forms in the blood
of alcoholics and heavy smokers and is a powerful initiator
of dangerous free-radicals as well as being a cross-linking
compound. A combination of certain sulfur amino acids
and vitamin C gave 100 percent protection against a standard lethal dose of acetaldehyde in laboratory rats. Dr.
Fred R. Klenner (see Chapter 6) has used vitamin C in
high doses for years to detoxify many poisons, including
snake venom, successfully.

Vitamin C Cleans Cholesterol from
Arterial Walls

Vitamin C regulates, in part, the amount of cholesterol circulating in the blood. If you have a deficiency of vitamin
C, your body's ability to convert cholesterol to bile is impaired; the cholesterol, instead of being properly used,
accumulates in the bloodstream. Vitamin C tends to nor-
malize the blood-cholesterol level and consume the cholesterol deposited in the arteries: vitamin C can clear
cholesterol from arteries and cure atherosclerosis!

Perhaps the greatest research in this area has been done by Dr. Emil Ginter, director of the Biochemical Department of the Research Institute of Human Nutrition in Bratislava, Czechoslovakia. In 1959 Dr. Ginter and his associates began a detailed study of the metabolic consequences of chronic vitamin C deficiency. Their research earned them worldwide recognition, yet the American medical profession has not followed up the studies. Dr. Ginter set out to see if there was a relationship between vitamin C deficiency and atherosclerosis. He chose the guinea pig for his experimental model because, like man, the guinea pig does not make its own vitamin C. Ginter noted that others had made similar studies, but the results could not be trusted (although they agreed with the concept) because the animals were made completely deficient in vitamin C and developed scurvy, which produced drastic changes in the animals' biochemistry. Ginter made his animals only slightly deficient so as to avoid scurvy.

In 1965 Dr. Ginter conducted an experiment with two groups, each composed of 30 guinea pigs. The control group was fed a normal diet which contained 5 mg of vitamin C. The experimental group was depleted of vitamin C for two weeks and then fed one-tenth of the vitamin C fed the controls. Both diets were low-fat diets. The amount of cholesterol deposits after one year averaged 30 percent higher in the vitamin C-deficient experimental group. A second experiment was designed to see what effect a high-cholesterol diet would have. Again two groups of guinea pigs were used, but the amounts of vitamin C were increased to handle the extra dietary fat. The control group received 50 mg, while the experimental group received 5 mg. Again after one year, an average of 550 mg of plaque had accumulated in the aortic wall in the group receiving the lower amount of vitamin C, as opposed to an average of only 400 mg in the group receiving the higher. Dr. Ginter's group set out to find why the vitamin C deficiency caused cholesterol deposits and found that this vitamin is required in the process that converts cholesterol into bile (*Science,* 1973).

Professor R. Knox of the University of Birmingham,

England, has compared the cardiovascular-disease statistics in regions in England and Wales having high and low levels of vitamin C. The low dietary vitamin C areas had high heart-disease mortality rates as opposed to the low rate of heart-disease deaths in the higher vitamin C intake areas.

Dr. Constance R. Spittle, a pathologist at Pinderfields General Hospital in Wakefield, Yorkshire, England, suggested in a 1971 letter to the editor of the *Hospital Tribune,* "Humans taking large doses of vitamin C will not necessarily get a fall in serum cholesterol—indeed, they may get the reverse, because they are mobilizing their arterial cholesterol. The actual serum level is not relevant when they are taking the vitamin, since the cholesterol is being channeled in the right direction—away from the arteries."

Dr. Spittle first noticed the "washing out" of cholesterol from artery walls when she observed that her own blood cholesterol would increase after taking vitamin C, regardless of her fat or cholesterol intake. She recruited a group of volunteers for a follow-up experiment that lasted twelve weeks. Fifty-eight healthy volunteers and twenty-five patients with atherosclerosis participated. For the first 6 weeks, the volunteers received no vitamin C supplementation to their normal diets; they took 1 gram of vitamin C daily during the second 6-week period. In the healthy volunteers under twenty-five years of age, most had decreases in their blood cholesterol levels, with an average decrease of 8 percent. All but five of the atherosclerotic volunteers had a rise in serum cholesterol averaging nearly 10 percent, as arterial cholesterol was dissolved. Similarly, some of the expected rise in blood cholesterol level was found in the volunteers over forty-five years of age. The volunteers between twenty-five and forty-five showed mixed results, presumably because in some, cholesterol was being washed out of their arteries while others, who had nearly "clean" arteries to begin with, were undergoing a lowering of blood cholesterol. Dr. Spittle's report was published in *Lancet* (December 11, 1971).

Dr. Boris Sokoloff reported in the *Journal of the Amer-*

ican Geriatic Society (1966) that long-term use (five to six months) of vitamin C resulted in moderate to impressive improvements in fifty out of sixty atherosclerotic patients receiving doses of 1 to 3 grams daily.

Vitamin B Complex Curbs Heart Disease

The B-complex vitamins are critical in avoiding heart disease. Vitamin B_6 is probably the single most important member of the family because it is used in making the cholesterol solublizing compound lecithin, and because it is in short supply as it is not added back to "enriched" flour. Nicotinic acid, vitamin B_{12}, choline, PABA, and inositol are other key members of the B-complex family of vitamins important in the prevention of heart disease.

Vitamin B_6, like most of the B-complex vitamins, is used in the formation of coenzymes that metabolize the fat and sugar in our diet. The large increase in sugar consumption has been associated with increased blood levels of triglycerides and heart disease. Vitamin B_6 is also part of the coenzyme that helps form lecithin in our bodies. Even when we eat lecithin itself, which is a good practice, we still need vitamin B_6 and the trace mineral, magnesium, to help put the lecithin molecule back together after it has been broken apart during digestion.

Choline can be made in the body and is widely available in foods. I recommend taking some extra choline daily: heart disease is such a killer that sometimes it is advisable to forget scientific conservatism and go a little overboard, just to be sure. One of the better sources of choline (which is used in making lecithin in your body) is lecithin itself.

Lecithin is like a detergent, for it keeps cholesterol soluble in the blood; it is widely available in foods, but don't consider yourself a fanatic if you decide to supplement your diet with extra lecithin as insurance. Remember, I said that taking extra vitamin E isn't insurance; it is a necessity; *not* taking extra vitamin E is a form of suicide. Taking extra lecithin is not necessary, but is a form of insurance. Later in this chapter I show how Dr. J. Rinse has improved the health of thousands with lecithin.

Choline is one of the components of lecithin, but vitamin B_6 is needed to put the components together. Another important component of lecithin is linoleic acid, an essential polyunsaturated fatty acid. The best sources of linoleic acid are wheat-germ oil, whole milk, nuts, seeds, eggs, soybeans, and, of course, lecithin itself. You can only make as much lecithin in your body as you have the least available components and coenzyme to make the whole lecithin molecule. Relying on one source of choline and another source of linoleic acid may not give you an optimum balance. Incidentally, **one of the problems with drinking skim milk is that the linoleic acid has been removed.** Another is that skim milk doesn't have cholesterol, which is needed by infants to make myelin sheaths for nerve fibers. Nature has always provided ample lecithin in the same foods that contain cholesterol, which may partly account for the reason that eating high-cholesterol foods has not been found to cause heart disease. Lecithin also increases the capacity of bile salts to remove cholesterol. Three times more of the lecithin-cholesterol complex than cholesterol alone can be incorporated into the bile salts.

Dr. C. Pries of the Gaubius Institute in Leiden, Holland, has analyzed the blood of 48 men between forty and sixty years of age. Half of them were known to have atherosclerosis, the other half were free of symptoms. Those men having a lecithin content of 36 percent or higher in the blood fats showed no atherosclerosis, whereas those with 34 percent or lower *all* had the disease. Dr. Pries concluded, "One should, based on the results of our investigation, increase the phospholipid percentage of the blood and the lecithin percentage of the fats."

By now you know that I don't stress blood-cholesterol level at all, but you might be interested to know that several of the B-complex vitamins have been shown to lower high blood-cholesterol levels to some degree. Over a thousand scientific papers have been written about nicotinic acid alone, which is one of the three natural forms of vitamin B_3—niacin and niacinamide are the others. Nicotinic acid was found by Dr. Mark C. Altschule to speed normal oxidation of cholesterol to its degradation products. Dr. Altschule and Dr. Abram Hoffer (see Chapter 7) have published extensively on the action of nicotinic acid and niacin on blood-cholesterol levels.

Other Factors Affecting Heart Disease

The minerals in drinking water, other vitamins, the amount of fiber or indigestible bulk in the diet, and refined sugars all play an important part in heart disease; it would take another book to discuss this subject in detail. I have shown that cholesterol is not a problem for the healthy person and that **any imbalance in the diet can cause heart disease.** I believe that the most critical factors are the ones in which we have the greatest deficiencies. Vitamin E is the prime factor, selenium next, vitamin C third, vitamin B_6 next, and so on. I have shown that the deficiencies can cause heart disease; now I want to show how Supernutrition will cure many forms of disease.

The Heart Disease Cure

I know of many hundreds of people who have been freed from heart disease for years by an improvement in their nutrition. Earlier, I told how Dr. Jacobus Rinse, a consulting chemist, was struck by heart disease although he had followed all of the rules; that was in 1951. The good news is that at this writing, twenty-four years later, Dr. Rinse, now seventy-five years old, is free from all signs of heart disease and enjoying his semi-retirement in Vermont.

The following account by Dr. Rinse tells how he over-

came heart disease when he discovered his own Supernutrition. Dr. Rinse's account first appeared in the July
1973 issue of *American Laboratory* and is presented here
with the magazine's permission.

An attack of angina pectoris in 1951 at the age of 51 initiated an inquiry by me into possible reasons for the occurrence
of atherosclerosis. Starting with a hypothesis that deficiencies
in my food could be causative factors, dietary changes were
explored, resulting eventually in the complete alleviation of
angina and related heart diseases. This paper describes the
evolution of the successful dietary changes, explores details of
the hypothesis, and cites some recent work supporting important aspects of the hypothesis.

Following the 1951 attack of angina pectoris with attendant
violent heart aches, the attending heart specialist predicted
that I might have another 10 years to live if all physical
exercises were avoided. I was completely puzzled, because in
my case none of the known causes was valid. I did not smoke,
was not overweight, had no special tensions, had sufficient
physical exercise, and had no family history of the disease. . . .

Early 1957 and later in October of that year, I experienced
attacks with heavy heart pains, which subsided after an hour
or so. The angina pains remained after the second attack,
especially walking up stairs. At the same time, spasms and an
increase of 50 strokes in the pulse rate were observed frequently.

At that time, I read about a series of experiments with rats
and rabbits who got lecithin . . . with the result that the cholesterol content in the blood was lowered. I decided to add a
tablespoon [of lecithin] to my cereal breakfast, which contained . . . other additives also.

Results appeared in a few days because the [heart] spasms
stopped and the increased pulse rate diminished slightly
but definitely. The improvement continued until after three
months, all symptoms of angina pectoris, even after exercising,
had disappeared. One year later, the capacity for heavy out-
door work and running had returned. This result seemed to
be too good to be true, and in the beginning, I would not
believe it. But it appeared to be a fact, because I have had no

recurrence of angina or other diseases since—now 16 years (1957–1973) later.

MORE EXPERIENCES Following the advice of a Dutch physician (Dr. W. L. Ladenius), I put my experiences in writing and gave copies to people who were interested. In December, 1960, a colleague, Dr. W., who had survived a cerebral thrombosis and a heart infarct at the age of 53, decided to take the food supplements [see page 110]. One half year later, he was again working full time and he has had no relapse since. He is convinced that the breakfast has helped to cure him. At the same time, a 69-year-old executive of Dutch industries (S.) had a blood clot in one of his legs, used anticoagulants, and followed a strict diet without eggs or butter. Learning about my experience, he cured himself rapidly and even has started a new industry. . . .

After a second chemist (D. W.) also found his condition improved with the breakfast, we wrote a short note for the Dutch paper *Chemisch Weekblad* titled "Is Atherosclerosis Reversible?" Shortly afterwards, *Chemical Week* (in the U.S.A.) published two of my letters to the editor about the same subject. The results of this publicity began to spread a year later in several letters, mostly from people we had not met. One letter written by a man of 72 years (J.) who suffered from a series of heart attacks and angina pectoris explained how he cured himself in three months' time and was able to take long walks again, which had been impossible during six years. Another letter was from a Dutch mechanical engineer (R.) who, at the age of 48, had such severe angina pectoris that he had to stop working and found no relief by drugs prescribed by several heart specialists. He did not believe that our breakfast could help him, but after the insistence of a friend he tried it and was back to work in two months' time. He can run again, and works at times in deep-freeze storage rooms without any bad effects. A 72-year-old consulting chemist (W.) from Texas had suffered from heart attacks, read the letter in *Chemical Week*, and improved rapidly. He stopped using the prescribed medicines and is again at work. A lady of 70 years (Mrs. P.) in Manchester, Vermont, had survived blockings in the neck artery and partial paralysis. In December, 1967, she started with the food supplements, which tasted exceedingly good to her. Her health improved rapidly and she has had no recurrences. Clinical tests showed that all cholesterol deposits had disappeared. Numerous similar cases could be cited.

Besides those individual reports, I received an invitation to meet a Dutch internist (Dr. K.) and I saw him in May, 1963. He told me that he prescribed the breakfast to numerous older patients with spectacular results. Many of them had resumed their activities, even after having been invalids for a long time. Six years later, Dr. K. was still enthusiastic about the supplements. . . .

Our working hypothesis is that food deficiencies are the main cause for atherosclerosis, and therefore all other known influences, such as tension, smoking, obesity, and maybe also heredity, are only contributory. Lack of exercise makes it difficult to detect atherosclerosis in an early stage.

Smoking deactivates vitamins. The abnormal way of life of people who push themselves too much affects either the nervous system or the blood vessels, or frequently both. These people can protect their arteries by using food supplements. Their bodies use more vitamins, and, therefore, must receive supplements. It should be instructive to investigate whether people who are atherosclerotic because of heredity (familial hypercholesterolemia) can be cured by the food supplements. We know of one case of two brothers whose parents died because of atherosclerosis. One brother used the supplements and remained healthy. The other was stricken but has now recovered after using the supplements. . . .

SUMMARY   The personal experiences of a considerable number of chemists, physicians, and other individuals whom I [Dr. Rinse] know suggest the following preliminary conclusions, which are offered here for consideration and continued investigation:

1.   Atherosclerosis is a deficiency disease, which can be counteracted successfully by the use of food supplements, in particular of lecithin.

2.   Atherosclerosis is a complicated chemical problem, which

should be studied along basic chemical lines, and by application of existing knowledge about antioxidants, free-radicals, liquid crystals, etc.

3.   Atherosclerosis can be accelerated by contributory factors, such as smoking, mental stress, heredity, obesity, and lack of physical exercise.

4.   It probably is unnecessary and even undesirable to replace all fats by unsaturated oils.

5.   Diet additives act favorably on many other diseases in addition to atherosclerosis. . . .

DR. J. RINSE'S FOOD SUPPLEMENT FOR PREVENTION AND CURE OF ATHEROSCLEROSIS* The following combination of vitamins and minerals has proved to be beneficial for the cure and prevention of atherosclerotic complications, such as high blood pressure, angina pectoris, cataract, obstructions in the arteries of neck, legs, arms, and kidneys. Consequently, heart infarcts and cerebral thrombosis become avoidable.

A mixture is made of one tablespoon each of soybean lecithin, debittered yeast, and raw wheat germ and one teaspoon of bone meal (ash). (It is recommended to prepare a larger quantity for storage.)

Mix in a bowl:

Two tablespoons of the above mixture,

One tablespoon of dark brown sugar,

One tablespoon of safflower oil or other linoleate oil, e.g., soybean oil.

Add milk to dissolve sugar and yeast.

Add yogurt to increase consistency.

Add cold cereal for calories as needed or mix with hot cereal such as oatmeal or porridge. Raisins and other fruits can be added as desired.

For severe cases of atherosclerosis the quantity of lecithin should be doubled.

Finally, it is recommended to take daily:

500 mg (½ g) of vitamin C and 100 I.U. vitamin E and one multivitamin-mineral tablet.

* Reprinted with permission from *American Laboratory*, May 27, 1973.

Any other normal food may be used, including eggs and butter, but high-melting fats (regular margarine) must be avoided. Soft (linoleate-containing) margarines are helpful, but butter is preferred, because it contains medium-chain-triglycerides (MCT fat).

The above given supplements act as follows:

(a) Linoleate-containing lecithin, after being reconstituted in the liver, combines with cholesterol and forms a blood-soluble lipid, removable from the body by excretion. In this way, the arteries become widened again.

(b) Antioxidants, vitamins C and E, prevent oxidation of linoleate in the bloodstream and, therefore, cross-linking of tissues and loss of flexibility. Also colds and other virus diseases may be prevented by these vitamins.

(c) Supply the metabolism with ingredients for the production of enzymes, the catalysts for numerous reactions in the body. They comprise many vitamins, metals, and trace metals, also iodine and sulfur.

Atherosclerosis appears to be caused by food deficiencies and aggravated by smoking, obesity, heredity, lack of exercise, and mental tension.

12

Hypoglycemia and the Dangers of Sugar

Hypoglycemia is common yet unrecognized by many physicians. The symptoms include fatigue, sudden hunger, weakness, and shakiness or trembling. Sometimes headache, cold sweats, dizziness, rapid heartbeat, numbness, irritability, confusion, blurred vision, or insomnia occur. Severe cases cause depression, hostility, anxiety, and violence. Several of these symptoms are so commonly experienced that they are all too often accepted as the natural result of modern lifestyles. Yet they are all indications that something is wrong—perhaps something with serious consequences to our health if not treated.

I am sure you are aware that a person describing these symptoms to a physician would in all likelihood end up with a prescription for tranquilizers; if a tired housewife complains of these symptoms, it is nearly automatic for the physician to mention boredom and tension while writing the prescription. Tranquilizers prescribed in such cases have frequently been the beginning of the use of "uppers" and "downers," a pattern that has hooked too many middle-aged, middle-class women.

Fortunately, several excellent books on hypoglycemia and frequent TV discussions of the disease by formerly afflicted TV personalities have educated physicians and the public alike. More and more people are recognizing that they have the symptoms and are requesting glucose-tolerance tests to determine if they have hypoglycemia. **If you discover that the Supernutrition program does not make you feel noticeably better, the reason might well be hypoglycemia.** Hypoglycemia can cause schizophrenia and alcoholism.

Hypoglycemia—The Cause

The "Western diet" with its refined flour and sugar, empty calories, and processed food taxes the adrenals and pancreas too much, often causing an overproduction of insulin that reduces the blood-sugar (glucose) level. Glucose is needed by the brain for proper function; when the blood doesn't supply adequate glucose, symptoms ranging from nervousness to coma occur. Caffeine in coffee and colas, strong tea, and nicotine from smoking can also cause hypoglycemia.

You may ask how eating sugar lowers blood-sugar levels. It doesn't at first. Eating empty-calorie foods that are simple, refined sources of sucrose cause the sugar to be digested quickly. The simple sugar is quickly absorbed and the blood level of glucose shoots up rapidly. Then the pancreas pumps insulin into the blood to control the blood-sugar level faster than the blood-sugar-level information can be fed back to the adrenal gland, and thus insulin is dumped to excess before it is shut off.

Next, the liver must convert stored glycogen to glucose to raise the blood-sugar level to normal—or the individual may feel tired, irritable, anxious, shaky, or faint. The liver continues to release glycogen until its store runs low; then the liver becomes stingy with its glycogen, responding only to stress situations. The constant overshooting of insulin depletes the liver of glycogen and insufficient blood-sugar levels result.

People suffering from hypoglycemia (like everyone else) imagine they receive quick "pick-me-ups" from candy bars, coffee, cigarettes and cocktails. But the satisfaction is only temporary, because soon extra insulin enters the bloodstream, driving the blood-sugar level still lower. A very harmful cycle has started. The individual craves sugar, chocolate, colas, coffee, and cigarettes, and can easily become addicted to alcohol, drugs, or sweets although people without these cravings may well have hypoglycemia.

Hypoglycemia—The Cure

It is fortunate that the cure requires only the avoidance or the drastic reduction of carbohydrates (especially refined sugars), caffeine, nicotine, and alcohol. It is necessary to eat frequent small high-protein meals and to snack often on high-protein foods such as milk, cheese, soybeans, and nuts. A typical dietary pattern might be as follows: juice or milk immediately upon rising, a high-protein breakfast, juice or milk two hours after breakfast, a high-protein lunch, milk or cheese three hours after lunch, juice or milk one hour before dinner, a high-protein dinner, milk or cheese three hours after dinner, milk or half a cup of nuts every two hours after that until retiring. This same high-protein, low-carbohydrate diet is excellent as a short-term weight-reduction diet. Once the body adjusts to the absence of sugar, the sugar craving stops and the diet can then be relaxed or normalized—but with sugars kept low.

In addition to eating frequent high-protein meals, vitamin supplementation is recommended. At least 1 gram of vitamin C, 800 IU of vitamin E, and 10 mg of each of the main B-complex vitamins (excepting vitamin B_{12}) are required to break the hypoglycemia cycle. Vitamin C is needed to protect the adrenal glands and fight stress, vitamin E is needed for proper energy utilization, and the B complex helps restore proper metabolism and effect nerve repair. The above regimen, along with the amino acid glutamine (available at health food stores), has helped cure many alcoholics.

For further information on hypoglycemia, the following books are all excellent:

E. M. Abrahamson and A. W. Pezet, *Body, Mind and Sugar* (Pyramid, 1971).

R. Adams and F. Murray, *Megavitamin Therapy* (Larchmont Books, 1973).

T. R. Blaine, *Mental Health Through Nutrition* (Citadel Press, 1969).

C. Fredericks, *Low Blood Sugar and You* (Constellation International, 1969).

P. J. Steincrohn, *The Most Common Misdiagnosed Disease: Low Blood Sugar* (Regnery, 1972).

Charles Weller, M.D., and Brian Boylan, *Hypoglycemia* (Doubleday 1968, Award Books, 1970).

R. J. Williams, *Nutrition Against Disease* (Bantam, 1973).

J. Yudkin, *Sweet and Dangerous* (Wyden, 1972).

Sugar—The Sweet Killer

It wouldn't make sense to have discussed heart disease without considering the indications that sugar is a major factor in its onset. Most people find that when they exclude refined sugar from their diets, it is relatively easy to control their weight and practice sound nutrition. However, often they find that if they eat one or two pieces of candy, their restraint vanishes and they then crave more sugar. Soon they are eating many empty calories and are overfed but undernourished. **When a person overeats, the fatty materials in the blood (triglycerides) increase, and this is more of a factor in heart disease than is cholesterol.** Refined sugar appears to be a much greater heart-disease problem than cholesterol and saturated fats. Studies by Dr. John Yudkin, professor of nutrition and dietetics, University of London, and his colleagues show that **a person eating four ounces of sugar daily, from all sources,**

**has more than five times the chance of having heart disease
than someone eating only half as much sugar.**

Refined Foods Are Dangerous

One of the difficulties arising from the consumption of
sugar is that simple refined sugar replaces the natural-
complex starches that have key functions in the body.
These complex starches are not as easily absorbed and
add bulk (roughage) to the diet; this bulk stimulates natural digestive mechanisms, lowers blood cholesterol levels,
and reduces the incidence of colon and rectal cancer. The
increased annual use of sugar (reported to have *averaged*
102 pounds of white sugar and 14 pounds of corn sugar
per person in 1970), the 88 pounds of refined white flour
(in which 90 percent of the crude fiber has been discarded
from the whole wheat flour) consumed by the average
person a year, and the trend toward eating processed foods
have all reduced the natural fiber that our bodies need.
Without this bulk, stools are smaller and require much
longer to pass through the intestinal tract, allowing bacteria time to turn bile salts into the cancer-causing agent,
deoxycholic acid. The use of processed foods and refined
carbohydrates continues to accelerate. The ratio of complex to refined sugars in the average diet has changed
from 2.90:1 in 1889, 1.98:1 in 1909 and 1.25:1 in 1932
to 0.91:1 in 1961.

The pioneer study of the inverse relationship between
roughage in the diet and colorectal cancer was made by
Dr. Denis Burkitt, English surgeon and Nobel laureate;
the direct relationship between refined sugar in the diet and
heart disease has been researched by Dr. Yudkin. If you
are not yet able to accept the relationship of refined foods
to poor health, I urge you to pursue the subject in the
books mentioned earlier.

Dr. Yudkin takes a strong stand against sugar, not just
what you add to your cereal or coffee, but the "hidden"
sugar in canned foods, sodas, instant cereals, snacks, and
almost everything in a manmade container. In his book,

Sweet and Dangerous, he states: **"If only a fraction of what is already known about the effects of sugar were to be revealed in relation to any other material used as a food additive, that material would promptly be banned. Sugar is the principal cause of heart disease, diabetes, and other killers."**

Professor Richard A. Ahrens of the Food and Nutrition Department of the University of Maryland concluded in his article "Sucrose (Sugar), Hypertension and Heart Disease" (*American Journal of Clinical Nutrition,* 1974):

(1) Although blood-cholesterol levels are elevated by an increase in dietary sucrose (sugar), such an elevation is of a much smaller magnitude than the concurrent rise in blood triglyceride levels that occurs. (2) High-sucrose diets reduce urine volume, causing filtration at the capillary level, which in turn increases the concentration of all blood solids, causing hypertension.

Drs. E. Cheraskin and W. M. Ringsdorf of the University of Alabama researched the question "How much refined carbohydrate should we eat?" and published the results in the May 1974 issue of *American Laboratory.* They concluded that "the input of 17 to 30 percent of one's calories from refined sugar generates four unmistakable nutritional problems. One, sugar is an empty food and does not contribute the essential vitamins, minerals, amino acids, or essential fatty acids which our bodies cry for to carry out growth, maintenance, and repair. Two, the consumption of sugar displaces foods which are rich in these essentials—meat, vegetables, fruit, milk, cheese, nuts, and seeds. Three, the body's utilization of sugar demands vitamins and minerals. These have to be stolen from other foods or from the body tissues and reserves. Four, eating lots of sugar and sweetened foods or drinks is a major cause of diabetes mellitus and hypoglycemia. Refined carbohydrates are also reported to play a role in the etiology and progression of these and other diseases—gout, kidney stones, urinary infection, peptic ulcer, cardiovascular disease, dental caries, periodontal disease, overweight, intestinal cancer, diverticulosis, indigestion, hormonal disorders, oral and vaginal infections, osteoporosis, alcoholism, and mental illness. In contrast, unrefined carbohydrates (high-starch foods) are vital to an optimal diet and do not contribute to these disorders.".

After studying over eight hundred doctors and their wives by comparing their health to their refined-carbohydrate intake, Drs. Cheraskin and Ringsdorf found that the more refined carbohydrate consumed, the greater amount of both types of diseases and severity of disease. They logically concluded that the ideal daily *refined*-carbohydrate intake may actually be zero.

Although the ideal intake of refined carbohydrates is zero, most people can or will not exclude all refined sugars from their diets. Supernutrition will provide the vitamins and minerals needed to metabolize refined carbohydrates, thus preventing the nutrient deficiencies that cause the multitude of diseases linked to refined-carbohydrate consumption. It is best to increase your intake of roughage as you follow the principles of the Supernutrition program. To provide bulk eat fruits, vegetables, bran, oatmeal, and whole wheat.

13

Cancer and Vitamin Therapy

Cancer is a word that strikes fear into more people's minds than words like heart disease, stroke, or paralysis. We are told that one out of four of us will eventually get cancer; this year more than 600,000 persons will be stricken; nearly 350,000 of the 1 million persons under treatment this year will die (American Cancer Society, *Facts and Figures,* 1974). That is far fewer than the million that will die from cardiovascular disease; but the fear of cancer comes not from the number that will die, but from the nature of the disease and the suffering involved. Since we cannot live forever, most people would rather leave this world via a quick heart attack rather than as a result of cancer.

Unfortunately, the cancer-death rate is still rising sharply. The mortality rate of most types of the disease, such as skin, prostate, pancreatic, colon, and rectal cancers, plateaued in the 1960s. Deaths from stomach cancer per 100,000 deaths have decreased steadily since before 1930. Deaths from lung cancer per 100,000 have, however, climbed rapidly during the same period. The reasons for

each give us a clue as to how cancer can be prevented.
Stomach cancers have declined possibly because of the
antioxidants, BHA and BHT, that have been added to our
foods. Lung cancer has increased as a result of cigarette
smoking and air pollution. Neither cancer involves a virus
but is caused by carcinogens, as can be demonstrated ex-
perimentally and will be discussed in later pages.

The National Center for Health Statistics attributes the
rising cancer rates to increased exposure to carcinogens
(cancer-causing chemicals) in smoking, and air, water,
soil, and food. The Center points out that in 1972 cancer
deaths rose at the fastest rate in twenty-two years. The
cancer mortality rate was 166.8 per 100,000 deaths in
1972 compared with 161.4 in 1971. This rate of increase
was 3.35 percent, about triple the annual average since
1950. There is a way to overcome the increased exposure
to carcinogens: use the antioxidant therapy described in
this chapter and don't smoke.

Supernutrition will reduce your chances of getting cancer. I have made a very conservative estimate which projects that, out of two groups—one group typical of the
general population and the other an equal number of
people practicing Supernutrition—the latter group will
have less than 70 percent of the control group's cancer
incidence and triple its cure rate. I admit that this is a
bold statement. Of course, it is unproved and will arouse
anger in some authorities. What gives me the confidence
to make it?

For openers, I make the projection based on animal
experiments that anyone can confirm. Several researchers
already have. A researcher can take a group of mice, feed
them a carcinogen, and, depending on the chemical used,
a typical experiment may induce stomach cancer or skin
cancer in 90 percent of the mice in four months. If, however, the mice are given antioxidant therapy along with
the carcinogen, only a few—typically less than 10 percent
—will get cancer. The good news is that the antioxidant
therapy consists of administering such common antioxi-
dant-type nutrients as vitamin E, vitamin C, and selenium.

You as easily can be protected to a large degree against carcinogen-induced cancers.

How did I learn of the prevention of cancer by antioxidant therapy? I was pushed into it by the results of my experiments to slow the aging process. A natural question was whether the increased life span was due to the retardation of the aging process, the protection from disease, or a combination of both; in my experiments I have complete autopsies on experimental animals performed routinely. The most striking observation I noted is that cancers or gross tumors were *never* found in the long-lived animals on high-antioxidant diets. Dr. Denham Harman of the University of Nebraska School of Medicine made a similar observation. Thus, I was almost compelled to pursue this investigation.

Free-Radical Attack on Cellular Membranes Can Cause Cancer

The membranes are primary suspects in allowing normal cells to become abnormal, as my studies have shown. Membranes contain a large amount of lipids (phospholipids) and thus are subject to free-radical attack and peroxidation. Without adequate antioxidant protection (primarily from vitamin E), the membrane surface can be altered. Topographical "holes" or "gaps" in the distribution of electronic charges can result in abnormal cellular chemistry. I believe that the regulation of nutrients through the membrane is as a result altered, encouraging either death (as in aging), if the nutrients cannot pass through the altered membrane, or irregular growth (as in cancer) if the nutrients enter into the cell uncontrollably. With the membrane surface altered, rapid cell growth may not be halted by feedback mechanisms dependent upon surface sensing. The ability of cells to "recognize" each other and maintain normal tissue patterns depends on the structural and immunological specificity of the cell surface. Also, membrane alterations may weaken antigens (sub-

stances that induce the formation of germ-killing antibodies), thus causing the immune system to fail in its
capacity to reject tumors.

Cancer-Causing Agents

Free-radicals may be involved in the activation or formation of carcinogens. My postulation as to how a free-
radical scavenger (inhibitor), such as the antioxidant vitamin C, can prevent carcinogen formation follows. A metabolic intermediate of the amino acid tryptophan, 3-hy-
droxyanthranilic acid, is readily converted to the carcinogen cinnabaric acid in urine that is antioxidant-deficient.
The presence of excess vitamin C in the urine interferes
with the conversion of 3-hydroxyanthranilic acid to cinnabaric acid and also interferes with the free-radical prop-
agating activity of any cinnabaric acid already present.
The presence of vitamin C along with available sulfhydryl
groups encourages the metabolic oxidation of 3-hydroxy-
anthranilic acid to 2-amino-β-carboxy-muconic acid. **The
high incidence of bladder cancer among heavy smokers
can be explained by the fact that their urine is often deficient in vitamin C and high in cinnabaric acid, free-radicals, and chemiluminescence.** Although the foregoing was
a postulation that I published in *American Laboratory* in
1973, I have since learned that Dr. J. U. Schlegel of
Tulane had earlier made the same postulation (*Journal
of Urology,* 1970). Still another example of an antioxidant preventing carcinogen formation was reported by Dr.
S. S. Mirvish of University of Nebraska Medical Center,
in a 1972 *Science* article, "Ascorbate-Nitrate Reaction
Blocks the Formation of Carcinogenic N-Nitroso Compounds."

Eating foods rich in vitamin C or adding vitamin C to foods
containing nitrates as preservatives can protect us from the
danger of the nitrates (harmless themselves) that form the
carcinogen nitrosamine in our stomachs. Nitrates are added to

meats to preserve their red color, especially to hot dogs, bacon, and luncheon meats.

In an *American Laboratory* article, "Cancer: New Directions" (June 1973), I suggested to nutritionists that they consider the "after-protection" of nutrients: nutrient antioxidants (vitamins C and E) should be taken often and in excess purposely to insure that some will be excreted. A moderate excess was defined as being well above present nutritional standards but well short of that which could cause medical problems. If excesses are excreted, they will be available in the bladder and colon to protect against carcinogen formation. As described, vitamin C, which is water-soluble, can protect the bladder, and vitamin E, which is fat-soluble and incompletely absorbed in the intestine, can protect the colon. The importance of adequate roughage in the diet cannot be overemphasized. The roughage moves waste along before it has a chance to putrefy.

Antioxidants Protect Against Cancer

As long ago as 1949, it was known that added dietary selenium reduced the incidence of cancers induced by dimethylaminoazobenzene. Several studies have now confirmed the relationship of low-dietary-selenium intake or low-selenium blood levels to an increasing cancer-death rate. As an example of such studies, the reader may wish to consult the following references: Dr. W. H. Allaway in *The Archives of Environmental Health* (1968); Drs. Raymond J. Shamberger and Douglas V. Frost in the *Canadian Medical Association Journal* (1969); and Dr. G. N. Schrauzer and his colleagues in *Experientia* (1969) and *Bioinorganic Chemistry* (1973). (The correlation is high for gastrointestinal cancer and Hodgkin's disease, but lower for other cancers.)

Dr. Ray Shamberger of the Cleveland Clinic Foundation has completed several experiments with either selenium or vitamin E (which interchanges with selenium in some functions) showing significant reduction of dimethylbenz-(a)anthracene (DMBA)-induced cancers in mice. Cancer reduction was accomplished by either dietary supplementation of selenium or application of either selenium or vitamin E to a skin area to which DMBA had been applied several days previously. **Cancer reduction varied with antioxidant concentration, but typically showed a 15 percent reduction with 0.1 part per million (ppm) sodium selenite added to the diet, and 50 percent reduction with 1.0 ppm dietary sodium selenite.** Recent experiments produced similar results with fluorenyl-acetamide (FAA)-induced cancer in rats.

Dr. S. Jaffe has reported reduction by wheat-germ oil (rich in vitamin E) of methyl-cholanthracene (MCA)-induced cancer in laboratory animals. (*Experimental Medicine and Surgery,* 1946.) Vitamin E proved effective in reducing cancers from injected MCA. However, Dr. S. S. Epstein found that vitamin E and several other antioxidants were not effective in reducing dibenzpyrene (BP)-induced cancers (*Life Sciences,* 1967). More recently, Dr. Lee W. Wattenberg of the University of Minnesota Medical School had great success with either butylated hydroxyanisole (BHA), butylated hydroxytoluene (BHT), or ethoxyquin in reducing BP- or DMBA-induced stomach cancers. BP-induced cancers were reduced from 100 percent incidence in controls to 17 percent with 5 mg/g of dietary BHA, and to 22 percent with 5 mg/g of dietary BHT. Dr. Wattenberg's results were reported in the *Journal of the National Cancer Institute* (1972).

BHT and BHA are antioxidants used in many of our foods to prevent spoilage. Diets containing 2 mg of BHA and/or BHT per day are not uncommon. According to Dr. Wattenberg's studies, this could protect the stomach from up to 0.5 mg of carcinogen per day. It is not surprising to note, as I wrote earlier, that the death rate from stomach cancer has decreased from 30 per 100,000 population in 1930, when antioxidants were introduced in our food supply, to less than 10 deaths per 100,000 population in 1970. The United States has the lowest stomach-cancer death rate; Western European nations have intermediate rates; and Poland, Hungary, Czechoslovakia, Austria, and Bulgaria the highest rates of twenty-four countries studied. The rate in Bulgaria was four times greater than the United States rate (*World Health Statistics Annual*, WHO, 1972).

Peroxidation: Another Source of Cancer-Causing Free-Radicals

Free-radicals are produced by several processes in the body. The healthy body normally can neutralize the self-produced free-radicals before an excessive rate of damage occurs. However, polyunsaturated fatty acids form highly reactive self-propagating free-radicals when initiated by a "starter" free-radical. Whenever the intake of polyunsaturated fatty acids greatly exceeds that necessary for function, the risk of rancidity (lipid peroxidation) increases. Table 9.1 lists the saturated and unsaturated fats and oils (Chapter 9). If this is true, today's trend toward increasing the ratio of polyunsaturated fats to saturated fats needs close examination.

I have voiced this concern along with my concern for unbalancing normal diets in trying to avoid dietary cholesterol. Cholesterolophobia has caused many people to increase their polyunsaturated-fat intake far beyond that advised by physicians; the "average" American today ingests about two or three times the polyunsaturated fats of Americans twenty years ago. A large number of studies alarmingly show proportionate increases in cancer (especially mammary) with increasing dietary polyunsaturate levels. Epidemiological studies of several countries show high cancer incidence in countries where considerable quantities of fish and less quantities of eggs and dairy products are consumed (*Lancet*, 1971). Drs. Pearce and Dayton have reported that humans consuming four times the polyunsaturates of those in control groups developed a significantly higher number of cancers: 31 cases of cancer in 174 people as opposed to 17 cases in 178 people.

To be objective, other tests have been conducted that cast doubt on some of the tests showing a direct link between high polyunsaturated fats and human cancer, according to Dr. Jean Mayer in his syndicated column, 1974—but at least fourteen tests still show a valid relationship. Other tests have implicated "fats" without distinguishing between saturated and unsaturated fats. Further analyses will probably show that these, too, implicate excess polyunsaturates.

This is not to say that polyunsaturates *cause* cancer. It is to emphasize the need for a balanced diet and a balance of antioxidants and polyunsaturates. Nor is it to say that polyunsaturates are harmful, or that they should necessarily be reduced if one's diet is balanced. It is important to have adequate polyunsaturates for proper nutrition; some people do not get enough of the three essential polyunsaturates. (The body has enzymes in the liver to convert the saturates to unsaturates.) But extreme measures to drastically change the polyunsaturate/saturate ratio of your diet, especially without adding the required antioxidants, appear to run you a great risk.

It should be stated here, as it was in the chapter on heart disease, that a continued adequate intake of vitamin E is required, because the polyunsaturates stay in the body for such a long time. Otherwise, the vitamin E can be used up while the polyunsaturates are still available. Typical animal experiments show that DMBA-induced cancer rates increase with polyunsaturates and decrease with added vitamin E. Dr. Raymond Shamberger of the Cleveland Clinic found that adding corn oil to the DMBA carcinogen promotor, croton resin, greatly increased the number of cancers (*Journal of the National Cancer Institute,* 1972). Applying either selenium, vitamin E, or vitamin C several days later reduced the number of new cancers. Saturated oils (such as coconut and olive) did not increase the cancer incidence. Dr. Denham Harman has recently presented data showing that vitamin E decreased the tumor incidence of rats on a diet containing safflower oil as the sole source of fat (Annual Meeting of the Gerontological Society, 1972).

Sun-Induced Skin Cancer

Vitamin C, vitamin E, and selenium can protect against skin cancer from carcinogens. **In humans, the prime cause of skin cancer is sunlight.** Can antioxidant therapy protect against sun-induced cancer as well?

Drs. S. Wan-Bang Lo and S. Black of the Baylor College of Medicine have found that antioxidant therapy *does* protect against sun-induced cancer. They observed that after human or animal skin was exposed to ultraviolet light, cholesterol in the skin was oxidized to a compound called cholesterol alpha-oxide. Drs. Wan-Bang Lo and Black reasoned that the cholesterol alpha-oxide could be the carcinogen and wondered if the use of antioxidants could prevent the formation of cholesterol alpha-oxide. They found that vitamins C and E or the food preservatives BHA and BHT did prevent the formation of cholesterol alpha-oxide; more significantly, they prevented skin cancer without causing any side effects (*Science News*, 1973).

At this point it is obvious that a well-balanced diet supplying all the vitamins and trace minerals required will be helpful in preventing some types of cancers; a reasonable person might conclude that it makes sense to take extra amounts of vitamins C and E to prevent cancer. But there is still more evidence to consider, and yet other ways that vitamins prevent cancer.

So far I have pointed out that cigarettes cause cancer in many people and that polyunsaturates can be harmful in excess. Now consider X-rays as an additional factor to avoid whenever possible.

Radiation Can Cause Cancer

Animal experiments show that nuclear radiation and X-irradiation can increase cancer incidence and mimic aging.

Strong doses of either can cause whole-cell destruction and lead to radiation sickness and death. In fact, localized strong doses are used to destroy cancerous cells; in this process, all cells are destroyed, but cancer cells more readily, since highly proliferating cells have a more rapid DNA synthesis, which makes them more vulnerable to attack by radiation. Smaller doses of radiation do indirect damage by creating free-radicals and disrupting lysomal membranes. Many antioxidants—methionine and cysteine (sulfur amino acids), methylethylamine, selenourea, and selenocysteine—are excellent radiation protectors as well as good free-radical scavengers.

They are helpful because the several theoretical processes of cancer development all respond to the same preventive measure. Whether all the proposed causes are actual causes or only one is, the prevention mechanism of getting adequate antioxidant nutrients remains effective against cancer. As an illustration, let's look at the effect of smoking. The most serious effects may include: the effect of carcinogens such as benzopyrene directly on the lung tissue; the effect of oxidizing smoke compounds in destroying tissue stores of vitamin A, which in turn leaves lung tissue unprotected; the production of free-radicals in the urine explaining the high bladder-cancer incidence in smokers; the activity of Aryl Hydrocarbon Hydroxylase (AHH) in converting "harmless" hydrocarbons into "active" carcinogens; and radiation from radioactive dust in tobacco. All but the latter has been discussed.

Let's look at the last trouble source, radiation. Dr. Edward Martell of the National Center for Atmospheric Research at Boulder, Colorado, found preliminary evidence in 1974 to support the role of radioactive dust in lung cancer. Dr. Martell believes that radioactive dust collects on tobacco leaves and is introduced to the lungs in the tobacco smoke *(Nature,* 1974). In support of this theory, Dr. Edward Radford of Johns Hopkins University has found high concentrations of radioactivity in the lungs of heavy smokers who have died from lung cancer.

I believe that all the above mentioned mechanisms may cause cancer and that natural antioxidants such as vitamin

E, selenium, and vitamin C will protect us against these disease pathways, provided we have a balanced diet and only a minimum exposure to the carcinogens. These sources of cancer sometimes exceed the protective ability of the supplemental antioxidants and initiate precancerous cells. Still, a healthy body can prevent cancer even at this stage. We have the immune system to protect us.

Antibodies Essential to the Body's Immune System

Many scientists believe, perhaps with good reason, that cancer results when the body's immune system fails. It is logical to assume that cells grow wildly quite regularly but are detected and destroyed by our immune system. Conceivably, defective cells constructed with proteins produced by altered DNA or cells with defective membranes can grow uncontrollably. As long as nutrients are available, the cells will continue to grow and divide irregularly. Normally, antibodies (substances that provide immunity) are summoned and surround, isolate, and destroy the premalignant cells with the help of macrophages. If the body does not detect that the premalignant cells are foreign, or cannot produce adequate antibodies, or if the antibodies are blocked before they can do their job, then the cells develop their own blood supply and become malignant tissue.

The stimulation of the immune system is receiving increasing interest as a cure for cancer. Surgery, radiation, and chemotherapy techniques are effective, as a rule, only when the cancer has been detected early. Several medical researchers (Drs. Michael Hanna, Edmund Klein, William Terry in the U.S. and Lucien Israel in Paris) have been successful in stimulating antibody formation with standard smallpox or Bacillus Calmette-Guerin (BCG) vaccines, and have, as a result, cured or caused remission of cancer.

Previously, I discussed the protective action of vitamin E and selenium in terms of their antioxidant and free-radical scavenging activity. However, a recent Russian report by Dr. T. F. Berenhtein adds another possible mechanism. Sodium selenite with vitamin E produced higher antibody levels (to typhoid vaccine) than either one alone or neither. Selenium alone had some effect, but vitamin E alone had none. *(Zdravookhr.,* 1972.)

Dr. J. E. Spallholtz and his colleagues at Colorado State University have confirmed that vitamin E and selenium together increase the body's production of antibodies to various invaders *(Facet,* 1973). Without vitamin E or selenium, your body cannot defend itself against carcinogens or wild cells; with extra vitamin E and selenium, your body cannot be damaged by many invaders or wild cells.

Antioxidants Work Best in Combinations

You may have noticed that the compounds which are effective against cancer and have been discussed so far (vitamin E, selenium, BHA, and BHT) are the same compounds used successfully in my longevity experiments. The question is raised as to whether the increased longevity is because of the retardation of the aging process or because of reduction of cancer in a strain of animals particularly susceptible to it, or both. This is one reason that several different strains of animals are used in gerontological studies, with emphasis on the longer-lived strains. I have posed two questions: if a combination of antioxidants is synergistic in retarding the aging process, will a combination be more effective than a single antioxidant alone in preventing cancer? Can antioxidants effective at low concentrations be selected that will also be effective against all types of cancer?

One problem that I noted with single antioxidants is that although a given antioxidant may protect against carcinogen-induced cancer of one organ, it is ineffective if the cancer site has shifted to a different organ. Some antioxidants have given total protection at fairly high concentrations, whereas others have given only specific protection. For the past several years, I have placed great emphasis on discovering combinations of antioxidants that exhibit synergism and provide complete protection against carcinogen-induced cancers. But what about virus-induced cancers? Will the same formulations be effective in inhibiting them?

The Elusive Virus

Viral cancers can be readily demonstrated in some animals. Researchers are able to extract viruses from animal tumors, some of which can transfer cancer from one animal to another; other viral cancers have not yet been shown to be transferable. Particles resembling both DNA and RNA cancer viruses have been found in human cancer tissues and leukemia cells. Even though cancer clusters have been found and viruses have transferred cancer in animals, conclusive proof that any human cancer is viral has not been presented. Many, if not most scientists feel that the evidence for viral involvement is strong, and that conclusive proof will be demonstrated in a matter of time. The virologists themselves are divided as to several theories, however: oncogenic, reverse-transcription, and others.

The oncogenic (tumor-causing gene) theory postulates the activation of quiescent cancer genes by carcinogens, radiation, or hormones to produce malignant cells. The oncogenes, as postulated by Drs. Huebner and Todaro of the National Cancer Institute, are built into all cells at conception, rather than being introduced later. An oncogene may be originally derived from a C-type RNA virus particle, but is genetically perpetuated.

In April 1970 Dr. Bergs obtained a virus from a carcinogen-induced cancer that, when transferred to rats at birth, produced lymphoid leukemia (*Journal of the National Cancer Institute*, 1970). The rat mammary tumor-derived virus (RMTDV) was induced by the carcinogen DMBA. The oncogenic theory postulates that the carcinogen activates a gene which becomes or produces a cancer-causing virus. However, studies of identical twins show that not every human cell contains in its DNA a segment that codes for malignancy. Thus the oncogenic theory is not well supported. Simpler theories imply that the carcinogen would directly activate a viral genome (a set of chromosomes with the genes they contain) to start the transformation of normal cells to cancerous cells.

It was also in 1970 that the RNA-dependent DNA polymerase (also RNA-directed DNA polymerase or RDD) concept was advanced by Drs. H. T. Temin and S. Mizutani of the National Institutes of Health. This is the reverse-transcription theory in which RNA makes a DNA replication of itself (provirus); then the DNA provirus synthesizes the original RNA structure into a cell chromosome. The reverse-transcription theory differs from the oncogenic theory in that there is no pre-existing material waiting to be activated; instead the material is assembled by the RDDP enzyme. This enzyme has been found in several cancer cells by researchers including Baltimore, Green, Gallo, Spiegelman, Levinson, Martin, Vogt, and others, and explains how RNA tumor viruses can replicate.

However, an important consideration is that the RDDP enzyme has possibly been found in normal cells (by Todaro in 1971). If this is confirmed through more research, the only difference between normalcy and cancer may be the activation of the gene or DNA—whether inborn (oncogenic) or synthesized (reverse transcription)—by carcinogen, radiation, or free-radicals. If this is the case, **it is possible that all cancers can be prevented** by certain antioxidants which would prevent the required activation by previously described mechanisms. Of those mechanisms considered, the only one in which antioxidants definitely would be ineffective would be the direct "infection" by a cancer virus. This mechanism has comparatively little support among researchers.

Air Pollution Can Cause Lung Cancer

The air is often polluted with oxidizing chemicals such
as ozone and nitrous oxide. These compounds are present
in smog and harm the body in at least two ways. First,
they directly oxidize lung tissue, causing disease and reducing the body's ability to abstract oxygen from the air.
Second, the oxidizing chemicals destroy the vitamin A in
the lung tissue, thereby increasing the risk of cancer. Even
if you take adequate vitamin A, the lungs become deficient
because of the oxidizing chemicals in the air. Vitamin A is
required for the health of the mucous membranes; a deficiency of vitamin A decreases the efficiency of the lungs'
first line of defense against carcinogens, unless the lungs
are protected by supplementary vitamin E. Vitamin E, an
antioxidant, can protect the lung tissues, including tissue
stores of vitamin A.

In 1970 I filed a patent showing how vitamin E and
other antioxidants protected lungs against air pollution.
The amount of protection increased directly with the
amount of antioxidants and, to a degree, with the length
of time between taking the antioxidants and exposure. An
important distinction to note is that these studies showed
that vitamin E was progressively effective *beyond* nutritional requirements; the Supernutrition program offers such
additional protection over the RDA. In the case of moderate smog, it is projected that an *extra* 400 IU of vitamin
E daily can protect the lungs against 85 to 95 percent of
the damage from oxidizing chemicals. The need for a high-
protection level can be partially explained by the fact that
smog is a recent development, one which our ancestors
weren't exposed to; our bodies have no natural defense
against it. This is a point I made in a *Chemical and Engineering News* discussion (November 1974). By contrast,
other scientists have implied that vitamin E is effective
only insofar as it corrects nutritional deficiencies.

In the same *Chemical and Engineering News* discussion
I called attention to the fact that vitamin E can protect us

from the increasing amounts of ultraviolet energy that we are exposed to. This ultraviolet increase results from the decrease in high-altitude ozone, which is disappearing because of reaction with the great quantities of chlorinated hydrocarbons released from all those spray cans we have been using.

The Solution to Food Pollution

Many toxic chemicals have entered our modern food supply.

There are chemicals in meat that are residues from feed used to make animals grow faster. The steroid DES is one such compound; it has been proven to cause cancer, yet residues still are found in some meats.

Pesticides and herbicides have been shown to be toxic, but not necessarily carcinogenic (FDA news release, April 1973). However, some of the herbicide and pesticide break-down products (e.g., TCDD) are carcinogenic (*Environmental Health Perspectives,* 1973). Mercury has been found to be above safe limits in some foods. **There are over 1,000 food additives used, with the average annual additive intake three pounds per American in 1966, four pounds in 1971, and five pounds in 1974** (*Chemical and Engineering News,* 1974). Optical brighteners and other harmful complex chemicals have been found in drinking water (*Mutation Research,* 1971). Fortunately, the same antioxidant nutrients that protect us against some forms of heart disease and cancer and slow the aging process can also detoxify most of the poisons found in food, air, and water. Selenium detoxifies mercury, vitamin E protects against carbon monoxide and detoxifies chlorinated pesticides and solvents, and vitamin C detoxifies many other toxins, including lead, cadmium, and allergens, as proved by Dr. Fred Klenner of North Carolina (see Chapter 6).

Water Pollution

Many carcinogenic compounds are washed into our streams—their origin is in industrial waste products as well as in insecticides and herbicides used on farms and lawns. Some of these carcinogenic compounds were once thought to be harmless but are now known to react with the chlorine used to treat the water we drink to form dangerous carcinogens. The news media have widely publicized the Environmental Protection Agency's study of Mississippi's drinking-water supply and the Navy's study of the Potomac at Washington, D.C. *(Washington Post,* Nov. 12, 1974.) Both studies revealed carcinogens that are not removed by present purification methods.

We can protect ourselves against most of these carcinogens with antioxidant nutrients and help fight any carcinogen with the optimum health obtained through Supernutrition.

The Solution to Carcinogen Pollutants

Modern man can protect himself from modern poisons even if they are carcinogenic. He should avoid exposure to too much of any one particular poison and follow the Supernutrition program. He can control his exposure by not smoking, by avoiding needless X rays, and by not overusing spray cans. If the diet is varied, the intake of food additives and pesticides will also be varied, thus keeping any one poison from saturating the body's defense mechanism against it. Extra vitamin C and E aid the body's defenses.

Vitamin C and Other Vitamins Protect Against Cancer

Antioxidant therapy is a prime defense mechanism against cancer, but it is not the only way that vitamins protect us against this disease. Vitamin C can also help because of its function in the formation of the viscous intercellular "ground" substance (intercellular "cement").

The effect of vitamin B_{17} must be mentioned too. Vitamin B_{17}, a member of the B-complex group and found in many seeds (especially apricot pits), is better known as Laetrile or amygdalin. Seeds of apples, cherries, peaches, plums, and nectarines contain 2 to 3 percent of vitamin B_{17}. It has also been found in seventy plants used for foods. The vitamin is considered a drug in the United States by the FDA, and it is illegal to use it in cancer therapy. There are citizen groups that support the use of vitamin B_{17} and supply information about it to those that want it. Court cases occur from time to time, as some American physicians use it in their cancer therapy. Although many have been cured while undergoing vitamin B_{17} treatment, the cure rate is not dramatically different from standard therapies—it is better, just not sufficiently better to excite the FDA.

More importantly, vitamin B_{17} reduces the agony of cancer (Dr. Dean Burke of National Cancer Institute, 1973 Los Angeles Convention of Cancer Control Society). Physicians in Mexico, France, and Germany claim that vitamin B_{17} has a 10 to 30 percent effectiveness in extending the lives of those with solid cancers. The combination of easing pain and extending lives makes it a worthwhile weapon to have in our arsenal of anticancer agents. It has no harmful side effects, such as radiation and chemotherapy do. (Some authorities believe that the amount of cyanide in three or four B_{17} tablets can be lethal to children.) Occasionally, the extension of life has allowed natural remissions to occur that would never have had a chance otherwise. The vitamin has been tested in this country on mice, but it is difficult to measure freedom from pain in mice. Successful results were obtained at the Southern Research Institute in Birmingham, Alabama (1973), Sloan-Kettering Institute for Cancer Research in New York (1973), and Scind Laboratories of the University of San Francisco (1968). For those people wanting

more information on Laetrile (B_{17} or amygdalin), write
to one of the following organizations:

Cancer Control Society, 2043 N. Berendo, Los Angeles,
Calif. 90027

The International Association of Cancer Victims and
Friends, 155-d South Highway, Solana Beach, Calif.
92075. Also, 1810 Wantagh Ave., Wantagh, N.Y. 11793

Committee for Freedom of Choice in Cancer Therapy,
Palo Alto, Calif. 92070

March of Truth on Cancer, The Arlin J. Brown Information Center, P.O. Box 251, Fort Belvoir, Va. 22060

Vitamin A and Cancer

Last to be mentioned here, but not the least important, is
vitamin A. Several articles have been reported in the
Journal of the National Cancer Institute (1971) and the
American Journal of Clinical Nutrition (1973) relating
tests in which vitamin A inhibited carcinogen and virus-
induced cancers in laboratory animals. It is almost impossible to transplant cancer cells from animal to animal if
nutritionally excessive vitamin A is also given. On the
other hand, a vitamin A deficiency makes it a cinch.

At a November 1974 symposium scientists from the National Cancer Institute, Massachusetts Institute of Technology, Southern Research Institute at Birmingham, Alabama, Illinois Institute of Technology, and other major
research centers reported that vitamin A had considerable
cancer-protecting effect—regardless of whether a deficiency
existed or not (reported in *Science,* December, 1974).

Cancer Prevention

In summary, this chapter has stressed the prevention of
cancer, not its cure. Because the cancer mechanism is still

unknown or not agreed upon by scientists, all my explanations must be labeled speculative. However, the fact that antioxidant therapy reduces the incidence of carcinogen-induced cancers cannot be denied; nor can the fact that the B-complex vitamins and vitamin A have some inhibitory effect. It can be concluded that Supernutrition, which stresses higher-than-average intake of vitamins and minerals, most probably reduces the incidence of cancer.

It is also important to avoid smoking, excessive intake of polyunsaturates, and needless X-rays. Eat foods with a high roughage content or take alfalfa or methyl cellulose tablets. Reduce your exposure to food pollution by avoiding, as much as possible, artificially colored foods, and avoid too much of any one carcinogen by eating a diverse diet. Help your body work properly by maintaining a good activity level.

14

Supernutrition and
Staying Young Longer

Sufficient knowledge is available today to increase the
number of years that we exist, and, more importantly, to
guarantee an increase in the number of years that we *live*.
The single greatest inhibitor of enjoyment to most people
is *premature* old age. Some people at fifty years of age
look like seventy and feel like eighty; this need not be so.
Why is it that some people seem ageless? Science has
learned what causes the signs of old age and has also
learned to retard their advance.

Dr. Alex Comfort, England's leading gerontologist, in
1964 wrote in his famous treatise *Aging: the Biology of
Senescence,* "If we kept throughout life the same resistance to stress, injury, and disease that we had at the age
of ten, about one-half of us here today might expect to
survive in seven hundred years time."

Contrary to popular belief, neither the maximum life
span nor the average age of death for people living past
the age of twenty has increased significantly since 1800.
The average age at death increased steadily until 1950, but
this was due to an improved childhood mortality rate.

At first glance the life tables, calculated annually by the U.S. Bureau of Census, look impressive. The *estimated* average life-span for people born in this country in 1900 was 47.3 years. By 1950 the estimated average lifespan had reached 68.2. A second glance, however, shows that the life-span estimates haven't changed much in the last twenty-five years. We have been told again and again of the modern medical wonders developed in these years. Yet for people born in 1950 the estimated mean life span is 68.2 years; for those born in 1955, it is 69.6; for 1960, it is 69.7; for 1965, it is 70.2; and for 1970, it is 70.9.

Can the people who reach seventy years today expect to live longer than people reaching that same age in previous decades? If you examine the percentage of people living to eighty-five years after they have reached seventy years, you will note little increase in the last twenty-five years. Based on the number of survivors reaching a given age out of each 100,000 live births, we find that the percentage of seventy-year-olds reaching eighty-five was 23 in 1950, 24 in 1960, and 24 in 1968 (the latest official figures available).

In terms of estimated years of life remaining for an individual reaching fifty-five years, there is only a difference of two years between the figures for 1900 and those for 1968. For someone reaching sixty years of age, there is only a one-year difference in life expectancy between the eighteenth century and today.

Age Is Not an Accurate Index of Health

Although growth proceeds at predictable rates, aging does not. Some people are old at forty; others are young at sixty. Measuring one's age chronologically has its limitations. It does not describe a person's appearance, vigor, or life expectancy accurately. Dr. Robert E. Rothenberg, author of the book, *Health in the Later Years* (1965), points out that it would be more logical to determine the present health of a person carefully and estimate the number of years left to him. If this were the practice, then the person of sixty with twenty years of life left could be said to be ten years younger than the forty-year-old with only ten years remaining.

Studies conducted at the University of Maryland indicate people with high blood pressure may be twenty years older physiologically than people of the same age with normal blood pressure, according to Dr. Nathan Shock of the Gerontology Research Center of NIH. Hardening of the arteries (arteriosclerosis) was at one time believed to be associated with aging. This is often true, but arteriosclerosis actually results from a chemical imbalance and not because of chronological aging. Many very old people, including octogenarians and nonagenarians, are free from arteriosclerosis and have normal blood pressures. These people are also "young" in spirit and vitality. Studies similar to those conducted at the University of Maryland have revealed that much of the human deterioration once believed to be the result of time is due to disease. Older people are more prone to most diseases; but as knowledge from gerontological studies is applied to larger and larger segments of the population, it is expected that many currently prevalent diseases will disappear completely. Then, nearly perfect health until a natural disease-free death occurs at the end of the maximum life span will be a reality—many diseases will have been avoided, not by specific treatment, but by improving the body's own defense mechanisms.

Why Slow the Aging Process?

Long life does not interest most of us unless we can be reasonably sure we are going to continue to be vital. The potential cumulative effect and benefit of having the population increase its percentage of able and mature people, still active in the pursuit of a better world, is, however, immense. By slowing down the aging process, we can succeed in preserving the quality of life. Crippling diseases due to neglect and undernutrition can be decreased, postponed, or eliminated by slowing the aging process. Arthritis, once thought to be age related, is related more to deficiencies of vitamins B_6, C, and pantothenic acid. It is not a matter of answering the question, "Why do you want to live longer?" It is a question of "Why should you want to die sooner?"

Critical Stages in the Aging Process

From birth to about fifteen or sixteen years of age, human growth is quite rapid. At the age of approximately twenty-five, the human body reaches its maximum strength and physical skill. Normally, this strength and physical skill diminish slowly until about forty-five years of age, the critical point in aging. From this point on, the aging process begins to accelerate. At fifty-five, the aging rate again increases its momentum significantly until age seventy or so, when the aging rate levels off. Table 14.1 lists a few of the body changes normally observed with increasing chronological age.

During youth, cells that are spent or "die" are replaced by an equal number of new cells. In early youth, there is actually an excess of new cells which causes growth. HGH, the human growth hormone, controls the rate of production of new cells. Although growth proceeds at predictable rates, aging does not. Aging reduces the number of healthy cells in the body and leads to a loss of reserve in body functions, meaning that the body is less able to withstand a challenge or shock. As a person ages, his blood sugar level may remain fairly constant, but his ability to handle the challenge of a large amount of sugar, as measured by the glucose tolerance test, diminishes. Other values (blood volume, red-cell content, and osmotic pressure) that seem to be constant throughout life under resting conditions show the same tendencies. The rate of blood pH returning to normal after the administration of a standard dose of bicarbonate is slower in the older person. The same is true of the other variables, concerning their recovery to normality, when challenged. Thus, an obvious and fundamental conclusion is that one of the

Table 14.1 Body Changes with Age

	Young (25–35)	Old (70–90)
Skin		
Texture	smooth	rough
Color (white skin)	even	grayish, yellowish pigmented areas
Elasticity	good	poor
Surface	smooth	wrinkled
Healing ability	normal	slowed to one-third
Digestive System		
Teeth	full	loss
Taste	normal	loss
Gastric juices	normal	loss (12% per 10 yrs.)
Intestine	normal	Increased frequency of diverticulosis
Circulatory System		
Cardiac output	normal	decreased (about 1% per yr.)
Kidney		
Filtration rate	normal	decreased (1% per yr.)
Renal plasma flow	normal	decreased (3% per yr.)
Nervous System		
Brain weight	3.0 lb.	2.7 lb.
Nerve impulse/speed	normal	decreased (0.5% per yr.)
Visual acuity	normal	decreased (2% per yr.)
Hearing	normal	decreased (3% per yr.)
Reflexes	normal	decreased (0.3% per yr.)
Respiratory System		
Vital capacity	normal	decreased (2% per yr.)
Maximum breathing rate	normal	decreased (3% per yr.)
Basal metabolic rate	normal	decreased (0.5% per yr.)

characteristics of physiological aging is this reduction in reserve capacities. Besides the decline in production of numerous body components such as hormones and enzymes, it has been established that a number of enzymes also increase in concentration as the body ages.

Many view aging as occurring when cells die out. As Dr. Comfort, in a January 1970 issue of *Gerontologia* puts it: ". . . like so many lights on a theater marquee [the cells die], eventually shutting off the entire network." Others prefer to view aging as the biological mechanism that occurs prior to, and is responsible for, the cells dying out. Cellular aging underlies aging of the whole person. The body consists of some sixty trillion cells of various types.

These cell types age at different rates and by different mechanisms.

Dr. Charles Barrows of the Gerontology Center, a section of the National Institute of Health, wrote in *Parade* in 1970: "We know, from animal studies, that death of cells in certain organs and tissues accompanies age." We can count the cells and note the reduction. It is as great as 55 percent in the skeletal muscles of extremely old rats. We know also that the weight of a seventy-five-year-old man's brain is less than that of the brain of a thirty-five-year-old, due to cell loss. This cell loss is greatest in nerve, muscle, kidney, and glands, which accounts for the gradual loss (about 0.6 percent per year) of their functions. Dr. Comfort wrote in his article "Experimental Gerontology and the Control of Aging," which appeared in the March 1970 issue of *Geriatrics,* "The consensus at the moment appears to be that aging represents the loss of biological information. This is only another way of saying that, with aging, the stability of the living system is progressively impaired, but by putting it in this way, we may become more alert to the kind of loss which is taking place and to its possible site."

The loss of biological information by the body components that reproduce and control the body is then responsible for aging. Obvious questions begging to be asked by this explanation include: What causes this loss of information? Can this information loss be restored, or at least stopped? What is the mechanism causing the information loss? In order to answer the first two, the last question has to be answered first. The aging process appears very complex when viewed as a group of specific chemical reactions, but one simplified view is to concentrate primarily on the loss of information in the molecules responsible for reproducing the body's proteins.

The Underlying Cause of Aging

Fundamentally, the free-radical theory first conceived by Dr. Denham Harman of the University of Nebraska states that in the body, the random and irreversible reactions initiated by free-radicals (highly reactive chemical groups) produce a multiplicity of harmful reactions. The damage occurs from the primary reactions of free-radicals with DNA (the body's genetic material and protein synthesizer) and other enzymes or cell membranes, as well as by secondary damage.

The Importance of Undamaged DNA

Proteins are the indispensable constituents of life. The chief reason they hold this key position is that all enzymes are proteins and cause physiological reactions to proceed at rates compatible with life. The job a particular protein is delegated to do in a cell depends upon its structure and seemingly small differences produce major consequences. Experiments at NASA with a mutant of a micro-organism, Neurospora, showed that the mutant DNA had miscoded (missynthesized or made wrongly when copying from the parent DNA) a single amino acid in the sequence of structural protein in the membrane. As a result of this seemingly minor alteration, the entire membrane was defective. Mutants, whether they be of individual cells or of entire membranes, can be caused by free-radicals that enter chemical reactions with the chromosomes of the cell and break the chromosomes, destroying some of the genetic information carried by them. The destroyed information may range over any part of the genetic message, but sometimes it alters that portion which controls the replication of the cell. In that case, uncontrolled replication of mutated cells may begin and a cancer may be produced.

If the DNA molecule loses information, for example, by alteration of one or more of its nucleotides, life is impaired and an important body function is destroyed. The alteration results in either no protein or a wrong protein ("clinker") being built. A "clinker" inflicts damage by causing an immunological reaction, by using up required nutrients, and by strangling cells with waste material.

Missynthesized Proteins Speed the Aging Process

It is important to realize that the aging process is a snow-balling, self-aggravating process. The feedback mechanism involved in protein missynthesis can theoretically cause more and more missynthesized protein to be formed, which in turn would activate the feedback mechanism more strongly, producing more and more missynthesized protein, etc. The proteins produced by DNA change as amino acids are misspecified. When proteins are sufficiently different from normal sequences synthesized by young cells, they may be recognized as foreign antibodies, which then begin immunological reactions. When more of what is produced is defective, you have to produce still more to get enough that is correct.

Dangerous Cross-Linking Caused by Free-Radicals

In 1941 Dr. Johan Bjorksten noticed similarities between aging human skin and the tanning of leather and prepara-tion of industrial protein films. He reasoned that since the latter processes can be controlled, then possibly human aging can also. Chemical "tanning" is actually caused by a "cross-linkage" of cells, in which one cell is chemically united to a neighboring cell by a bridge or bond between an atom of one cell and atom of another cell. Dr. Bjorks-ten speculated that the cross-linkage could be the result of an unusual biological side reaction. He suggested that the cumulative cross-linking of body proteins is the con-dition known as old age.

In the June 1964 issue of *Chemistry*, Dr. Bjorksten wrote, "Whether or not such cross-linking is fatal depends on the importance of the large molecules involved, how many of the cross-linkages have been formed, and in what positions." Dr. Bjorksten pointed out in the *Chemistry* article that "many of these cross-linked molecules lead to agglomerates which cannot be broken down by any body enzyme, but will increase in the cell and gradually crowd out other constituents, thereby causing a continual decline in the cell's activity and ability to cope with stresses."

The Danger of Free-Radical Attack

One result of partially degraded enzymes is the accumulation of age pigments with the resultant congestion of cells. Lipofuscin (age pigment) occupies 10 to 30 percent of the volume of "old" cells; it is not present in new cells. This percentage is enough to "strangle" a cell.

Most cells (skin cells, blood cells, etc.) are regenerated very often, and the alteration of the DNA affects the aging of these cells the most. Other cells, principally nerve cells, are not regenerated. These cells are most subject to damage from the accumulation of age pigment (lipofuscin). Additionally, cells are destroyed when their membranes become defective. Thus free-radical attack on membrane lipids kills entire cells. This type of free-radical destruction—lipid peroxidation—is a self-perpetuating reaction.

Retarding the Aging Process

My approach to aging research is aimed, first, at finding ways to slow the aging process. This approach is simpler, safer, and has a higher probability of producing relatively rapid results than direct rejuvenation attempts. After slowing the aging processes, we can then seek to reverse them. Gerontologists such as Bjorksten are presently seeking to reverse the aging process.

A simple solution to the aging process is to destroy the free-radicals before they can do harm to DNA, enzymes, or other macromolecules in the body. Antioxidants are scavengers (inactivators) for free-radicals. Since collagen, which makes up 30 percent of the body's protein, is very subject to cross-linking initiated by free-radical attack, it is easy to see that neutralizing the free radicals with vitamin E and promoting the growth and health of collagen with vitamin C will help slow the aging process. Several researchers (including Drs. Denham Harman and Alex Comfort and myself) have increased the mean life spans of rats and mice significantly by feeding them antioxidants.

A combination of radiation absorbers and antioxidants would do more to slow the aging process. Chemicals in the body that can absorb radiation before it reaches critical body components will protect them and prevent free-radicals from being initiated. In addition, the presence of antioxidants will back up the radiation protectors by squelching the reaction in the oxidation stages. Of course, these solutions do not help the body components already destroyed by free-radical attack or radiation. They only prevent or minimize further deterioration.

The aging process cannot be significantly altered without controlling either the missynthesized material or repairing the damaged body components. The latter hasn't been accomplished yet and shows little promise that it will be, but several scientists are pursuing this research as part of science's continuing routine and thorough investigation.

Missynthesized Proteins Must Be Repaired

The approach dealing with repairing the missynthesized components, treated as foreign bodies by the body, has met with reasonable success. At least two different theories exist concerning the probable mechanisms for breaking up the missynthesized material into its basic building blocks, e.g., amino acids. Though the proposed mechanisms are vastly different, the practical means of achieving the desired results are identical. The key seems to be in adding selenium, or selenoamino acids, and sulfur-containing amino acids to the diet (see Table 14.2). I believe these materials encourage the breaking up of the misformed proteins into their primary components that again

Table 14.2   Important Nutrients and Their Sources

Nutrient	Natural Sources
Selenium	Eggs, onions, tuna, brewer's yeast, wheat germ, bran, broccoli, cabbage, tomato
Sulfur-amino acids	Eggs, cabbage, muscle meats, onions
Vitamin E	Wheat-germ oil, leafy vegetables, eggs, muscle meats, fish, whole wheat, vegetable oils
Vitamin B complex	Brewer's yeast, liver, sprouts, wheat germ, citrus fruits, berries, sprouted seeds
Vitamin C	Citrus fruits, berries, sprouted seeds

Source: Passwater in American Laboratory, May 1971.

become food materials for the body's primarily undamaged DNA.

Missynthesized proteins greatly different from normal proteins can cause adverse immunological reactions. Fortunately, these missynthesized proteins are not rapidly integrated into cells because of stereochemical misfit and abnormal conformation changes; they are thus exposed to agents such as selenium, seleno- and sulfur-containing amino acids, sulfhydryl-disulfide exchange catalysts, and folic acid for relatively long periods, increasing the possibility of degradation to the protein's basic components. Vitamin E and selenium, when acting together, stimulate the immune response, which in turn may destroy the defective cells clogging proper body functions.

Antioxidant therapy alone should add five to ten years to the human life span; radiation protection alone should add two to five years; and success with protein missynthesis re-sorting alone should add five to ten years. The three protection mechanisms together will act synergistically, potentially producing a life span increase of thirty to forty years of youthful life.

Ingredients can be selected so that each chemical performs at least two of the above functions and each enhances the action or lowers the toxicity of another ingredient. As an example, certain combinations of water-soluble and lipid-soluble antioxidants (including vitamins C and E, selenium, BHA and BHT) can stabilize cell membranes and, by free-radical scavenging, protect body components against unwanted free-radical attack and lipid peroxidation. They also break up radical chains as well, thereby terminating a self-propagating reaction.

A companion antioxidant, vitamin C, can work in the water-based fluids as vitamin E works in the fat-based membranes. Both vitamins C and E help circulation, so that cells are nourished and remain vital. Vitamin C also helps regenerate used vitamin E. In addition, vitamin C is needed for healthy collagen, the protein substance that makes up more than 30 percent of our body. A deficiency in vitamin E results in abnormal collagen which constricts blood vessels and chokes off adequate blood supply to the tissues. The diminished blood supply reduces the nutrients reaching the tissues, resulting in cell death and loss of reserve. The loss of cells from any cause results in aging. Environmental poisons, including air pollution, some food additives, smoking, and alcohol can all cause cell loss. Vitamins C and E both help secondarily to protect against these environmental poisons. There are other factors affecting aging, including mental attitude, exercise, and genetics, but they should be discussed more fully as separate topics.

Sulfur compounds that are excellent radiation protectors are also free-radical scavengers, peroxide decomposers, and catalysts of sulfhydryl-disulfide exchange; possibly they can implement repair of damaged sites. Sulfhydryl compounds and vitamin E also increase the body's tolerance to selenium, so that quantities normally toxic can be used to protect against free-radicals.

Selenium Compounds Protect Against Radiation

Selenium and certain organic-selenium complexes help the body assimilate vitamin E (a natural antioxidant), are free-radical scavengers themselves, and may play a key role in protein missynthesis re-sorting.

An analogy often used by gerontologist Dr. Alex Comfort in his 1970 *Gerontologica* paper is that the taking of chemicals such as antioxidants and radiation protectors guard the cellular-synthesis program "like protecting a phonograph record by lubricating the needle to reduce scratching with use that would make it unplayable."

Vitamin E Breaks Radical Chains

Dr. Bernard Strehler of UCLA said in a 1969 speech before leading gerontologists at Santa Barbara, California: "Auto-oxidation appears to play a key role in aging; experiments have shown a striking increase in the longevity of laboratory animals whose diet was supplemented with antioxidants such as BHT (a food preservative). The natural antioxidant vitamin E also seems to be important in the maintenance of cellular function. There appears to be little reason to doubt that the judicious use and development of dietary supplements and restriction of caloric intake to optimum levels will add significantly to healthy life-expectancy."

Also at the 1969 Santa Barbara Conference, Robert W. Prehoda, author of *Extended Youth* (1967), stated, "Free radicals have been associated with somatic mutation and extracellular biological damage. They can be neutralized by various antioxidants, such as butylated hydroxytoluene (BHT) and vitamin E. Controlled studies have demonstrated that treatment with BHT will extend the average life span of mice by 50.3 percent; comparable results in humans would increase our life expectancy to 105 years."

BHT and other antioxidants can be cheaply produced in quantity. BHA and BHT are used extensively in foods as additives, but are not yet available as drugs for human use.

The Effect of Vitamin E on Aging

In gerontology there are many theories and not enough gerontologists. However, it is easy to prove the effect of antioxidant vitamins such as vitamin E on animal health and life span. Thirty to forty (control group) mice may be raised on a normal and nutritionally adequate diet, another thirty to forty mice on a vitamin E fortified diet, and a third thirty to forty mice on a vitamin E deficient diet. I have undertaken this experiment and so have other scientists; most experiments have yielded the following observations:

1.   Vitamin E deficient diets lead to premature death.

2.   Vitamin E supplemented diets lead to longer actual mean life spans (the age at which 50 percent of the original group has died), but so far, yield no significant increase in *natural* maximum life spans (the length of time the animal should live, if in an optimum environment).

I think an analogy with humans is valid, but of course, the correlation may never be proved. With a balanced diet, people should live closer to the natural mean life span of eighty-five years. With a balanced diet and vitamin E supplementation, people should live closer to the potential natural maximum life span of 120 years. In essence, vitamin E, in addition to a balanced diet, overcomes many problems that arise because we do *not* live under perfect conditions.

Research with animals and other laboratory models indicates that vitamin E is related to the aging process in two primary and several secondary ways. The two primary ways are through protection of cell membranes and through the deactivation of free-radicals. Protection of cell membranes is essentially a nutrition function, wherein a deficiency of vitamin E causes membrane damage, while an excess of vitamin E offers little additional membrane protection. The deactivation of free-radicals, on the other hand, is related to total vitamin E concentration and appears to offer additional benefits above the level of vitamin E required for nutritional purposes. Few scientists would question the role of vitamin E in membrane protection, but its role as a free-radical scavenger is not as widely known.

Vitamin E Extends Cell Life Span

Recently scientists have learned to grow living tissues in laboratory containers. The tissues grown in this manner are known as cell cultures, and they allow scientists directly to study interactions between chemicals and cells, without the complicating interactions that may occur within a host animal.

In normal cell cultures, cells have a definite life span. Human embryonic lung cells will divide and reproduce about fifty times before they die. However, in a vitamin E enriched medium cell lives are dramatically extended; physiologists Drs. Lester Packer and James R. Smith of the Lawrence Berkeley Laboratory have found that cells have divided 120 times and are still dividing at this writing (October 1974); moreover, the cells are young and healthy. Thus, vitamin E has unquestionably retarded the normal aging process in laboratory-cultured human cells. The researchers reported their full findings in the December 1974 *Proceedings of the National Academy of Sciences.* Dr. Packer has been quoted by reporter Robert Joffee in the September 29, 1974, issue of *The Washington Post* as saying, "Cells might not necessarily have a finite life span, but their death might be influenced by compounds called free-radicals that combine to form such large, insoluble molecules that cells become clogged." Dr. Packer went on to say, "We don't know how vitamin E works, but it seems that damage which accumulates in the cells is reduced [by it], thus enhancing their chances to live."

I have reached several conclusions about aging based on laboratory experiments and human observations.

1. A deficiency in vitamin E (or any nutrient) will cause

premature aging. Vitamin E is more critical than others because it is involved in membrane protection; it is lacking in most diets. Vitamin E's possible role in slowing the aging process is not accepted as fact by all scientists, even though they are aware of such experiments as described above.

2. Vitamin E will protect the body against many pollutants and poisons. This too is not accepted as fact by all scientists, although it can be demonstrated by animal experiments and "uncontrolled" clinical studies.

3. Vitamin E will protect cell membranes, aid circulation, and reduce cell loss; a deficiency will cause greater cell loss, and a slight excess over the suggested RDA will add greater protection because of better replacement efficiency. A larger excess will not give greater membrane protection, but may play other roles. Some scientists argue against this strenuously, although the work of Dr. Lester Packer has confirmed it.

4. In my opinion, if everyone received adequate amounts of vitamin E, the *actual* mean life span of seventy years would increase. In summarizing the above three points, I conclude that the role of vitamin E in aging is twofold: a deficiency causes accelerated aging; a nutritional excess may inactivate free-radicals. Although vitamin E supplements may shift the *actual* mean life span, they will not significantly shift the *natural* mean life span, the life span of those individuals living under perfect conditions.

Vitamin E and Aging in Perspective

Those who say that there is no *direct* evidence that vitamin E increases the human life span or slows the human aging process are literally correct. The evidence for humans is not available, and the required double-blind tests on humans will probably never be run, as such tests would be prohibitively expensive, difficult to control (test individuals would have to follow a protocol throughout their lifetime), and the tests would span several lifetimes. Without the tests, there can be no evidence; but it does not take an intrepid scientist to conclude from the available evidence derived from animal studies that vitamin E decelerates the rate of "premature" aging.

You may wish to read more on this subject. Of the several good books for laymen, I feel that two are outstanding: *Slowing Down the Aging Process* by Dr. Hans J. Kugler (Pyramid, 1973), and *Vitamin E and Aging* by Dr. Erwin Di Cyan (Pyramid, 1972). Each discusses the free-radical theory as well as other theories on aging in an entertaining manner, and gives sound advice on staying younger longer. Their advice is pretty much the same as I have given you: eat balanced diets, take extra vitamins—especially vitamins C and E—keep trim, be active, don't smoke, learn to cope with stress, and enjoy life.

15

Supernutrition Is Essential to Optimum Health

Why MDRs and RDAs Are Poor Nutritional Guides for You

There is no scientific method that predicts the proper amount of vitamins that *you* require. Minimum daily requirements (MDR) and recommended daily allowances (RDA) are thought to be indications of need by many, but they aren't. First of all, MDRs and RDAs are changed every time the RDA committee of the National Academy of Sciences meets to establish them. Second, they are based on short-term animal studies and aren't reliable even for the animals. Third, they are influenced by the prejudice (and the source of grants) of the scientists on the committee.

But the most important reasons why MDR and RDA are meaningless to *you* is that they represent the levels of vitamins required to prevent immediate *recognizable* deficiencies in the *average* animal or person. The MDR and RDA do not take into account biochemical individuality, an individuality proved by Dr. Roger J. Williams, University of Texas (see *Nutrition Against Disease* [Bantam] and *Nutrition in a Nutshell* [Dolphin]). They do not seriously consider differences in life-style, environment, height, weight, occupation, temperament, emotional stress, illness, metabolic error, bad habits, activity, and the like, even though they claim to do so. They consider only the lowest nutrient level required to keep the idealized nonexistent "reference man," who is supposed to be the average healthy person, free from signs of deficiencies. You deserve better!

You *are* different. Your heart or stomach is not exactly like the ones you see in the textbooks; no two organs are alike in shape, size, and location; you may have a different number of arteries or muscles; your fingerprints, earprints, and voiceprints are unique. Dr. Williams explained the importance of biochemical individuality in the autumn 1973 issue of *Perspectives in Biology and Medicine* in this manner: "We can list the quantity of a nutrient required by the majority of adults. We could then compile a list of five nutrients, each with the quantity required by the majority of adults. However, few adults would have their needs met with the quantities listed. The data would necessarily only apply to 3 percent of the adult population."

The mathematical explanation is that 499 out of 1,000 adults may require more of the first nutrient than that listed. Of the 501 remaining adults, 250 may need more of the second nutrient than the figure listed. With the third, fourth, and fifth nutrients, 125, 62, and 31 additional individuals may be successively eliminated from the original 1,000 adults. The remainder is only 33 of the original 1,000 having their needs met by all five quantities of nutrients. If the example had included a larger number of nutrients, say thirty, the number of people receiving the right vitamin quantities would be virtually zero. If, rather than calculating quantities required for the majority of adults (51 percent), one determined quantities to satisfy 80 percent of the adults, the collective estimates would apply to only one in 806 adults.

Dr. Williams pointed out in the same article that "If individual needs were clustered around narrow limits, it would not be so much of a problem, but the range for at least ten nutrients is very wide."

Senator William Proxmire of Wisconsin, in an article in a 1974 issue of *Let's LIVE*, called the RDAs "unscientific and illogical." The senator pointed out: "The RDA standard is established by the Food and Nutrition Board of the National Research Council which is influenced, dominated, and financed in part by the food industry. It represents one of the most scandalous conflicts of interest in the federal government."

Furthermore, Senator Proxmire revealed that "the board is both the creature of the food industry and heavily financed by the food industry. It is in the narrow economic interest of the industry to establish low official RDAs because the lower the RDAs the more nutritional their food products appear. The present chairman of the Food and Nutrition Board, for example, occupies an academic chair funded by the Mead-Johnson baby food company. He appeared at the FDA vitamin hearings not only as an FDA-government witness but also on behalf of such firms and groups as Mead-Johnson and Abbott Laboratories. He was also scheduled to appear on behalf of the Pet Milk Company and Distillation Products. His research was funded to the tune of about $40,000 by the FDA and he had additional government grants of about $90,000 in the year he appeared for the FDA."

In the same article, Senator Proxmire discussed the constant fluctuations of the RDA values and the nutrients on the list. He reasoned that since the 1968 RDA list has undergone fifty-five changes in value, varying from 20 to 700 percent from the 1964 RDA list, and similar changes were involved in the 1974 RDA list, the list can only be regarded as unstable and suspect. Senator Proxmire summed up the RDAs very accurately: **"At best the RDAs are only a 'recommended' allowance at antediluvian levels**

Table 15.1   Magnitude of Benefits From Nutritional Research

Health Problem	Magnitude	Potential savings from improved diet
Heart and Vasculatory	Over 1,000,000 deaths in 1967.	25% reduction.
Respiratory and Infectious	141 million work days lost in 1965–66; 166 million school days lost.	15–20% fewer lost days.
Mental Health	5.2 million people are severely or totally disabled; 25 million have manifest disability.	10% fewer disabilities.
Early Aging	About 49.1% of population have one or more chronic impairments: 102 million people.	10 million people without impairments.
Reproduction	15 million with congenital birth defects.	3 million fewer children with birth defects.
Arthritis	16 million afflicted.	8 million people without afflictions.
Dental Health	½ of all people over 55 have no teeth; $6.5 billion public and private expenditures on dentists' services in 1967.	50% reduction in incidence, severity and expenditures.
Diabetes and Carbohydrate Disorders	3.9 million overt diabetic deaths in 1967; 79% of people over 55 with impaired glucose tolerance.	50% of cases avoided or improved.
Osteoporosis	4 million severe cases; 25% of women over 40.	75% reduction.
Obesity	30 to 40% of adults; 60 to 70% over 40 years.	75% reduction.
Alcoholism	5 million alcoholics; ½ are addicted; annual loss over $2 billion	33%

Health Problem	Magnitude	Potential savings from improved diet
	from absenteeism, lowered production and accidents.	
Eyesight	48.1% or 86 million people over 3 years wore corrective lenses in 1966; 81,000 became blind every year; 103 million in welfare.	20% fewer people blind or with corrective lenses.
Allergies	22 million people (9%) are allergic; 16 million with hayfever asthma; 7–15 million people allergic to milk.	20% of people relieved; 90% of those allergic to milk.
Digestive	About 20 million incidents of acute condition annually; 4,000 new cases each day; 14 million with duodenal ulcers.	25% fewer acute conditions; over $1 billion in costs.
Kidney and Urinary	55,000 deaths from renal failure; 200,000 with kidney stones.	20% reduction In incidence and deaths.
Muscular Disorders	200,000 cases.	10% reduction In cases.
Cancer	600,000 persons developed cancer in 1968; 320,000 persons died of cancer in 1968.	20% reduction in incidence and deaths.
Improved Growth and Development	324.5 million work days lost; 51.8 million people needing medical attention and/or restricted activity.	25% fewer work days lost.
Improved Learning Ability	Over 6.5 million mentally retarded with I.Q. below 70; 12% of school age children need special education.	Raised I.Q. by 10 points for persons with I.Q. 70–80.

designed to prevent some terrible disease. At worst they are based on the conflicts of interest and self-serving views of certain portions of the food industry. Almost never are they provided at levels to provide for optimum health and nutrition."

Since there is no way to predict how much you need, you may decide to take large doses of vitamins to insure that you get enough; this is better than taking the MDR if you are sure that you are not poisoning yourself. But you still may not be getting all that you need for your best health, and such a procedure is wasteful and expensive. If we all took more vitamins than we needed, it would probably create shortages that would drive vitamin prices up, as well as reduce the chances that the poor and elderly could afford the supplements they need.

The *only* way that we can determine the proper amount of vitamins we need to be at our best is by the practical test of taking increasingly higher quantities and observing the results. The old concept—that a body is like a cup and once the cup has been filled the additional vitamins run out—has been disproved. Chemical reactions of the body can be influenced by a supersaturation (an abundance above the standard amount) of certain vitamins. This is especially true in cases of enzyme deficiencies, the aging process, and stress. Therefore, you should experiment to find the nutrient levels you need. Self-discovery is more accurate than the dictates of "experts." Yet you will be guaranteed by the syndicated columns of Harvard's two "spokesmen" nutritionists that you need only the RDA.

The Effect of Wise Health Practices

Health improvements can be realized by eating properly and practicing wise health habits. I have observed this in surveys of nutritionally oriented groups, and recently others have begun to conduct larger surveys in greater detail. Studies have been made of religious groups such as the Mormons, Seventh-Day Adventists, and the Amish section of Mennonites (Pennsylvania Dutch) that emphasize well-balanced diets, wholesome grains, and moderation in the use or avoidance of tobacco, alcohol, coffee, tea, and addictive drugs.

Dr. James E. Enstrom, of the School of Public Health of the University of California at Los Angeles, reported in 1974 that the Mormons appear to have the lowest cancer mortality rate of any American group, except possibly the Seventh-Day Adventists. Mormons comprise some 73 percent of the 1.1 million people in Utah, whose rates of death from cancer and from all causes are the lowest for any state in the nation. The state's rate of death from all cancer is about 25 percent less than the national rate. In Utah County, which is 90 percent Mormon, the death rate from all cancers is 35 percent less than the national rate for males and 38 percent less for females. In 1970, the crude death rate (total deaths divided by total population) for Mormons in Utah was 33 percent less than that of non-Mormons; the same rate (for Mormons contrasted with non-Mormons) was 40 percent less in Idaho, 48 percent less in California, and 51 percent less in Nevada.

Still further data comes from an all-California study based on Mormon church records for 1970. The study of 350,000 California Mormons showed the observed mortality for cancer was about half the expected mortality for all causes and for all cancer sites. For several cancer sites, the observed mortality was substantially less than half the expected mortality. Particularly interesting, Dr. Enstrom says, is the low observed mortality for cancer sites such as stomach, colon, rectum, breast, uterus, prostate, kidney, and lymphomas. (None of these cancers has been clearly related to risk factors like smoking and drinking.)

In 1974, the Associated Press reported on a five-and-a-half-year study of 7,000 Californians by Dr. Lester Breslow and his associates at the University of California. They studied seven health habits and found that people who get adequate sleep, eat breakfast, stay lean, avoid empty-calorie snacks (pastries, soda pop, candy, cookies), don't smoke, exercise regularly, and abstain from or go easy with alcohol are rewarded with superior health.

Dr. Breslow concludes, "The physical health of men in

their mid-50's who follow 6 or 7 [of the above listed] good health habits is on the average about the same as men 20 years younger who follow 3 or fewer of the good habits. For men 65–74 who have followed [all] seven good health habits, the likelihood of dying is about the same as the men 45–54 who ignored most of those practices.

"Those who followed all of the good practices were in better health at every age than those who followed one or few. Poor health habits were more closely related to mortality than was income."

The specific effect of nutrition on the entire population has also been studied.

Dr. Edith Weir of the USDA reported in August 1971 that the health benefits from better nutrition would include the following:

1. 300,000 lives could be saved from heart disease and stroke each year.

2. 150,000 lives could be saved from cancer each year.

3. Death rates for unborn children, infants, and mothers giving birth could be cut in half.

4. The 250 million cases of respiratory infections causing 80,000 deaths each year could be reduced by 20 percent.

5. Substantial reductions would occur in mental illness, arthritis, allergies, alcoholism, dental problems, diabetes, digestive ailments, blindness, kidney disease, muscular disorders, and obesity.

6. Improvements would occur in life span, learning ability, and personal appearance. See Table 15.1.

My research and the research presented in this book indicates that even more impressive gains can be made with Supernutrition. These projections show that 500,000–1,000,000 lives would be saved each year if those people followed the Supernutrition plan.

1. Heart disease would be reduced by 60–80 percent.

2. Cancer would be reduced by 30–40 percent.

3. Air-pollution damage would be reduced by 95 percent.

4. The cure rate for schizophrenia would increase by 500 percent.

5. Individual IQ and mental alertness would increase by 5–8 percent.

6. Most individuals would live better longer and stay younger longer.

7. Their bodies would awaken to total sensual fulfillment.

8. Most individuals would be happier and less moody.

9. Arthritis and other crippling diseases would be reduced by 40 percent.

10. The incidence and severity of all types of diseases would be reduced by 50 percent.

Millions Are Needlessly Suffering from Chronic Diseases

According to the National Health Education Committee, Inc., the ten chronic diseases that affect the greatest portion of the American population are:

1. heart and circulatory disorders
2. allergic disorders
3. mental and emotional disorders
4. arthritis and rheumatic diseases
5. hearing impairments
6. mental retardation
7. visual impairments
8. diabetes mellitus
9. neurological disorders
10. cancer

The 1968 statistics, abstracted from the NHEC's *Facts on the Major Killing and Crippling Diseases in the United States Today* (1971), are as follows:

1. Heart and Circulatory Disorders
   a. Heart disease and hypertension in adults
Hypertensive heart disease	12,670,000
Coronary heart disease	3,650,000
Rheumatic heart disease	1,510,000
Hypertension without heart disease	8,370,000
	26,200,000
   b. Cerebrovascular disease — 2,000,000

2. Allergic Disorders
a. Asthma and/or hay fever	16,000,000
b. Others	6,000,000
	22,000,000

3. Mental and Emotional Disorders
a. Alcoholics	9,000,000
b. Criminals and delinquents	1,300,000
c. Narcotic addicts	60–100,000
d. Mentally ill persons	2,579,000
	13,800,000

4. Arthritis and Rheumatic Diseases
a. Under medical care	16,000,000
b. Not under medical care	50,000,000
	66,000,000

5. Hearing Impairments
a. Totally deaf	236,000
b. Some degree of hearing loss	20,000,000
	20,236,000

6. Mental Retardation
a. Capable of becoming self-sufficient	4,800,000
b. Capable of becoming partially self-sufficient	600,000
c. Completely dependent	600,000
	6,000,000

7. Visual Impairments
   a. Legally blind persons　　　　　　435,000
   b. Persons with impaired vision　　5,390,000
   　　　　　　　　　　　　　　　　　5,825,000

8. Diabetes Mellitus　　　　　　　　　4,000,000

9. Neurological Disorders
   a. Epilepsy　　　　　　　　　1–2,000,000
   b. Parkinson's Disease　　　　1–1,500,000
   c. Cerebral Palsy　　　　　　　　　75,000
   d. Multiple Sclerosis　　　　　　　500,000
   e. Muscular Dystrophy　　　　　　200,000
   　　　　　　　　　　　　　　　　　3,525,000

10. Cancer　　　　　　　　　　　　　960,000

Supernutrition can prevent others from joining this awesome list of ill Americans; it can reduce the suffering of millions and cure many thousands; it will prevent the premature death of a half-million to a million U.S. citizens each year. In 1969, 1,921,990 Americans died. Heart disease killed over 800,000, cancer 300,000, stroke 210,000, accidents 117,000, pneumonia and influenza 69,000, and diabetes 39,000.

Douglas Gasner pointed out in the January 1975 *Family Health* that 20 percent of the annual number of premature deaths (400,000) could be prevented by attention to diet and reasonable habits alone. For example, you have to remember to take vitamin pills regularly and you should study a little bit about nutrition. If you do this, then you save time that would otherwise be lost to illness—time that would be lost from work and pleasure, time waiting in doctors' offices and at prescription counters. You will save money as well. Supernutrition appears expensive at first—buying pills and books—but soon you perform better at work, accomplish more, and earn more; you don't have as many doctor and hospital bills; you are in better health for more years; you reap great dividends from a minor investment of time and expense. The extra cost is less than cigarette or beer money and much less than losing a day's pay or footing a hospital bill.

In our youth, our bodies compensate for nutritional inadequacy. Our rate of cell replacement exceeds the rate of cell death. In the summer of our lives, we notice among our peers the difference between the average and the well-nourished. In the fall of our lives, the more poorly nourished are in "spotty" health or have died, while the better-nourished are still enjoying life. The extra cost of the vitamin supplements you require beyond RDA amounts may run to only $5 per month, based on 1975 prices. It is less money than a cola a day or one evening's supply of cocktails.

It is interesting to compare animal nutrition to human nutrition. Farming is a business. Farmers must get a good return for their investment. They get the most milk, wool, or meat they can from their animals because they supernourish them. The animal RDA levels would not allow them to be champion producers—and animal RDAs are more generous than human RDAs. The farmer learns in college or from his father that Supernutrition pays. He has no intention of throwing money away or of wasting nutrients. He is scientific in nutritional programs. He knows the animals' Supernutrition points.

Lee Fryer, co-author of *Food Supplement Dictionary* (Mason & Lipscomb, 1975) and many books on farming and food-crop production, has pointed out to me the importance of nutrition in crop health and food production. "In scientific agriculture, the amount of fertilizer required to produce maximum crop yield is determined, and this amount is arbitrarily divided into ten equal portions called 'Baule' units." Corn growing in a field may yield from between less than a bushel to more than 150 bushels per acre. "Typically, a crop farmed at one Baule unit will yield about 50 percent of its potential maximum yield. When farmed at two Baule units, a crop can be expected to produce 75 percent of its potential. Applying fertilizer at a rate of three Baule units would produce 88 percent of its potential, and so on with each Baule unit adding about one-half again of the yield of the preceding Baule unit. I see similarities between the Baule system and your Supernutrition curves. I am sure that you have found the Supernutrition curve, for each nutrient is affected by the other nutrients, and that maintaining a balance will lessen the toxicity of each."

Well, Lee Fryer is right! Use the Supernutrition score to measure progress. (See Chapter 16.) Your progress will vary according to your needs, and finding the amount of each nutrient to best fulfill your needs will establish the proper balance for you.

You automatically will get the highest score when your nutrient intake is precisely balanced. Generally it is not just one or two vitamins that are keeping people from obtaining their Supernutrition point, but entire groups or classes of nutrients that are insufficient. Nutrients are balanced in nature, with each food group supplying an entire class of nutrients. If you are deficient in one vitamin because of avoidance of a particular food group, you are generally deficient in the other members of the vitamin class as well. Vitamins B_6, C, and E are exceptions to this rule, however. Vitamin B_6 is an exception because it is not returned to white flour in so-called enrichment. Vitamin C is an exception because it may be more than a vitamin; it may be considered a missing metabolite lost because of a genetic mutation in early man. Vitamin E is an exception because it is stripped away from grains, flours, and oils for various reasons and is essentially unavailable to us through our diet. Each of these three exceptions, vitamins B_6, C, and E, is particularly important because a deficiency of one or the other is involved in the major killing and crippling diseases: heart disease, cancer, mental illness, and arthritis. There is a high probability that your Supernutrition plan will consist of a generalized and balanced moderate supplementation of vitamins and minerals, with larger amounts of vitamins B_6, C, and E.

If you want to take large amounts of the vitamins discussed in the preceding chapters without following the program, go ahead—but don't call it the Supernutrition plan or say that I recommended it. Some people just can't take certain vitamins—A, B, C, D, E, K, or whatever. Some people may have adverse reactions caused by illness or genetic differences. Your own Supernutrition program is a long-term project. A short-cut short-changes you. Decide what you are going to do—gamble and not take vitamins at all—gamble and take large doses of vitamins —or do it *correctly*.

It is better to experiment step by step and learn what each vitamin does for you. Start with a given level and vary one vitamin at a time for weeks or months and measure your health by adding up your Supernutrition score. Some factors are more important than others and are given "weighted" values in the score. Blood pressure increases are not always bad, and blood pressure decreases are not always good, but it is generally safe to conclude that such is the case. The effect of blood pressure on longevity has been studied by the Metropolitan Life Insurance Company and is summarized as follows:

Age	Blood Pressure	Added Life Expectancy (years)	
		Men	Women
35	120/80	41.5	?
	130/90	37.5	?
	140/95	32.5	?
	150/100	25	?
45	120/80	32	37
	130/90	29	35.5
	140/95	26	32
	150/100	20.5	28.5
55	120/80	23.5	27.5
	130/90	22.5	27
	140/95	19.5	24.5
	150/100	17.5	23.5

You should throughout the program keep taking measurements of your blood pressure and pulse rate and check with your doctor; otherwise you might miss the improvements in blood chemistry. Don't assume what works best for most people works best for you. You are the important one.

George Allen, coach of the Washington Redskins football team, has told me that "we will be successful because we have a program. Some organizations do not have a program . . . they play it by ear, first doing this, then doing that. We have a definite program that we adhere to and it pays consistent dividends. If it didn't, of course, we would change it; but we picked a sound program and gave it a chance. If we saw progress we stuck to it. We didn't change just because we didn't win the championship overnight. But with a program, we saw consistent progress and knew where we were heading." Coach Allen has a health program too. Always under stress and working eighteen or nineteen hours a day, his health could easily suffer. But he exercises properly and consistently, and he began the Supernutrition program in 1973.

16

Your Supernutrition Plan

The Supernutrition Score

To begin your Supernutrition plan, you need two things:
(1) a quantitative measurement of your present health
and (2) an examination by your physician. If you are not
presently under the guidance of a physician oriented toward prevention of disease rather than merely body repair,
you may wish to inquire at several health-food stores for
the names of nutrition-minded physicians. The personnel
in these stores are often in contact with such physicians
because they may supply many of the recommended supplements. Alternately, you may write to the International
Academy of Preventive Medicine, 871 Frostwood Drive,
Houston, Texas 77024 or the Huxley Institute at 1114
First Avenue, New York, New York 10021, both of which
maintain lists of physicians throughout the United States
and Canada who are trained in nutrition and preventive
medicine. You need the quantitative measurement of your
present health so that you will know where you were at
the start and how you are progressing; you need the physi-

cal examination for certain health measurements and to detect any valid organic reasons as to why you should not take certain vitamins and minerals—i.e., serious kidney disease, metabolic defects, etc. The measurement is called a Supernutrition score and the means of determining your score is with the Supernutrition quiz and scorecard.

The quiz is merely three series of questions that you use to measure your body's performance. One series of questions of major importance determines 40 percent of your total Supernutrition score. These questions concern a combination of subjective and objective measurements. A second group of indicators is mostly subjective but allows you to see the subtle improvements you might otherwise miss. The final group must be obtained through an examination by your physician. The examination provides an independent objective measurement that insures that you are making real progress and are not doing harm to yourself. It removes all doubt.

You determine your score by answering each question and putting a check in the appropriate box on the "Start" section of the scorecard. After filling in the proper boxes corresponding to your present condition, you convert the boxes into a numerical score by using the instructions immediately following the scorecard. Your scorecard becomes a permanent reference. After two weeks on the Supernutrition plan, you repeat the procedure using the "2-week" portion of the scorecard, and tally the score to determine your improvement. You repeat the process periodically until you have reached your highest consistent Supernutrition score.

A Word of Caution

Some people invariably become overinvolved or worry about their physiological measurements. Physicians often hesitate to tell patients what their blood-pressure or blood-chemistry values are because these patients worry themselves needlessly. Yet an informed person can keep the values in perspective and use the information constructive-ly. Please be informed that because of biochemical individuality and other genetic differences, many people with blood chemistry values above the range considered "normal" for the majority of people have perfect health. Therefore, deviations from "normal" do not always indicate a problem. The purpose of the Supernutrition scorecard is to monitor the *trend* of your blood chemistry to see if you are improving with increased vitamin consumption or not.

You might also worry needlessly because your blood pressure or blood chemistry doesn't fall into the best category of the Supernutrition scorecard. If you are not yet in superior health, you still may be in far better health than 80 percent of the people considered "healthy." The scorecard is designed to give, on a "weighted" basis, increasingly higher points for the better values, and few if any points for values just outside of average. Therefore, an "average" person will have a very low score, not far above a "sick" person's score. The *trend* of the Supernutrition score is higher as a person reaches his or her best values, whatever they may be.

A third needless worry may be the tests themselves. Many people experience anxiety when they have their pulse or blood pressure taken, thus increasing heartbeat and blood pressure. As you get used to taking these readings, your anxiety will disappear. Try resting for a few minutes before taking them, and, immediately before taking them, take two (and only two) deep breaths. If your readings are high, don't worry, because you are now starting a program that will improve them. Women should not attempt to find their Supernutrition points while pregnant.

The only three physical measurements you need to take are weight, pulse rate, and blood pressure. If you can't take your blood pressure, you may skip it.

Monitoring Your Weight

I assume that you weigh yourself regularly. Compare your weight to the "ideal" weight listed in Table 16.1 to find

Table 16.1   Weights for Men and Women Aged 25 and Over
(in pounds according to height and frame, in indoor clothing)

	Height		Small	Medium	Large
	feet	inches	Frame	Frame	Frame
	(1-inch heels)				
MEN	5	2	112–120	118–129	126–141
	5	3	115–123	121–133	129–144
	5	4	118–126	124–136	132–148
	5	5	121–129	127–139	135–152
	5	6	124–133	130–143	138–156
	5	7	128–137	134–147	142–161
	5	8	132–141	138–152	147–166
	5	9	136–145	142–156	151–170
	5	10	140–150	146–160	155–174
	5	11	144–154	150–165	159–179
	6	0	148–158	154–170	164–184
	6	1	152–162	158–175	168–189
	6	2	156–167	162–180	173–194
	6	3	160–171	167–185	178–199
	6	4	164–175	172–190	182–204
	(2-inch heels)				
WOMEN	4	10	92–98	96–107	104–119
	4	11	94–101	98–110	106–122
	5	0	96–104	101–113	109–125
	5	1	99–107	104–116	112–128
	5	2	102–110	107–119	115–131
	5	3	105–113	110–122	118–134
	5	4	108–116	113–126	121–138
	5	5	111–119	116–130	125–142
	5	6	114–123	120–135	129–146
	5	7	118–127	124–139	133–150
	5	8	122–131	128–143	137–154
	5	9	126–135	132–147	141–158
	5	10	130–140	136–151	145–163
	5	11	134–144	140–155	149–168
	6	0	138–148	144–159	153–173

your percentage variance from the ideal. The simple calculation is as follows:

Step 1: Subtract your "ideal" weight from your present weight. (If your present weight is the same or less than your "ideal" weight, enter a check in block A of question 8. Otherwise proceed to step 2.)

Step 2: Divide your ideal weight into the difference that you obtained in step 1. Multiply this answer by 100 to convert to percentage. Check the appropriate block in question 8.

Example:	Step 1:	present weight	168
		ideal weight	140
		difference	28

$$\text{Step 2: (a)} \quad 140 \,\overline{)28.00}^{\,0.20}$$

$$\text{(b)} \quad 0.20 \times 100 = 20\%$$

Monitoring Your Pulse Rate

To determine your pulse rate, take a reading at your wrist or neck for a full minute. The full minute will give you the accuracy needed to differentiate between the closely grouped values in question 7. The full minute will also give you time to become at ease while taking the measurement. Be sure that you haven't been exercising or moving around much during the fifteen minutes preceding the measurement; it is not valid to compare your pulse rate after sleeping with that after walking upstairs. Your scorecard is meaningful only if conditions are constant, and reproducible each time.

Monitoring Your Blood Pressure

Similar caution applies to taking your blood pressure. Eighty percent of seventh-grade students can be taught to take accurate blood pressure measurements; you can too.

If you don't have a sphygmomanometer (the instrument used for measuring blood pressure), consider getting one —it's a good investment. Taking your blood pressure once a month could possibly save your life, or prevent you from dying twenty years too soon because of undetected hypertension. Good sphygmomanometers cost about $20 and can be bought at drugstores, hospital-supply stores, or through catalog sales from major stores such as Sears and Wards. You will also need a stethoscope for accurate readings. They can be purchased from the same stores and cost only a few dollars.

It is simple to take someone else's blood pressure but it requires practice to take your own. Your mate or a friend and you can learn the procedure in ten to fifteen minutes by following the manufacturer's instructions. If you do take your own blood pressure, don't get carried away and take it every hour or so, or walk around with a stethoscope glued to your heart. Relax. Use the measurement as a guide. Remember, it will probably improve soon, especially if you learn not to worry about it.

If you decide not to invest in a sphygmomanometer, skip question 1, and enter this information in Section II when you have your medical checkup. When using the score-card, you can decide not to use a certain value or question by crossing the category out. Do not use a category sometimes and not at other times, because that will distort the score. Alternatively, you can use only one section of the quiz if you so choose. Answer all questions based on your health during the past three years.

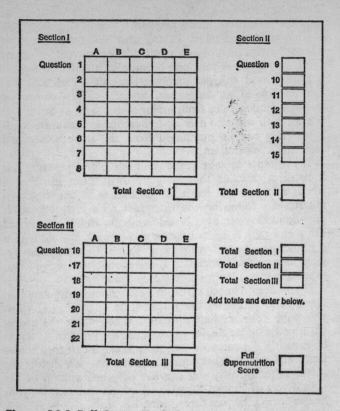

Figure 16.1 Full Score—To find your short-term percentage of relative health, which is independent of disease and long-term factors (such as resistance to colds), divide your *full* Supernutrition score by 5 (or multiply by 0.2). A perfect Supernutrition score of 500 indicates 100 percent of the best "variable" health for the mythical "normal" person. Your best health may be reached at a somewhat lower value.

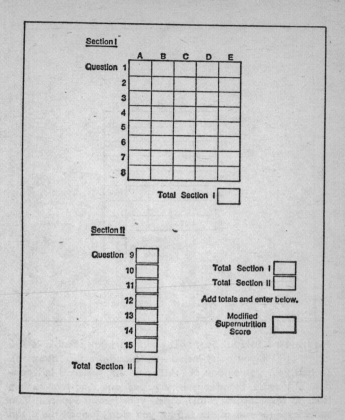

Figure 16.2 Modified Score—To find your approximate short-term percentage of relative health, which is independent of disease, blood-chemistry values, and long-term factors (such as resistance to colds), divide your *modified* Supernutrition score by 3.6 (or multiply by 0.28). If you did not include the blood-pressure question, divide your score by 3.4 (or multiply by 0.3). A Modified Supernutrition score of 360 (without blood pressure, 335) represents the approximate best "variable" health for an average person. Your best health may be reached at a lower value.

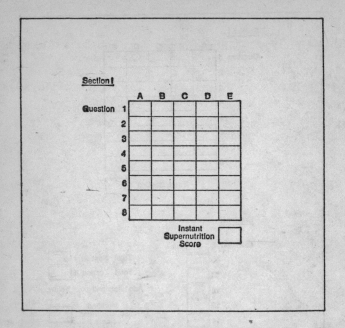

Figure 16.3 Instant Score—The highest total possible is 200 points (180 if you don't include the blood-pressure question). To find your percentage of relative health, which is independent of disease, blood-chemistry values, and long-term factors (such as resistance to colds), divide your *instant* Supernutrition score by 2 (or multiply by 0.5). If you didn't include the blood pressure question, divide by 1.8 (or multiply by 0.6). Your best health may be reached at a value somewhat less than 100 percent.

The Supernutrition Quiz

SECTION I. Major (Choose only one letter for each question.)

1. Blood pressure (normals from 90/60 to 140/90). (If not known, leave question 1 blank.)

   Is your blood pressure:
   a) 120/80 or less
   b) between 121/80 and 125/85
   c) between 126/85 and 140/90
   d) between 141/90 and 165/95
   e) above 165/95

2. Energy level

   Do you normally feel:
   a) peppy, zesty
   b) alert
   c) average
   d) tired, sluggish
   e) exhausted

3. Mood

   Are you:
   a) thrilled with life
   b) happy
   c) average, OK
   d) blah
   e) depressed, moody

4. Stamina

   Is your endurance:
   a) excellent
   b) good
   c) average
   d) fair
   e) poor

5. Bowel regularity

    Are your bowels:
    a)   very regular
    b)   mostly regular
    c)   almost regular
    d)   poorly regular
    e)   constipated

6. Headaches

    Do you have headaches:
    a)   no more than once or twice a year and mild
    b)   seldom
    c)   occasionally
    d)   often
    e)   often and severe

7. Pulse rate (after 15 minutes of rest; normals 65 to
    90, average 75)

    My pulse rate is:
    a)   below 65
    b)   between 65 and 70
    c)   between 71 and 75
    d)   between 76 and 85
    e)   above 85

8. Obesity

    My body weight is:
    a)   less or the same as "ideal" weight (according to
         height/weight table)
    b)   less than 10% above "ideal"
    c)   between 11 and 15% above "ideal"
    d)   between 16 and 20% above "ideal"
    e)   more than 20% above "ideal"

Enter one checkmark in the appropriate block on your
Scorecard for each question in Section I. Total the number

of checks under each letter. Multiply by the following factors: 25 points for each *a* answer, 15 points for each *b*, 10 points for each *c*, 5 points for each *d* and zero for each *e*. Enter the total at the bottom of the Scorecard. Maximum score for Section I is 200.

SECTION II. Subjective

9. Chronic pain

Answer yes or no:

sinus	yes	no
back	yes	no
neck	yes	no
eye	yes	no
shoulder	yes	no
elbow	yes	no
finger	yes	no
when urinating	yes	no
muscle cramps	yes	no

Give yourself 1 point for each "no" answer (maximum 9 points). Enter total here ___7___ .

10. Swelling

Answer yes, reduced since the last time you answered the question, or none:

face	yes	reduced	none
hands	yes	reduced	none
ankles	yes	reduced	none
joints	yes	reduced	none

Give yourself 2 points for each "none" answer and 1 point for each "reduced" (maximum 8 points). Enter total here ___6___ .

11. Skin, hair, and nails (Improved refers to the time since you last answered the question.)

	Column a	Column b	Column c
skin	(smooth)	improved	rough
veins showing in face	none	reduced	(yes)
veins showing in legs	none	reduced	(yes)
nails, color	(normal (pinkish))	—	discolored or pale
hair, condition	(glossy)	—	dry and brittle
hair, amount	normal or regrowing	—	balding
hair, color	normal or returning	—	(graying)
eyes	bright and clear	—	dull or red (blood vessels)
circles under eyes	(none)	reduced	yes
bruise easily	(no)	—	yes

Give yourself 2 points for each answer in Column a and 1 point for each answer in Column b (maximum score 20). Enter your total here _____.

12. Oral

	Column a	Column b	Column c
gums	(healthy)	improved	diseased
tongue, color	(normal)	—	pale or red
tongue, surface	(normal)	—	rough or swollen
breath	odorless	—	(halitosis)
mouth sores	(none)	improved	yes

Give yourself 2 points for each answer in Column a and 1 point for each answer in Column b (maximum 10 points). Enter score here _____.

13.   Circulation

Answer yes or no:
leg cramps, restless legs,
    intermittent lameness
    (especially at night or
    after walking)   (yes)   no
shortness of breath   (yes)   no
tightness in chest   yes   (no)
cold feet or hands   (yes)   no
hands or feet "go to sleep"
    easily or become numb   (yes)   no
muscle twitches   yes   (no)
extreme sensitivity to
    weather changes   yes   (no)

Give yourself 3 points for each "no" answer (maximum
21 points). Enter your score here ____.

14.1   *For females only*

Answer yes or no:

	Column a	Column b
irregular periods	yes	(no)
premenstrual tension or premenstrual depression	(yes)	no
painful menses or painful breasts	(yes)	no
menopausal hot flashes	yes	(no)

14.2   *For males only*

Answer yes or no:

prostate trouble	yes	no
frequent night urination (after bedtime)	yes	no
dribbling or difficult urination	yes	no
sexual staying power	not as desired	as desired

Give yourself 4 points for each answer in column b (maximum 16 points). Enter your score here ____.

15. Miscellaneous

	Column a	Column b
dizziness or fainting spells	(yes)	no
buzzing or ringing in ears	yes	(no)
allergy	yes	(no)
cough (chronic)	(yes)	no
indigestion or heartburn	yes	(no)
weakness if meals delayed	(yes)	no
hard stools	yes	(no)
poor appetite	yes	(no)
nausea	yes	(no)
trouble sleeping	(yes)	no
stiff joints	(yes)	no
hemorrhoids	(yes)	no
diarrhea	yes	(no)
urine (does not refer to color but transparency)	cloudy	clear
urination frequency	more than six times daily	six times daily or less
reflexes	slow	(fast)
vision	blurred	clear
sex, enjoyment	(average or poor)	good or excellent
sex, frequency	less than first 2 years of relationship	same or more than first 2 years of relationship

37 4/8

Give yourself 4 points for each answer in column b (maximum 76 points). Enter score here ___44___.

Total score of Section II, questions 9–15 (maximum 160 points). Enter score here ___81___.

SECTION III. MEDICAL

16. Blood pressure (normals from 90/60 to 140/90).
    (Enter again even if answered in question 1.)

    Is your blood pressure:
    a) less than 120/80
    b) between 121/80 and 125/85
    c) between 126/85 and 140/90
    d) between 141/90 and 165/95
    e) over 165/95

17. Cholesterol (normal values 149 ± 36)

    Is your blood-cholesterol level:
    a) 175 or lower
    b) between 175 and 200
    c) between 201 and 235
    d) between 236 and 275
    e) 275 and over

18. Triglycerides (normal values 10 to 200, or your age
    plus 110; values can go to 4,000)

    Is your blood triglyceride level:
    a) less than 100
    b) between 101 and 150
    c) between 151 and 200
    d) between 201 and 300
    e) 300 and over

19. Hematocrit (normals: men, 47 ± 7; women 42 ± 5)

    Is your hematocrit:
    a) between 40 and 43.9 (men)
       between 37 and 39.9 (women)
    b) between 44 and 46.9 (men)
       between 40 and 41.9 (women)
    c) between 47 and 49.9 (men)
       between 42 and 44.9 (women)

   d)   between 50 and 54.9 (men)
         between 45 and 47.9 (women)
   e)   above 54 or below 40 (men)
         above 47 or below 37 (women)

20. Uric acid (normal 3–5)

   Is your uric acid level:
   a)   4.0 or less
   b)   more than 4.0 and less than 5.0
   c)   5.0 or more and less than 6.0
   d)   6.0 or more and less than 7.0
   e)   7.0 or more

21. Blood urea nitrogen (BUN) (normal 8–20)

   Is your blood urea nitrogen:
   a)   more than 10 but less than 14
   b)   14 or more but less than 16 (or more than 8
         but less than 10)
   c)   16 or more but less than 18
   d)   18 or more but less than 20
   e)   21 or more

22. Blood glucose (normal 80–120)

   Is your blood glucose:
   a)   more than 90 but less than 105
   b)   105 or more but less than 120 (or more than
         80 but less than 90)
   c)   120 or more but less than 128 (or 72 or more
         but less than 80)
   d)   128 or more but less than 133 (or 67 or more
         but less than 72)
   e)   less than 67 or more than 133

23. Reference points

   The following measurements are a significant part of
   your medical history but do not enter into the Supernutrition score. Record them each time that you record numbers 16–22.

- Body temperature (normal 97.0–99.1)
- Coagulation time (Lee-White) (normal 6–12 minutes)
- Prothrombin time (Quick) (normal 10–15 seconds)

Total each column in Section III.

Give yourself 20 points for each *a* answer
Give yourself 15 points for each *b* answer
Give yourself 10 points for each *c* answer
Give yourself 5 points for each *d* answer
Give yourself 0 points for each *e* answer
Maximum score is 140.

Total your scores for Sections I, II, and III (maximum score is 500). Enter your Supernutrition score here _____.

Multiply by 0.2 (or divide by 5) to obtain your Relative Health Percentage.

See page 275 for the interpretation of your score.

If You Can't Check with a Doctor

Of course, some of us do not have easy access to physicians or cannot afford visits to the doctor for the purposes of preventive medicine. This is unfortunate, but it is insufficient cause to prevent an effective measure of health improvement. If you are not under a doctor's care, you will have fewer facts and, therefore, your quiz will be less accurate than it could be. But the "modified" Supernutrition score and "modified" relative health percentage can be calculated in the following manner:

Your maximum score in this modified version is 360 rather than 500. Add your scores from Sections I and II together. How does the total compare to the maximum?

You can find your "modified" relative health percentage either by multiplying by 0.28 or dividing by 3.6.

Without the information normally obtained in Section III and the surveillance of your family physician, be sure to look for danger signs such as extreme nervousness, eye whites turning yellow, unusual fatigue, unexplained diarrhea, irritability, heart palpitations, cloudy urine (not colored, but cloudy). Any of these symptoms may be due to lack of sleep, illness, excitement, overstimulation from too rapid an increase in vitamin intake, or a severe nutrient imbalance. Try cutting back for a three- or four-day period until the symptoms disappear. If they don't disappear in three or four days, see your physician. They are due to something else.

The Supernutrition Plan

An organized program, not a prescription, the Supernutrition plan outlines a scientific procedure to reach *your* Supernutrition point. Your guidance comes from your Supernutrition score, not from me, from your physician, or from anyone else. As you exercise your right to alter your dietary intake constructively so that you reach your best health, your score will reflect your success or slippage.

The objective of the plan is to reach your best health by regularly measuring your Supernutrition score while systematically increasing your vitamin and mineral intake. The surest way to reach success is by a slow, steady, and safe progress. Start with a good foundation by having a blood-chemistry test and minor checkup by your family physician (an expensive and complete examination isn't needed, but it certainly won't hurt). The next step is to take your initial Supernutrition score as previously explained; then examine the individual Supernutrition curves for each nutrient listed in the appendix and choose a moderate level for a starting point. In choosing your starting levels of vitamins, you will find it convenient to select standard strengths that are commercially available. It is wise to start with low doses rather than high ones; step-by-step suggestions follow in the next section. Again, pregnant women should not attempt to find their Supernutrition point.

After two weeks, you should measure your progress by taking your Supernutrition score again. The amount of progress will depend on how good your health was to begin with, dosage selected, and how reliably you have followed the dosage suggestions listed on the Supernutrition curve.

If your starting health was near perfect, you will not see measurable progress for some time, but your health will progressively become optimized. On the other hand, if your initial health was far from ideal, your progress will be swifter and more noticeable right from the start. In the first two weeks you will notice dramatic improvements in energy, spirit, bowel regularity, and overall alertness. Instead of being weary, you will have drive; instead of dropping off to sleep at nine or ten, you will have the energy to see the late shows on TV if you wish, and to exercise.

A Few Words About Vitamin Selection

Supernutrition is based on a diet of good foods, yet compensates for the fact that we do not always eat what we should. Our diet should be varied, balanced with the seven basic food groups, and consist primarily of whole, fresh, unprocessed foods whenever possible. We do not have to eat "organic" foods, but they will generally taste better (if fresh) and often be less contaminated by food additives or insecticides. If nutritional gaps occur in our food selection we can fill them with excellent food concentrates, such as wheat germ, desiccated liver, brewer's yeast, lecithin, yogurt, protein concentrates, etc.

A single capsule or tablet of a food concentrate taken daily is not going to make much difference in your health. (Only vitamin and mineral supplements are significantly effective in single-pill quantities.) There are, however, several reasons for taking food concentrates in substantial quantities: (1) to add to your diet undiscovered nutrients the concentrates may contain; (2) to add known nutrients deficient in your normal diet (e.g. essential polyunsaturated fatty acids that occur in vegetable oils and nuts); (3) to add nutrients to balance a poor assortment of specific nutrients in your normal diet (e.g., one or more essential amino acids to allow utilization of other nonessential amino acids provided by poor quality proteins sometimes, for example, found in vegetarian diets deficient in lysine); and (4) to provide certain foods in a more acceptable form. (Those who dislike a particular food, for example, liver, usually have no objections to the taste of the concentrate.) Generally, one or two tablespoons daily of each food concentrate will be helpful. The amounts recommended in Dr. Rinse's Breakfast (Chapter 10) are ideal. More would be even better, but be sure to consider calorie content and reduce the junk food in your diet by the *same* calorie amount.

There are people who prefer not to take food concentrates. Their hope for balanced nutrition generally lies in vitamin and mineral supplements. Individual needs may vary from just a single multiple-vitamin pill each day to a variety of high-potency pills; the Supernutrition plan provides a guide to determining your needs. The program recommends starting at a low dosage and progressively increasing it. *Minimum* quantities are suggested for each step of the plan; please note that these minimum quantities are not the *recommended* amounts. The formulations that you buy should contain *at least* the minimum amounts of each nutrient suggested. You will *not* find the exact formula suggested because each manufacturer provides a slightly different proportion of vitamins and nutrients. If the formulation you buy has at least the quantities suggested, it will work well. If you can't find a formulation with the minimum quantities that I list, buy the one closest to it that you can. As long as the minimums are met, you don't have to worry about "balance." Your body will take what is required and leave what is not needed, except in the cases of vitamins A and D, discussed below.

Several formulations are recommended in the Supernu-

trition program: a "complete" vitamin-mineral formula, a
"B-complex" formula, a "vitamin C" formula, a "vitamin
E" formula, and a "mineral" formula. In combination,
these formulas will allow you to select the right proportion
of nutrients to fit your needs, without creating any imbalance. Don't try to get by on the "complete" vitamin-
mineral formula alone by taking several in order to reach
the suggested minimum levels of the various vitamins.
There are two important reasons for not doing this. First,
you may take toxic amounts of vitamins A or D. Second,
you will be stuck with the ratio of nutrients selected by
a single manufacturer. Let your body judge what is best
for you, not what is convenient or least expensive for a
particular manufacturer.

You may discover that you do not tolerate a particular
formulation well. One may use an oil base that is wrong
for you, causing an allergic reaction or indigestion. Another, instead of using niacinamide, may use niacin, which
can cause "flushing" (reddening of the face) (see "Niacin"
in the Appendix). Change formulations if either is the
case. Health-food store personnel can often help you to
match formulations to your specific body tolerances.

You will find that you will get better results if you
start with products of reliable quality. Once you have
reached your highest Supernutrition score, you can experiment with less expensive formulations, if you wish. But
do not try to build health with vitamins or minerals of
unreliable quality.

Natural Vitamins Versus Synthetic Vitamins

VITAMIN C   Quality high-potency vitamin formulations are
a combination of natural-food concentrates, extracts from
natural sources, and synthetics. For example, 1,000 mg
vitamin C tablets can be purely synthetic (all ascorbic acid
from a wholly industrial source) or partly natural (a mixture of synthetic ascorbic acid and ascorbic acid that has
been extracted from rose hips or acerola cherries). This
type of tablet is usually labeled "Ascorbic Acid with Rose

Hips." It is not practical for a manufacturer to produce a single tablet containing 1,000 mg of vitamin C unless it is predominantly synthetic ascorbic acid; a 1,000 mg pill of rose hips or acerola extract would be too large to swallow. Acerola extract (prepared by drying the juice from crushed acerola cherries) is the most compact natural form of vitamin C available, yet pure acerola extract tablets are not available in amounts greater than 50 mg of vitamin C because of the size problem, according to the largest supplier of the acerola fruit, Nutra-lite Corporation. Since 5,000 mg of dried acerola extract are required to yield 1,000 mg of vitamin C, one would have to swallow twenty of the 50 mg tablets to obtain 1,000 mg of vitamin C.

There is continuing debate concerning the preference of natural over synthetic vitamin C. Vitamin C activity is due to the ascorbate ion that comes from ascorbic acid; this ascorbate ion is handled by the body in the same way, whether it comes from synthetic or natural sources—the body cannot detect any difference because there is none. But this is only part of the story. Natural sources may provide us with a vitamin C-"complex"—a combination of nutrients that work together synergistically. Although they are not recognized as essential by the FDA, these tag-along nutrients of the natural vitamin C-"complex," such as the bioflavonoids, have been shown in several studies to help the body utilize vitamin C or lower the body's requirement for it.

Some high-potency vitamin C formulations have bioflavonoids and other natural factors—such as rutin and hesperidin complex—added. There may be additional benefits from these natural substances but there is no conclusive evidence on them. The only fact we do have is that less ascorbic acid is required to do the same job when bioflavonoids are present. Generally, 20 percent less natural ascorbic acid (which contains partner nutrients forming a vitamin C-"complex") is required.

It makes sense to take vitamin C supplements (which come in tablets, capsules, powder, and liquid) along with the companion nutrients provided by nature. One sure way of doing this is to add the vitamin C in its pure chemical powder form to citrus-fruit juice as Dr. Pauling prefers to do, or to take the pills along with a glass of juice.

VITAMIN E Tocopherol (vitamin E) exists in several chemical structural forms called isomers: alpha, beta, gamma, and delta. Each has a different activity. This is why vitamin E pills are labeled according to total biochemical activity (in International Units) rather than simply according to weight (in milligrams). There is still another complicating factor with this vitamin. Each isomer can appear in two variations called enantiomorphs; one is designated dextro (D-), the other levo (L-). Nature makes only the D-enantiomorph; the body has evolved to use this D- variation. When tocopherols (vitamin E) are made synthetically, a mixture of the D- and L- variation of each isomer is produced. The presence of synthetic vitamin E in a pill is usually indicated without noting the fact that it is a mixture of the D- and L- variations, which is designated as DL-. Thus when we see the most active isomer, alpha tocopherol, written on a label without the D- prefix, we do not know if it is D-alpha tocopherol (the natural variation) or DL-alpha tocopherol (the synthetic variation). Since there is an advantage to listing D-alpha tocopherol (natural vitamin E can be sold for a higher price), we can assume that when we do not see it specified, what we have is the synthetic DL-alpha tocopherol.

There is evidence that some of the functions of vitamin E can be partially fulfilled with the L-alpha tocopherol, and we have no evidence that L-alpha tocopherol interferes in any way. Since vitamin E is sold by units rather than by weight, it should make no difference whether natural or synthetic vitamin E (a mixture of D- and L-forms) is used. But my feeling is that not all of the facts are in, so I take the natural variation (D-) because there is a chemical difference. The same argument can be applied as to which isomer to take. Since nature makes several isomers, it may be that each serves a purpose. There are no facts to support this reasoning beyond the knowledge that each isomer is absorbed differently and persists in the body for different times. I prefer to switch back and forth between natural D-alpha tocopherol and the complete family of natural D- mixed tocopherols in a single pill (D-alpha, D-beta, D-gamma, and D-delta tocopherols). Regardless of which you choose, the Supernutrition score will tell you which gives you the best health.

VITAMIN B COMPLEX   B-complex natural vitamins contain all of the eleven known members of the B complex, and possibly others; synthetic B-complex formulations hardly ever do, but generally contain only six or seven. However, good high-potency B-complex formulations are generally a mixture of a natural food concentrate (yeast and/or liver), natural extracts, and synthetic B vitamins.

In general, adding synthetic vitamins to a formulation reduces both the cost of the high-potency tablets and the size of the pills, so many people prefer them. When synthetic vitamins are taken in combination with natural vitamins and a balanced diet, they are useful. However, you should use synthetic vitamins by themselves only if you have no other choice.

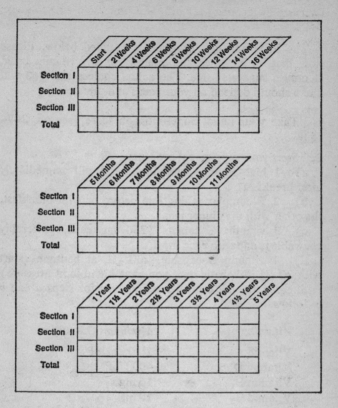

Figure 16.4 Supernutrition Scoreboard

The Step-by-Step Details

The Supernutrition program is outlined below. Please note that, in all cases, the quantity of any vitamin listed is only a suggested one. The actual choices that you will make should depend on your needs and preferences.

1. Take your initial Supernutrition score (see pp. 207–15).

2. *Start* your supplement program:

a) 1 high-potency vitamin-mineral pill immediately after breakfast

b) 2 B-complex tables, one before or with breakfast, the other with the dinner meal

c) 3 vitamin C tablets (250 mg each, preferably chewable), one with each meal

d) 1 vitamin E capsule, 200 IU, at bedtime (start with 30 IU if diabetic or if you have high blood pressure)

Suggestions, not critical requirements for steps *a* and *b* as follows:

Vitamins	Minimum Quantities
Vitamin A	10,000 USP
Vitamin D	400 USP
Vitamin B_1	10 mg
Vitamin B_2	10 mg
Vitamin B_6	5 mg
Vitamin B_{12}	4 mcg
Niacinamide (B_3)	50 mg
Pantothenic acid	10 mg
Choline	10 mg
Biotin	2 mcg
Folic Acid	0.1 mg
Inositol	5 mg
Vitamin C	75 mg
Vitamin E	5 IU

Minerals	Minimum Quantities
Iodine	10 mcg
Manganese	1 mg
Magnesium	2 mg
Potassium	2 mg
Copper	1 mg
Zinc	1 mg
Iron	10 mg

Vitamin B Complex	Minimum Quantities
Vitamin B_1	10 mg
Vitamin B_2	10 mg
Vitamin B_6	10 mg
Vitamin B_{12}	4 mcg
Niacinamide (B_3)	10 mg
Pantothenic acid	20 mg
Other B-complex	
choline	desirable
biotin	desirable
folic acid	desirable
inositol	desirable

3. After two weeks, take your Supernutrition score again, using the same values for Section III as you used when you took your initial Supernutrition quiz.

4. Increase your supplements in accordance with the following schedule:

a) 1 high-potency vitamin-mineral pill immediately after breakfast

b) 3 B-complex tablets, one before or with breakfast, a second with dinner, and a third soon before bedtime

c) 4 vitamin C tablets (250 mg each), one with each meal and one at bedtime

d) 1 vitamin E capsule, 200 IU, at bedtime

If dieting, pills should be taken 5 to 10 minutes before meals with a glass of water to help control hunger (by partially filling the stomach).

5. After two more weeks (1 month total since starting), take your third Supernutrition score, again using the same values for Section III as you used in your first Supernutrition quiz.

6. Increase your supplements to the following:

a) 2 high-potency vitamin-mineral pills, one immediately after breakfast, another at bedtime

b) 4 B-complex tablets, one before or with each meal plus a fourth at bedtime

c) 6 vitamin C tablets (250 mg each): 2 with breakfast, one with lunch, two with dinner and one at bedtime

d) 2 vitamin E capsules (200 IU each), one with breakfast, one at bedtime

7. After two more weeks (6 weeks after starting), take your fourth Supernutrition score, again using the same values for Section III as you used in your first quiz.

If your Supernutrition score is lower than previous score (step 5) go back to step 4 and repeat steps 4, 5, 6, and 7 in proper sequence. If for the second time the score from step 7 is lower than step 5, step 4 is your optimum level.

If your Supernutrition score is higher, then advance to step 8.

8. Increase your supplements to the following:

a) 2 high-potency vitamin-mineral pills, one immediately after breakfast, another with dinner

b) 5 B-complex tablets: 2 before or with breakfast, one before or with lunch, one with or near dinner, and 2 soon before bedtime

c) 2 vitamin C pills (1,000 mg each), one with breakfast, another with dinner

d) 3 vitamin E capsules (200 IU each), two with breakfast, another at bedtime

e) A mineral tablet at dinner or bedtime

A typical mineral tablet might contain the following:

Mineral	Minimum quantities
Calcium	125 mg
Magnesium	100 mg
Zinc	15 mg

Potassium	10 mg
Iodine	5 mcg
Manganese	1 mg
Copper	1 mg

It would be beneficial if the mineral tablet contains 200 USP of vitamin D and 100 mg of betaine hydrochloride.

9.   Take your fifth Supernutrition score after 2 weeks (8 weeks after starting), again using the same values in Section III as you used in your first Supernutrition quiz.

If your Supernutrition score is lower than it was in step 7, go back to step 6 and repeat steps 6, 7, 8, and 9. If for the second time the score of step 9 is lower than that of step 7, step 6 is your optimum level.

If your Supernutrition score is the same as in step 7, repeat steps 8 and 9.

If your Supernutrition score is higher, advance to step 10.

10.   Increase your supplements to the following:

a)   2 high-potency vitamin-mineral pills, one immediately after breakfast, another with dinner

b)   2 high-potency B-complex pills, one before or with breakfast, another soon before bedtime (or 8 regular B-complex pills). The high potency B-complex tablet should have at least 50 mg of each of the major B vitamins.

c)   3 vitamin C pills (1,000 mg each), one with breakfast, a second with dinner, a third at bedtime with a glass of milk

d)   4 vitamin E capsules (200 IU each), 2 with breakfast, 2 at bedtime

e)   a mineral tablet at bedtime

11.   The amounts in step 10 should bring most people to their Supernutrition point (highest score). Take your sixth Supernutrition score after 2 weeks (10 weeks after starting), again using the same values for Section III as you used in your initial Supernutrition quiz. Repeat the same pattern as in steps 5, 7, and 9, according to whether your Supernutrition score is better, the same, or worse.

12.   Maintain the same level of supplements as in steps 10 and 11.

13.   After 2 weeks (12 weeks from the start), take your seventh Supernutrition score. This time visit your doctor and get your second blood-chemistry and minor checkup.

14.   Continue to adjust your supplement program, making variations only (plus or minus) in B-complex, vitamin C, vitamin E, and mineral levels until you find your Supernutrition point—this will be the highest score achieved in periodically taking the quiz. After vitamin and mineral levels are determined, you can experiment with other supplements such as lecithin, yeast, etc.

Blood chemistries and minor checkups are suggested at
—start
—12 weeks
—9 months
—18 months
—once yearly after that

When your Supernutrition score decreases, decrease dosage until an increase is seen or until it returns to the previous high. Be sure to increase the dose again to see if the decrease in score was real or a result of an unrelated event stemming from overwork, emotion, stress, illness, or whatever. You may not have sensed an illness because, rather than being sick in bed, you experienced only a decrease in energy. If the decrease in score appears again, decrease dosage—you have just passed your Supernutrition point. If the score increases, continue—you experienced an unrelated event or had a temporary response to the larger dose. Minimum variances in the score of less than 15 points may be disregarded.

The Supernutrition principle has built-in safety factors, both in terms of protecting your health and in preventing you from making mistakes or misinterpretations. The program includes "trend" and "repeat" principles to prevent false conclusions. If you are feeling good and your score is moving upward, it must be *sustained* or it is false and meaningless; if you are feeling good because of natural emotional cycles or psychological factors, you may get a sudden but temporary increase in your Supernutrition score—this is a false peak and will disappear. A true Supernutrition peak follows a long upward trend and is sustained—within reasonable limits—at all times. A decrease might make you conclude that you have gone too high. The "repeat" principle requires you to confirm this by repeating the dosage. The plateau may occur at a point where your body has not learned to utilize beneficially the higher dose, but with time and continued improved health, the body *can* utilize that dose. The "repeat" may reveal that you have passed your plateau.

Don't be discouraged if you catch a cold three weeks after starting your program; it takes much longer to build up resistance. Also, unrelated events, such as a skin rash caused by a fungus, should not enter into the Supernutrition score. Because not everything is known about nutrition and many of the changes are long-term, the Supernutrition program is not perfect. But it is better than taking the RDA or taking vitamins haphazardly. It is the *best* program of vitamin supplementation *known today*.

The Supernutrition Curves

To guide you in maximizing your Supernutrition score and optimizing your health, use the discussions, suggestions, and Supernutrition curves in the following section—"Vitamin Guide with Supernutrition Curves." Each critical nutrient is discussed separately, and a guide is provided to show you relative relationships between the RDA, optimum intake, and toxicity diseases.

The Supernutrition curve illustrates the relationship between health and nutrient intake. The horizontal axis represents nutrient intake, with greatest amounts on the right; the vertical scale represents health, the best being at the top. The object is to optimize your health—to find the nutrient level that gives you the highest Supernutrition score, which is the peak at point *D* on the curve. This is called the Supernutrition point. Point 4 directly below the

Supernutrition point, on the straight line *BE*, represents the amount of nutrients that you should take for best health. Point 1 is the official RDA, point 2 is a typical Supernutrition starting point, point 3 is the point at which one generally begins to feel the effects of the program, and point 5 is the level at which toxic effects begin to show in some people. Point 6 is a dangerously toxic level.

You now have the facts to help you find your best health—a SUPERIOR health. The Supernutrition score will tell you how well you are doing, and the Supernutrition curve will tell you what you need to know about each vitamin as you improve your health.

This is a start. The information is here for you to construct your supplement plan; suggestions (not prescriptions) are offered, and facts about the use of Supernutrition are given. The rest is up to you. Do not become a fanatic or a "health nut," but *do* read all you can to learn more about how nutrition affects your health; it is a good idea to subscribe to one or two nutrition magazines. A few of the more popular magazines available in the United States are listed below for your convenience.

Bestways Magazine, 466 Foothill Boulevard, La Canada, Calif. 91011

Food & Nutrition Magazine, Food & Nutrition Service U.S. Department of Agriculture, 500 12th Street, S.W. Washington, D.C. 20250

Let's LIVE, 444 Larchmont Blvd., Los Angeles, Calif. 90004

National Health Federation Bulletin, 212 West Foothill Blvd., Monrovia, Calif. 91016

Nutrition Today, Box 465, Annapolis, Md. 21404

Prevention, Rodale Press, Emmaus, Pa. 18049

APPENDIX:

Vitamin Guide with Supernutrition Curves

Vitamin A (Retinal or Retinol), Provitamin A (Carotene)

Vitamin A is a fat-soluble vitamin with known toxicity. Although its toxicity has been exaggerated, it is a factor well worth consideration. Carotene is converted in the body to vitamin A (retinol); it comes from vegetable sources (carrots, peas, lettuce, sweet potatoes, and tomatoes). Retinol comes from animal sources (liver, eggs, and dairy foods).

Agreed function: Vitamin A is necessary to normal growth and to skeletal development. It is also important in maintaining the health of the cells of mucous membranes and skin and in the normal functioning of all tissue. It is essential to the regeneration of visual purple in the eye and thus especially critical to night vision.

Speculative function: There are legitimate signs that vitamin A is essential to tissue health, especially in preventing precancerous cells from becoming cancerous. Simi-

231

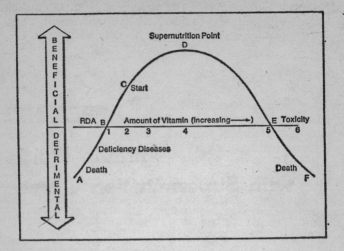

Figure A.1 Supernutrition Curve: Vitamin A

Typical Values

Points	Values
1.	RDA is 5,000 IU.
2.	Supernutrition starting point is 10,000 IU.
3.	20,000 IU.
4.	25,000 IU to 35,000 IU.
5.	75,000 IU.
6.	200,000 IU.

lar evidence indicates that vitamin A plays a role in the prevention of colds and other viral infections.

Reference chapters: 2, 6, 13.

Deficiency signs: Gross deficiency of vitamin A causes night blindness (nyctalopia), dry, rough skin, and a thickening of the cornea of the eye (xerophthalmia), which may lead to ulceration and blindness.

Toxicity signs: Dry, rough skin, yellowing of skin and eye whites, painful joint swellings, and nausea.

Precautions: None known.

Preferred forms: (1) mixture of vitamin A (retinol)

palmitate plus carotene; (2) vitamin A (retinol) palmitate; (3) fish oils; and (4) carotene (vegetable oils).

Dosage advice: Absorbed best if taken with meals.

Vitamin B₁ (Thiamine)

Thiamine is a water-soluble vitamin with no known toxic
effects if taken with other members of the vitamin B complex. Good sources are meat, fish, poultry, eggs, whole-
grain breads, and cereals.

Agreed function: Thiamine is essential to appetite and to

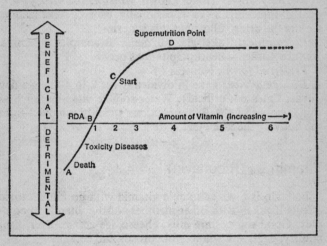

Figure A.2 Supernutrition Curve: Vitamin B₁
Typical Values

Points	Values
1.	RDA is 1.5 mg.
2.	Supernutrition starting point is 10—25 mg.
3.	50 mg.
4.	100 mg.
5.	Does not apply.
6.	Does not apply.

enable the body to use sugars and other carbohydrates. It is also necessary for the proper functioning of the nervous system.

Speculative function: To correct certain enzyme deficiencies and improve mental processes.

Reference chapters: 7.

Deficiency signs: Fatigue, insomnia, irritability, loss of appetite, irregularity. Also heart and circulatory disturbances, digestive disturbances, muscle tenderness, weight loss, neuritic pain, forgetfulness, lassitude, mental inadequacy. Gross deficiency results in beriberi, a fatal heart disease.

Toxicity signs: None known when taken orally. Repeated injections have occasionally caused sensitization. Colors the urine yellow but this is normal.

Precautions: Take with all major B-complex vitamins. Reduce dosage if heart palpitations occur.

Preferred forms: None.

Dosage advice: Take in divided doses 2 to 4 times a day (exact times not critical). Water-soluble vitamins, such as this member of the B complex, are quickly removed from the body by the kidneys.

Vitamin B₂ (Riboflavin)

Riboflavin is a water-soluble vitamin with no known toxic effects if taken with other members of the vitamin B complex. Good sources are milk, cheese, ice cream, liver, fish, poultry, eggs, and whole-grain breads and cereals.

Agreed function: Riboflavin is necessary in the oxidative process of metabolism.

Speculative function: To correct certain enzyme deficiencies and improve mental processes.

Reference chapters: 7.

Deficiency signs: Riboflavin deficiency produces mouth irritation, dry scaling of the red surface of the lips and corners of the mouth, magenta-colored tongue, dermatitis, abnormal intolerance of the eyes to light, the release of tears, and eye redness.

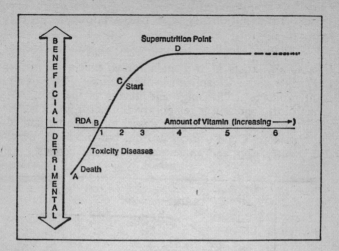

Figure A.3 Supernutrition Curve: Vitamin B₂

Typical Values

Points	Values
1.	RDA is 1.8 mg.
2.	Supernutrition starting point is 10–25 mg.
3.	50 mg.
4.	100 mg.
5.	Does not apply.
6.	Does not apply.

Toxicity signs: None known.

Precautions: Take with all major B-complex vitamins. Reduce dosage if heart palpitations occur.

Preferred forms: None.

Dosage advice: Take in divided doses, 2 to 4 times daily (exact times not critical).

Vitamin B₃ (Niacin, Niacinamide, Nicotinamide, Nicotinic Acid)

Vitamin B₃ exists in two main forms, niacin (or nicotinic acid) and niacinamide (or nicotinamide). The niacin form produces a "flushing" and itching of the skin. Although this condition is temporary and occurs only when niacin is first taken in higher doses, most people find it objectionable. Good sources are nut butters, meat, liver, fish, poultry, eggs, and whole-grain breads and cereals.

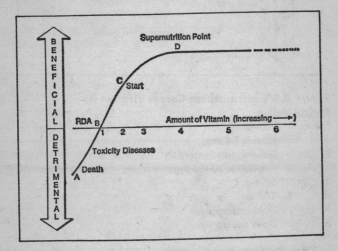

Figure A.4 Supernutrition Curve: Vitamin B₃

Typical Values

Points	Values
1.	RDA is 20 mg.
2.	Supernutrition starting point is 50 mg.
3.	100 mg.
4.	250 mg–3 grams.
5.	Does not apply.
6.	Does not apply.

Agreed function: Vitamin B₃ is related to protein and carbohydrate metabolism.

Speculative function: To facilitate the cure of mental disturbances by correcting certain enzyme deficiencies.

Reference chapters: 7.

Deficiency signs: Loss of appetite, nervousness, mental depression, soreness and redness of the tongue, skin pigmentation, ulceration of the gums, and diarrhea. Gross deficiency results in pellagra.

Toxicity signs: None known.

Precautions: Be sure to include other B-complex vitamins with the Vitamin B₃. Reduce dosage if heart palpitations occur. Niacin causes skin flushing and sometimes itching when first taken in higher doses—niacinamide does not. Use with caution if you have glaucoma, severe diabetes, impaired liver function, or peptic ulcer.

Preferred forms: Niacinamide (or nicotinamide).

Dosage advice: Take in divided doses, 2 to 4 times daily (exact times not critical).

Vitamin B₅ (Pantothenic Acid)

Pantothenic acid is a water-soluble member of the vitamin B complex. Good sources are whole-grain cereals, legumes, and animal tissues.

Agreed function: Pantothenic acid is involved in adrenal gland function and is required to fight stress.

Speculative function: To correct certain enzyme deficiencies and improve mental processes. To help cure arthritis.

Reference chapters: 7.

Deficiency signs: Headache, fatigue, muscle cramps, and reduced coordination.

Toxicity signs: None known.

Precautions: Be sure to include other B-complex vitamins with pantothenic acid.

Preferred form: Calcium pantothenate or pantothenic acid.

Dosage advice: Take in divided doses, 2 to 4 times daily (exact times not critical).

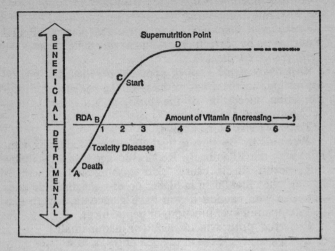

Figure A.5 Supernutrition Curve: Vitamin B$_5$

Typical Values

Points	Values
1.	RDA is not given; a reasonable estimate would be 5–10 mg.
2.	Supernutrition starting point is 10–20 mg.
3.	25–50 mg.
4.	100 mg.
5.	Does not apply.
6.	Does not apply.

Vitamin B$_6$ (Pyridoxine, Pyridoxol, Pyridoxal, Pyridoxamine)

Vitamin B$_6$ is a water-soluble member of the vitamin B complex. It exists in three forms and often occurs in nature as a mixture of these three forms. This family was originally called pyridoxine, but more recently has been called pyridoxol—currently biochemists favor the term pyridoxol while nutritionists favor the term pyridoxine. The three forms of vitamin B₆ are pyridoxal, pyridoxol, and pyridoxamine. Good sources are liver, ham, lima beans, and corn.

Agreed function: Vitamin B₆ is involved in protein, fat, and sugar metabolism and is intimately concerned with the metabolism of the central nervous system.

Speculative function: The utilization of vitamin B₆ in the coenzymes used to make lecithin in the body and convert cholesterol to cholesterol ester may make vitamin B₆ im-

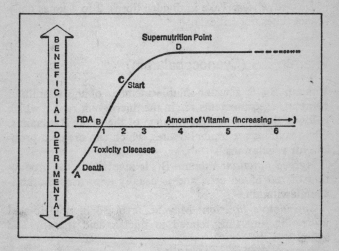

Figure A.6 Supernutrition Curve: Vitamin B₆
Typical Values

Points	Values
1.	RDA is 2 mg.
2.	Supernutrition starting point is 10–25 mg.
3.	50 mg.
4.	100 mg.
5.	Does not apply.
6.	Does not apply.

portant in preventing heart disease. It also helps cure arthritis.

Reference chapters: 7, 9, 11.

Deficiency signs: Loss of appetite, diarrhea, skin and mouth disorders, blindness.

Toxicity signs: None known (may turn urine yellow but this is normal).

Precautions: Be sure to include other B-complex vitamins with vitamin B_6. Reduce dosage if heart palpitations occur.

Preferred forms: None.

Dosage advice: Take in divided doses, 2 to 4 times daily (exact times not critical).

Vitamin B_{12} (Cyanocobalamin)

Vitamin B_{12} is a water-soluble member of the vitamin B complex. Requirements are in the microgram range, which is lower than the milligram range of the other B vitamins. Good sources are animal tissues, which can create a problem for vegetarians.

Agreed function: Vitamin B_{12} is involved in the production of red blood cells and is usually known as the anti-anemia vitamin.

Speculative function: May be involved in nucleic-acid utilization and thus related to nucleic-acid therapy and aging.

Reference chapters: 6, 13, 14.

Deficiency signs: Anemia and degeneration of the nervous system.

Toxicity signs: None known.

Precautions: Be sure to include other B-complex vitamins with vitamin B_{12}. Reduce dosage if heart palpitations occur.

Preferred forms: None.

Dosage advice: Take in divided doses, 2 to 4 times daily (exact times not critical).

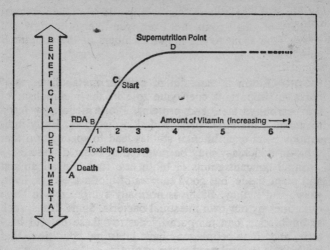

Figure A.7 Supernutrition Curve: Vitamin B$_{12}$
Typical Values

Points	Values
1.	RDA is 3 mcg.
2.	Supernutrition starting point is 5–10 mcg.
3.	75 mcg.
4.	100 mcg.
5.	Does not apply.
6.	Does not apply.

Important Members of the Vitamin B Complex

Five members of the vitamin B complex (biotin, inositol, folic acid, PABA, and choline) are often overlooked. They can be considered minor members of the family only because they are often omitted from the less expensive formulations. Human needs for them are just as great as needs for any other vitamin. Often these minor B-complex vitamins are in commercially short supply. Biotin and inositol are acutely scarce, although it is hoped that the supply will appreciably increase by 1980. Good natural sources of this group are liver, yeast, eggs, and whole grains (the same as the major members of the vitamin B complex).

BIOTIN Biotin is essential to cellular metabolism, as it plays an important coenzyme role in the metabolism of fats, carbohydrates, and proteins. Biotin deficiency leads to anemia, muscular pain, and skin disorders. Early indications from experimental studies lead to speculation that a biotin deficiency may be involved in heart disease.

Small concentrations of biotin are found in all animal and plant tissue, but good sources of biotin are eggs, liver, yeast, and kidney. Biotin is normally synthesized in large quantities by our own intestinal bacteria. Some drugs, such as antibiotics, can temporarily destroy these helpful bacteria, and some people may have intestinal conditions that inhibit this natural production of biotin.

Vitamin formulations vary markedly in biotin content. Often they change as the availability of biotin varies. Typically, a good multivitamin formulation may contain 2 to 50 mcg of biotin, a good B-complex formula may contain 10 to 50 mcg and a "super" B-complex 10 to 75 mcg. There is no known toxicity. It is estimated that a healthy person eating a balanced diet makes and ingests a total of 150 to 300 grams daily. Normal production and ingestion from foods overwhelm the minute amount available in vitamin pills. Personally, I use the biotin content of pills to judge the completeness of the formula.

INOSITOL The precise role of inositol is unknown. Animals deficient in inositol grow poorly and show hair loss. No human vitamin function is yet claimed for inositol, thus the FDA does not recognize it as an essential vitamin. You may, however, remember that the FDA did not recognize vitamin E as an essential vitamin until 1957.

Inositol occurs naturally in fruits and cereals. Good sources are yeast, citrus fruits, wheat germ, lima beans, peas, and organ meats. It is possible, though not certain, that we may synthesize some inositol with the aid of our intestinal bacteria. Good vitamin formulations typically contain 10 to 500 mg of inositol in multivitamins and 50 to 1000 mg in B-complex formulations—if they contain any.

FOLIC ACID   Folic acid is really a family of several complex chemicals, but is generally referred to as one substance. It is present in all green-leaved vegetables, eggs, liver, kidney, wheat germ, and yeast. Folic acid is limited by the FDA to 0.4 mg per pill for adults and children over four years of age. Exceptions are pills specifically labeled for pregnant or lactating women, which may contain 0.8 mg each, and pills limited to prescription sales, which may contain 1.0 mg each. The FDA limits are applied not because of possible toxicity or any real danger, but solely to allow simpler diagnoses of pernicious anemia—when vitamin B_{12} is deficient, but folic acid is present in adequate amounts, pernicious anemia develops without its normal telltale signs in the blood cells. Thus the disease develops but can't be detected until it is too late to prevent irreversible damage. The FDA reasons that if B_{12} is deficient because of faulty assimilation by the body, this deficiency might be masked by the folic acid in vitamin pills. But then what about the folic acid in a regular diet?

The exact human daily requirement for folic acid is not known, but it is probably in the 0.1 to 2.0 mg range. There is no known toxicity.

PABA   Para-aminobenzoic acid (p-aminobenzoic acid or PABA) is an important growth factor for many microorganisms and a deficiency causes a loss of hair color in mice. However, no vitamin function has been shown in man, thus PABA is not yet recognized as an essential vitamin by the FDA. PABA is known in gerontology as an effective sun-screen to prevent skin-wrinkling and sunburn. In humans it has often restored gray hair to its normal color, but perhaps only in cases where graying was because of a vitamin B complex deficiency in the first place.

It is used by green-leafed vegetables to synthesize folic acid. As it is a part of folic acid, it can be found wherever folic acid occurs naturally. The best sources of PABA are liver, yeast, and rice. Vitamins typically contain 10 to 50 mg. There is no known toxicity.

CHOLINE   By definition, choline is not a vitamin. It is a nutritionally important, accessory food substance that for want of a better classification is grouped with the vitamins. It is widely found in nature with high levels in animal tissues and lower levels in vegetables and cereals. The best source of choline is eggs. Choline may be useful in protecting our livers, kidneys, and arteries.

The actual need for choline may be only 10 to 20 mg per day, but several hundred milligrams have to be eaten to supply the body with 10 mg; most ingested choline is destroyed by the intestinal bacteria. "Normal" balanced diets contain 300 to 1000 mg of choline; multivitamin pills contain 20 to 500 mg if they contain any, and vitamin B-complex formulas contain 50 to 100 mg. There is no known toxicity.

Biotin, choline, folic acid, inositol, and PABA are all safe in large quantities and are involved in protection against heart disease and stress. Several experiments have shown success in restoring natural hair coloring to those prematurely gray because of deficiencies in these vitamins—get as much of each as you can. A good B-complex formulation, liver, and yeast are your best sources.

Vitamin C (Ascorbic Acid)

Vitamin C is a water-soluble vitamin with no known toxicity. It is looked upon by some researchers as being more than a vitamin, as being actually a liver metabolite missing in humans as a result of a genetic accident. Good sources are citrus fruits, tomatoes, strawberries, cranberries, potatoes, and raw greens.

Agreed function: Vitamin C is necessary for the formation and renewal of the intercellular ground (or cement) substances which hold together the cells of all tissues, including bones, teeth, skin, organs, and capillary walls.

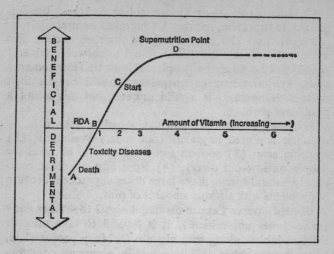

Figure A.8 Supernutrition Curve: Vitamin C

Typical Values

Points	Values
1.	RDA is 45 mg.
2.	Supernutrition starting point is 500—750 mg.
3.	2 g. (2,000 mg.).
4.	4 g.
5.	Does not apply.
6.	Does not apply.

Vitamin C detoxifies many poisonous substances, is important in healing processes and red blood formation, and is needed by the adrenal gland to fight stress.

Speculative function: Vitamin C has shown evidence of reducing the severity of cold symptoms. Several researchers claim evidence that vitamin C has antiviral and antibacterial properties. Vitamin C has been shown to reduce cholesterol deposits, and may help prevent cancer.

Reference chapters: 6, 7, 11, 13, 14.

Deficiency signs: Bleeding and receding gums, unexplained bruises, slow healing, and scurvy.

Toxicity signs: None known (often increases the frequency of urination, but this is a harmless natural sign).

Precautions: Cut back dosage if diarrhea occurs. The sodium ascorbate form (often found in chewable tablets) should not be taken by people on low-salt (low-sodium) diets. People taking anticoagulants should consult their doctors. Vitamin C is a mild diuretic, but this is not a significant problem.

Preferred forms: (1) calcium ascorbate, the form in which it is stored in glands (not widely available); (2) ascorbic acid; (3) sodium ascorbate (not to be taken by people on low-salt diets); (4) Rose hips, or other completely natural forms, make large doses impractical because of problems with sizes or amounts of pills.

Dosage advice: Take in divided doses, 2 to 4 times daily (exact times not critical). It is helpful to take milk or calcium tablets along with vitamin C. Many people claim better results when taking naturally occurring cofactors along with vitamin C; some, for example, prefer to drink natural citrus-fruit juice along with it. Be sure to take adequate vitamin B_{12}.

Vitamin D (Calciferol)

Vitamin D is present in nature in several forms, all of which occur only in animals. Provitamins D from vegetables can be converted in the body to vitamin D by the action of sunlight on the skin. Vitamin D is a fat-soluble vitamin with known toxicity. The two most common forms of vitamin D are vitamin D_2 (ergocalciferol or irradiated ergosterol) and vitamin D_3 (cholecalciferol). Good sources are sunlight and fish-liver oils.

Agreed function: Vitamin D is needed most during periods of growth for good bones and teeth. It is required throughout a person's life for calcium metabolism.

Reference chapters: 2.

Deficiency signs: Weight loss, loss of appetite, cramps, poor bone formation, and rickets.

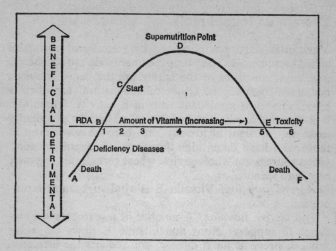

Figure A.9 Supernutrition Curve: Vitamin D

Typical Values

Points	Values
1.	RDA is 400 IU.
2.	Supernutrition starting point is 400–500 IU.
3.	800 IU.
4.	1,000 IU.
5.	40,000 IU (2,000 IU in children).
6.	300,000 IU.

Toxicity signs: Unusual thirst, urinary urgency, vomiting, and diarrhea.

Precautions: People with heart disorders or kidney disease should use vitamin D with caution; everyone should be aware of its possible toxicity.

Preferred forms: (1) irradiated ergosterol (ergocalciferol); (2) fish oils; (3) others.

Dosage advice: Best absorbed if taken with meals.

Vitamin E (Tocopherol)

Vitamin E activity is possessed by a family of chemicals called tocopherols. The prime member is alpha-tocopherol, and lesser members of the family are the beta-, gamma-, and delta-tocopherols. Other related natural tocopherols have not shown significant vitamin E activity. Vitamin E is a fat-soluble vitamin and hence viewed as potentially toxic, but no signs of toxicity have been observed even in those who have taken high dosages over several decades. Good sources are whole grains, wheat germ, nuts, legumes, eggs, and sprouts.

Agreed function: Vitamin E is vital to normal reproduction.

Speculative function: A number of researchers see evidence to support claims that vitamin E slows the aging process, prevents heart disease, and reduces the incidence of cancer.

Reference chapters: 7, 10, 13, 14.

Deficiency signs: Pigmentation, anemia. Other signs have been seen in animals, such as nutritional muscular dystrophy, testicle shrinkage, blood-vessel disorders, etc.

Toxicity signs: None known. Studies with growing chickens have shown growth abnormalities at very high dosages. One physician has reported increased fatigue associated with initiation of vitamin E therapy. If fatigue develops, check the creatine level monitored as part of your periodic blood analysis.

Precautions: People with overactive thyroids, diabetes, high blood pressure, or rheumatic hearts should proceed cautiously; start at 30 IU for a month, then increase by 30 IU each month until a tolerance limit is reached.

Preferred forms: (1) mixed tocopherols; (2) D-alpha-tocopheryl succinate or D-alpha-tocopheryl acetate; (3) DL-alpha-tocopheryl acetate or DL-alpha-tocopheryl succinate.

Dosage advice: Best absorbed if taken with meals or wheat-germ oil (one teaspoonful or 2 to 3 capsules, each 3 minims or more in size, of wheat-germ oil is adequate for this purpose). Try to take at times when you are not taking pills containing iron. Although the action of iron on vitamin E has been overemphasized, "free" iron in the same pill with vitamin E can destroy it. Chelated iron or strongly bound organic forms of iron will not attack vitamin E and the iron in food is usually chelated.

To double the blood content level of vitamin E, the dosage must be increased 40 times. Compared with the 100 IU level, a 500 IU level of vitamin E increases the blood level of vitamin E by only 9 percent.

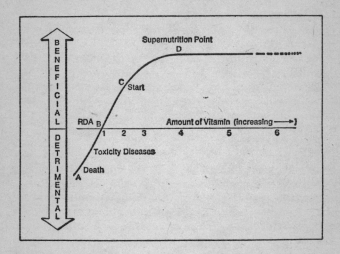

Figure A.10 Supernutrition Curve: Vitamin E
Typical Values

Points	Values
1.	RDA is 15 IU.
2.	Supernutrition starting point is 200 IU.
3.	400 IU.
4.	800 IU.
5.	No known toxicity.
6.	No known toxicity.

Glossary

ALPHA TOCOPHEROL. (*a*-TOCOPHEROL)

The principal form of vitamin E.

AMINO ACID.

1. A group of atoms containing an amine group and a carboyxl group.
2. The building block of protein.
3. 22 amino acids are considered essential for life and must be in our regular diet.

ANGINA PECTORIS.

1. Pain and oppression about the heart or chest.
2. Pain radiating from the heart to the shoulder and then to the left arm.
3. Heart disease due to cholesterol plaques in the walls of the coronary arteries.

ANTIBODY.

A substance in the body that provides immunity to disease by killing germs.

ANTIOXIDANT.

A substance that prevents oxidation (reaction with oxygen).

ANTITHROMBIN.

A substance that retards or prevents blood clots or coagulation.

ARTERIOSCLEROSIS.

A hardening of the arteries due to the presence of calcified deposits in the artery wall and inflammation of the tissue.

APOENZYME.

The protein part of an enzyme.

ATHEROSCLEROSIS.
1.   A type of arteriosclerosis.
2.   Deposits of cholesterol and fats in the artery wall.

BHA.
See BUTYLATED HYDROXYANISOLE.

BHT.
See BUTYLATED HYDROXYTOLUENE.

BIOFLAVONOIDS.
Naturally occurring substances believed to enhance the activity of vitamin C, primarily rutin, esculin, and hesperidin.

BUTYLATED HYDROXYANISOLE.
A synthetic antioxidant often used in foods as a preservative. It has been shown to reduce cancer incidence and extend mean life spans.

BUTYLATED HYDROXYTOLUENE.
A synthetic antioxidant often used in foods as a preservative. It has been shown to reduce cancer incidence and extend mean life spans.

CARCINOGEN.
A substance that causes cancer.

CATALYST.
A substance or agent used to speed or maintain a reaction in which it does not participate; thus it may be used over and over.

CHOLESTEROL.
A solid monatomic alcohol found only in animals, including man.

CHOLESTEROLPHOBIA.
The needless and unfounded fear and avoidance of cholesterol.

COENZYME.
1.   The nonprotein part of an enzyme.
2.   Usually a B vitamin.
3.   Forms the major portion of the enzyme.

COLLAGEN.
The main structural protein of the body, making up about one-third of the total protein content.

CORONARY THROMBOSIS.

Blockage in the coronary arteries thereby preventing blood from reaching the heart for its own use.

CROSS-LINKING.

The abnormal uniting of neighboring cells or molecules in a tissue, which affects tissue function. A handcuffing of vital components in a cell.

DEOXYRIBONUCLEIC ACID.

The basic genetic molecule and protein factory of the body, and the only substance that can reproduce itself.

DIASTOLIC.

The phase of greatest cardiac relaxation in which the heart-muscle fibers lengthen, the heart dilates, and the cavities fill with blood.

DIENES.

Oxidized fragments of polyunsaturated fatty acids formed because of an antioxidant deficiency.

DNA.

See DEOXYRIBONUCLEIC ACID.

EMBOLISM.

Blood clot obstructing a blood vessel.

ENZYME.

A large molecule that is a body-chemistry catalyst. Enzymes have two parts: an apoenzyme and the coenzyme. Enzymes speed and control the rate of reactions.

FREE-RADICALS.

Highly active fragments of molecules generally harmful to the body.

FREE-RADICAL SCAVENGER.

A substance that removes or inactivates a free radical.

GENE.

A factor that determines heredity.

HYPERCHOLESTEROLEMIA.

Excess blood cholesterol.

HYPERTENSION.

A condition in which one has a higher blood pressure than normal for his age.

HYPERVITAMINOSIS.

A condition caused by an excessive amount of vitamins.

Known to occur only with massive doses of vitamins A and D.

HYPOCHOLESTEROLEMIC.

Lowering of serum-cholesterol levels.

HYPOVITAMINOSIS.

A condition due to a deficiency of a vitamin.

INFARCT.

Death of tissue due to lack of blood.

INTIMA.

The innermost coating of a blood vessel.

ISOMER.

A chemical structure.

IU.

A unit of measure defined and adopted by the International Conference for Unification of Formulas. A different definition is applied to each nutrient, usually based on the amount required to produce a certain reaction or instrument reading.

LAETRILE.

Vitamin B_{17}. Used to reduce pain in cancer patients and may have reduced some tumors.

LIPID.

A fat or fatty substance.

LIPID PEROXIDATION.

Rancifying or spoiling of fatty substances.

MEAN.

The average.

MEDIAN.

The middle (not the average) number. There are as many lower numbers as higher.

MEGAVITAMIN.

Large doses of a vitamin, especially a water-soluble vitamin.

MEMBRANE.

A layer that separates one part from another, such as the surface or "skin" of a cell, or the layer of tissue which lines a cavity.

MICROGRAM.

Less than one-millionth of an ounce, more precisely one millionth of a gram.

MILLIGRAM.

Less than one-ten thousandth of an ounce, more precisely one thousandth of a gram.

ORTHOMOLECULAR.

The process of adding more oxygen to a substance than the normal oxides of that substance contain, generally leading to deleterious reactions.

PLACEBO.

A "dummy" inert pill (sometimes a sugar pill) used in controlled studies to confuse the patients so that they can't tell "who gets what."

POLYUNSATURATED FATTY ACID.

A fatty material, capable of readily combining with other atoms or molecular fragments. Generally, polyunsaturated fatty acids are either very soft or liquid at room temperature. Polyunsaturated fatty acids have two or more places capable of reactions or addition. Three polyunsaturated fatty acids are essential and must be in our diet: linoleic, linolenic, and arachidonic acids.

PUFA.

See POLYUNSATURATED FATTY ACIDS.

SCHIZOPHRENIA.

A psychotic disorder characterized by progressive withdrawal and deterioration of emotional response.

SELENIUM.

An antioxidant and essential mineral that can be toxic even at low concentrations. Found in brewer's yeast, most eggs, and grains grown in soils containing selenium.

SUPERNUTRITION.

The practice of taking the most beneficial amounts of nutrients as scientifically determined.

SUPERNUTRITION CURVE.

A graphic relationship showing the effect on health of different amounts of each nutrient.

SUPERNUTRITION PLAN.

The systematic increase in nutrient level as the Supernutrition score increases, until the proper amount of nutrient is found for each person.

SUPERNUTRITION POINT.

The highest point on the Supernutrition curve; it represents the best health for an individual and the proper amount of nutrients required to achieve it.

SUPERNUTRITION SCORE.

The result of several indicators that reveal the health of an individual. As the health improves, the Supernutrition score increases.

SYSTOLIC.

Pertaining to the heart cycle in which the heart is in contraction. This causes the first sound and is the greatest force exerted by the heart and the highest degree of resistance put forth by the arterial walls. The first number in blood pressure readings.

THROMBIN.

A substance in blood that combines with fibrinogen to form the fibrin needed to clot blood.

THROMBOSIS.

The formation of a blood clot.

TOCOPHEROL.

The family of compounds having vitamin E activity. The four principal isomers are alpha-, beta-, gamma-, and delta-. There are two possible forms of each isomer—dextro, D, which is the active form and levo, L, which is inactive.

TRIGLYCERIDES.

Fatty materials in the blood.

USP.

Units of strength determined by the United States Pharmacopeia.

VITAMIN.

An organic substance existing in foods in minute amounts, essential for life, and needed in minor amounts for metabolism. A shortage of any vitamin will cause a disease.

Bibliography and Suggested Reading

Chapter 6

Bartz, Fred H. *The Key to Good Health: Vitamin C.* Chicago: Graphic Arts Research Foundation, 1969.

Pauling, Linus. *Vitamin C and the Common Cold.* San Francisco: Freeman, 1970.

Stone, Irwin. *The Healing Factor: Vitamin C Against Disease.* New York: Grosset & Dunlap, 1972.

Webster, James. *Vitamin C: The Protective Vitamin.* New York: Award Books, 1971.

Chapter 7

Abrahamson, E.M., and Pezet, A.W. *Body, Mind and Sugar.* York: Pyramid, 1971.

Adams, Ruth, and Murray, Frank. *Megavitamin Therapy.* New York: Larchmont Books, 1973.

Blaine, Tom. R. *Mental Health Through Nutrition.* New York: The Citadel Press, 1969.

Cheraskin, E., Ringsdorf, W.M., and Brecher, A. *Psychodietetics.* New York: Stein and Day, 1975.

Fredericks, Carlton. *Low Blood Sugar and You.* New York: Constellation International, 1969.

Hoffer, Abram, and Osmond, Humphrey. *How to Live with Schizophrenia.* New York: University Books, 1966.

———. *New Hope for Alcoholics.* New York: University Books, 1968.

Kiernan, Thomas. *Shrinks, etc.* New York: Dial, 1974.

Steincrohn, Peter J. *The Most Common Misdiagnosed Disease: Low Blood Sugar.* Chicago: Henry Regnery, 1972.

Weller, Charles, and Boylan, Brian Richard. *Hypoglycemia*. New York: Award Books, 1970.

Chapters 8 and 9

Pinckney, Ed. *The Cholesterol Controversy*. Los Angeles: Sherbourne Press, 1973.

Chapter 10

Adams, Ruth, and Murray, Frank. *Vitamin E: Wonder Worker of the '70's?* New York: Larchmont, 1971.

Bailey, Herbert. *Vitamin E: Your Key to a Healthy Heart*. New York: ARC Books, 1964.

Ebon, Martin, *The Truth About Vitamin E*. New York: Bantam, 1972.

Shute, Wilfrid E., and Taub, Harald J. *Vitamin E for Ailing and Healthy Hearts*. New York: Pyramid, 1972.

Winter, Ruth. *Vitamin E: The Miracle Worker*. New York: Arco Publishing, 1972.

Chapter 14

Di Cyan, Erwin. *Vitamin E and Aging*. New York: Pyramid, 1972.

Hrachovec, Josef P. *Keeping Young and Living Longer*. Los Angeles: Sherbourne Press, 1972.

Kugler, Hans J. *Slowing Down the Aging Process*. New York: Pyramid, 1973.

Wade, Carlson. *The Rejuvenation Vitamin*. New York: Award Books, 1970.

General Nutrition and Specialties

Cheraskin, E., and Ringsdorf, W.M. *New Hope for Incurable Diseases*. New York: Arco Publishing, 1971.

Clark, Linda, *Stay Young Longer*. New York: Pyramid, 1961.

Editors of Executive Health Report. *The "Executive Health Report" Fitness Guide*. New York: Award Books, 1969.

Fryer, L., and Dickinson, A. *Food Supplement Handbook*. Mason & Lipscomb, 1975.

Garrison, Omar V. *The Dictocrats*. Chicago: Books for Today, 1970.

Jacobson, Michael F. *Eater's Digest*. Garden City, N.Y.: Doubleday Anchor, 1972.

————. *Nutrition Scoreboard*. Washington, D.C.: Center for Science in the Public Interest, 1973.

Williams, Roger J. *Nutrition Against Disease*. New York: Pitman, 1971.

————. *Nutrition in a Nutshell*. New York: Dolphin Books, 1962.

INDEX

Index

Acerola extract, 220
Acetaldehyde poisoning, 128
Acetyl-Co A, 95
Acrocyanosis, 124
Adventitia, 74
AEVIT, 43
Aging: the Biology of Senescence (Comfort), 166
Aging process, 2, 43, 147, 157, 166-82; critical stages in, 169-70; missynthesized proteins, 172-73, 175-77; underlying cause of, 171-72; vitamin C and, 175, 177; vitamin E and, 174-82
Agriculture, 193-95
Ahrens, Richard A., 33, 144
Air pollution, 2, 5, 147, 160-61, 177, 191
Albania, 91
Alcohol, 141, 177, 189
Alcoholics, 16, 68
Alfalfa, 165
Allen, George, 196-97
Allergens, 161
Allergic disorders, 191, 192
Alpha tocopherol. *See* Vitamin E

Altschule, Mark C., 133
American Heart Association (AHA), 84, 98, 102, 104, 105
American Medical Association (AMA), 1, 3, 5, 9, 32
American Schizophrenia Association, 65, 67
Amino acids, 8, 60, 61, 149
2-Amino-β-carboxy-muconic acid, 149
Amygdalin. *See* Vitamin B_{17}
Anderson, T. W., 53, 54
Anemia, 4, 18, 19, 115
Angina pectoris, 74, 122, 134-35, 137
Anitschkov, Nikolai, 75
Antibodies, 156-57
Antigens, 148-49
Antioxidant therapy, 6-7, 8, 21, 151, 155, 157, 159. *See also* Vitamin C; Vitamin E
Apoenzymes, 60, 61
Arachidonic acid, 109
Arteries, 74, 97, 101, 137
Arteriosclerosis, 74, 98, 168
Arthritis, 2, 3, 19, 169, 191, 192, 195

263

Instant Score (questions 1-8)	Modified Score (questions 1-15)	Full Score (questions 1-22)	Percentage of Total	Interpretation
192-200	346-360	480-500	96-100	Superior Health. You probably practice Supernutrition.
182-191	328-345	455-479	91-95	Good Health. Your health can improve noticeably.
172-181	310-327	430-454	86-90	Average Health Plus. Most will benefit significantly from Supernutrition.
162-171	292-309	405-429	81-85	Average Health. You probably need Supernutrition badly.

HEALTHY IS BEAUTIFUL
Shape Up Within & Without

Whatever your interests, whatever your needs,
Pocket Books has the best books to help you look good
and feel good.

_____82382	**BACKACHE: STRESS & TENSION** H. Kraus, M.D.	$2.25
_____42239	**BODYBUILDING FOR EVERYONE** Lou Ravelle	$2.25
_____41445	**CARLTON FREDERICK'S CALORIE & CARBOHYDRATE GUIDE** Carlton Fredericks	$2.50
_____41646	**COMPLETE ILLUSTRATED BOOK OF YOGA** Swami Vishnudevananda	$2.95
_____41759	**CONSUMER GUIDE TO A FLATTER STOMACH**	$2.50
_____83406	**DICTIONARY OF NUTRITION** Richard Ashley & Heidi Duggal	$2.50
_____41651	**FAMILY MEDICAL ENCYCLOPEDIA** J. Schifferes, Ph.D.	$3.50
_____82608	**FEEL LIKE A MILLION** Elwood	$2.50
_____83236	**HEALTH & LIGHT** John Ott	$2.25
_____41053	**HOW TO STOP SMOKING** Herbert Brean	$2.50
_____41763	**JOY OF RUNNING** Thaddeus Kostrubala	$2.25
_____41768	**TOTAL FITNESS IN 30 MINUTES A WEEK** Laurence E. Morehouse, Ph.D.	$2.50